Understanding Non-fiction Texts and Writers' Choices

Introduction

This section of Chapter 1 shows you how to

- explore a range of non-fiction texts and their features
- prepare to analyse texts in the exam
- practise a range of reading skills to boost your performance.

Why is the close reading of different texts important?

- In everyday life, we are surrounded by texts which attempt to influence us, so knowledge of how they work is vital.
- You will be tested on your understanding of non-fiction texts in the exam.

A **Grade C** candidate will

- understand and demonstrate how meaning and information are conveyed in a range of texts
- make personal and critical responses, referring to specific aspects of language, grammar, structure and presentational devices to justify their views.

C

A **Grade A/A★** candidate will

- develop perceptive interpretations of texts
- respond personally and persuasively to texts
- employ apt quotations to support detailed understanding
- comment perceptively on thoughts, feelings and ideas in texts.

A **A★**

Prior learning

Before you begin this unit, think about

- the many kinds of non-fiction texts you read in a day, and how and why they are different
- the different purposes of those texts
- what you learnt about non-fiction texts at Key Stage 3.

Can you list them all? What are the main features of each one?

Are they informing you, persuading you, entertaining you?

How many technical terms for features can you use: headline, caption, pull-quote?

Forms and conventions of non-fiction texts

ACTIVITY

In groups, list as many different forms of non-fiction text as you can think of.

Be specific: don't just write 'newspaper article' but try to think of all the types of newspaper article you might encounter – for example, a leader, a news report, a feature or a column.

What does non-fiction mean?

In the exam, you will have to answer questions on three non-fiction texts, which are likely to be from different **genres** or forms of non-fiction. There will not be any form of fiction such as a novel extract, short story, play or poetry.

Non-fiction forms include journalistic texts (newspaper reports, articles or leaders), leaflets and travel writing.

Checklist for success

Try to read a different kind of non-fiction text every day and ask yourself these questions:

- How do the presentational features and pictures attract the reader's attention?
- What is the audience for this text? How do I know?
- What does the writer want me to think about this topic?
- Is there anything interesting about the language used?

Focus for development: Conventions

Each form of non-fiction text has its own **conventions**. These are the typical features that help you recognise what kind of text you are reading. Conventions can be to do with **language** (style), **structure** (how the text has been organised) or **layout** and **presentation**.

Writers adapt these conventions according to their **audience** (who they are writing for) and their **purpose** (why they are writing).

Look at the two texts opposite. In groups, work out what form each text is, and pick out the textual and presentational features that tell you this.

Think about

- **language and style**
  What kind of words and phrases are used? Is the tone formal or chatty? Are the sentences long and elaborate, or short and snappy?
- **structure**
  Does the text use paragraphs or bullet points to organise the information?
- **presentation and layout**
  What presentational features do you notice – pictures, headlines and so on? Why are they used and how has the text been arranged on the page?

Use the annotations to help you.
Finally, try to explain why you think each text has been written, organised and presented in this way. What is its **purpose**?

English GCSE for AQA

English Language Targeting Grade A/A★

Contents

What's it all about?

Being able to analyse the different non-fiction texts that we meet every day is an important life skill. It helps you understand how writers try to influence their readers. For the exam, you need to be able to move beyond describing what a text is about into explaining how effects are achieved and analysing why particular features are effective. If you can interpret how language, structure and presentation are used by writers and are able to compare texts, you will be able to cope well with the demands of the exam.

How will I be assessed?

You will get **20% of your English Language marks** for your ability to deal with close-reading questions in the exam.

You will have to complete **four** questions based on your reading of **three** non-fiction texts. You will not have seen these texts before the exam.

The four questions will carry a total of **40 marks**.

This forms Section A of the exam paper and you will have **one hour** to complete it.

What is being tested?

You are being examined on your ability to

- read and respond to the texts, focusing on the questions asked
- select material from the texts to answer the questions
- interpret the texts
- use evidence from the texts to support your answers
- compare the language used in the texts
- explain and evaluate how writers use language, grammar, structure and presentational features to achieve effects and engage and influence the reader.

This chapter will develop and offer you practice in the necessary skills.

Today's television

SUNDAY 26 JULY

Star of show in remote and threatening setting – appealing to audience

Picks of the day

Programme title clearly highlighted

✳ **CHOICE**

RIVERS WITH GRIFF RHYS JONES
BBC1, 9PM

A new five-part series, in which Griff Rhys Jones explores how "the forgotten highways into the heart of Britain" have influenced our lives throughout history. He begins in Scotland, travelling upstream from Kinlochleven into one of the most remote areas of the country and following the course of the water downstream to Perth. He milks fish for their eggs, goes canyoning and canoes a fast-flowing river that pine trees, ripped from the banks, have turned into an obstacle course. An informative, enthusiastic perspective.

Why is the picture used?

What purposes are shown here?

What form of text does this indicate?

ASSESSMENT FOCUS

- Who do you think the texts have been written for? How do you know?
- Find details from the texts to support your answer.

Remember

- Analyse non-fiction texts by examining their most significant features.
- Discuss how their features are appropriate for their purpose and intended audience.

Adapting text conventions

Learning objective

- *To understand how conventions can be adapted to appeal to different audiences.*

What does adapting conventions mean?

Conventions are the features we usually expect to find in a particular form of text (for instance, a headline in a newspaper article, or a series of steps to follow in an instruction manual). The way writers adapt these features varies according to the audience and purpose of the individual text.

Focus for development: News report conventions

Read this report from a **broadsheet** newspaper.

ACTIVITY

What is a typical news report like? Think about how journalists use

- the opening paragraph
- presentational features like pictures and headings
- quotations
- text boxes
- the conclusion.

THE TIMES Wednesday November 25 2009

Flood victims will suffer trauma of a war zone, says GP

Cockermouth pictured from 2,000ft on Sunday. The flooding of the Derwent and Cocker rivers has cut people off from health services

BRITISH GEOLOGICAL SURVEY

Russell Jenkins

People in Cumbria may suffer depression and health problems as bad as if they were in a war zone, according to an expert in disaster medicine who practises in Cockermouth.

John Howarth, who has worked in Angola, Rwanda and Chechnya, said: "It is difficult mentally and physically for the victims of the floods. They have to pick themselves up off the ground. We have to be careful that no one else dies as a result of this major catastrophe. Depression is a major issue in these situations."

Heavy rain was forecast in the area last night, and the Environment Agency said that flooding was very likely in Cockermouth, Workington and Keswick. If the Calva bridge over the Derwent, declared unsafe by Cumbria County Council, collapses, it will cut the telephone lines to 1,000 households north of the river.

In Wales, the body of a young woman believed to have been swept away by the River Usk in Brecon has been identified. Kirsty Jones, 21, was found more than six miles downstream in Talybont-on-Usk.

Dr Howarth, who worked for Médecins sans Fron-

'We have to be careful that no one else dies as a result of this major catastrophe'

tières and now works in a practice in Cockermouth, said: "I have worked in war zones and flood disasters before, but I did not think I would need those skills here. These floods are going to make a large part of the county poorer and it will have a significant impact on the health of people living here."

Letters, page 33
Weather, page 78

ACTIVITY

What typical textual and presentational features of a news report can you find here?

Now read this report from a **tabloid** newspaper.

AFTER THE RAIN, HERE COMES

Supplies . . The Sun's Perrie with Agnes Bell

Drenched . . clear-up in Cockermouth yesterday

THE Sun joined the Cumbrian relief effort yesterday by helping people cut off by the devastating floods.

We took food to residents stranded when a raging river smashed the only bridge linking hundreds of locals with Workington.

The vulnerable and elderly like Agnes Bell have been particularly hard hit, so she was thrilled when we arrived with goodies from Asda. Great-gran Agnes, 84, said: "I am so pleased The Sun is helping us. When I heard that the bridge had gone I felt so alone.

"So many kind people have offered help. It makes you realise we have a great community."

Five hundred homes in Northside were cut off when the bridge over the Derwent collapsed on Friday, killing cop Bill Barker, 44.

It has turned a two-minute trip to town into a 20-mile detour.

Locals can collect food and toiletries from a supermarket-supported emergency aid station in the community centre.

Council officials have set up a Job Centre, GPs' surgery and a creche upstairs. Housing

By ROBIN PERRIE

officer Estelle Kent, 44, said: "People have been cut off, so we're bringing services to them."

Engineers fear the town's sinking Calva Bridge may collapse. If it goes, 1,000 homes will lose their phoneline.

Tory leader David Cameron described the damage as "biblical" yesterday on a visit to flood-ravaged Cockermouth.

Warnings

Asked if his party would help people in the county if elected next year, he said: "Of course we will. They're going to need help."

Residents and business owners, meanwhile, continued to return. Alison Watson, 37, of Al's Toys, said: "This couldn't have come at a worse time."

Locals were hoping the floods would not return after up to **FOUR INCHES** of rain in Cumbria yesterday. Eight roads and 21 bridges remained closed.

Across Britain, there were 15 flood warnings in place last night — ten in North West England, three in Wales and one each in the Midlands and the North East.

r.perrie@the-sun.co.uk

The Sun Says — Page Eight

Visit . . . Cameron in Cockermouth

Glossary

broadsheet: one of the larger-format newspapers (traditionally), such as *The Times* or the *Guardian*. They report national and international news in detail and offer in-depth coverage of 'serious' issues. They are also called **quality** newspapers.

tabloid: a smaller newspaper (traditionally), such as *The Sun* and *The Mirror*. They often cover less serious stories, for example, scare stories and celebrity news. They are also called **popular** newspapers.

In what ways are the broadsheet and the tabloid reports different? Copy and complete the table below.

Typical features	Broadsheet	Tabloid
pictures		
how the pictures are used		
captions		
other features to catch reader's eye		
language		
detail included		
opening		
ending		

Finally, look at this webpage:

CHOOSE YOUR NEWS

HELP ?
Use the drop down menu below to filter stories and videos the way you want - when you want it!

Popular UK News

Weather Warning For Motorists >

Pensioner Takes On 'Stupid' Trump >

Team Sky Gears Up For Launch >

Twelve Hurt In Town Centre Blast >

More Heavy Rain As Fears Grow Over Bridge

11:16pm UK, Tuesday November 24, 2009
Graham Fitzgerald, Sky News Online

Heavy rain has been falling on Cumbria again as fears grow that another key bridge may collapse.

Up to 100mm (3.9in) of rain has been predicted, raising river levels and putting the emergency services on flood alert.

Cumbria County Council said Calva Bridge, which has been declared unsafe, has dropped "several inches" more.

It warned Workington residents that if it collapses, 1,100 homes north of the river will lose their telephone connections.

But the Environment Agency said river levels were not expected to be as high as last week when some parts of Cumbria saw more than 305mm (12in) of rain in 24 hours.

Six bridges have already collapsed, causing major transport and logistical headaches for thousands of people.

As hundreds of residents of flood-hit Cockermouth were allowed back into their homes, work began shoring up flood defences.

UK NEWS IN PICTURES

The Daily Telegraph

All Monday's Front Pages >

Year 2009 In Business: The Photos >

Most Wanted Criminals On Run In UK >

WEATHER >

LONDON

Make my default location

Today   Tue   Wed   Thu   Fri

Ford S-MAX | Feel the difference

What main differences can you find between this text and the paper-based news reports above?

How does the use of conventions in each of these three texts appeal to their likely audiences? Consider:

- **presentation and layout:** images, captions, headlines, subheadings
- **structure:** length of paragraph, order of argument, any organisational features
- **language and style:** vocabulary chosen, tone, difficulty or ease of reading, sentence length and structure.

Remember

- Look at how conventions are used in different ways in similar texts.
- Decide how writers use conventions to match their purpose and audience.

Purpose

Learning objectives

- To explore writers' purposes.
- To read and analyse different kinds of travel writing.

What does purpose mean?

Whenever anyone writes a text, they have an **aim** or **purpose**. For example, they could be writing to entertain the reader or to inform them about an important issue. Or both.

Checklist for success

You need to identify

- the **purpose** of every text you read (**why** it has been written)
- which textual and presentational **features** make the text appropriate for that purpose
- how the writer tries to produce a particular **response from the reader**.

Travel writing for different purposes

Travel writing is a popular genre of non-fiction; typically, it deals with journeys, holidays, different places, customs and cultures. However, *how* an individual travel-writing text is written will depend upon its **purpose**.

Read this extract from a guidebook about New York.

GAZE AT THE STATUE OF LIBERTY & ELLIS ISLAND

The Statue of Liberty (p48), the gorgeous green woman, a gift from France, has welcomed millions of immigrants and inspires awe in all who see her. Sculptor Frederic Auguste Bartholdi built the 305-ft tall, 225-ton statue, but Gustave Eiffel contributed the skeleton.

Just next to Lady Liberty is Ellis Island (p48), formerly the holding tank, so to speak, for third-class passengers coming off immigrant ships from Europe. Ellis Island's exhibits include leftover trunks and bags from immigrants, pictures of gaunt, hollow-eyed arrivals (who might have left home in decent health but didn't always arrive that way after weeks crammed on a ship), and an interactive display that lets you search among a database of émigrés for your own relatives. It's well worth waiting in line for the ferry that takes you there.

New York: Encounter (Lonely Planet)

- With a partner, discuss and note down
  - the text's purpose or purposes
  - how the language supports this purpose (what does it make us think?)
  - who might read this text.

  Refer closely to the text in your answers.
- Imitate the style of the guidebook by writing about an interesting place to visit where you live. Use facts, interesting detail and vivid description.

Now look at this website about visiting New York.

ACTIVITY

With your partner, discuss and note down

- the general purpose of the text
- its more specific purposes, for example, what the writer hopes we will do after reading it
- what impression of New York it creates, and how
- whether you would be influenced by this text. Explain why or why not.

Next, film star Richard E. Grant writes about his first visit to New York.

A gloved hand opens the door [of my cab] and is getting my holdall and me into the lobby of the Algonquin Hotel pronto! Inside, it's a wood-panelled Edwardian gentleman's club. The loose sexy style, you'd never encounter anywhere else. Punters are cocktailing and clinking glasses and fur-coating up for the short walk to the theatres.

Up in the old elevator with the bell-boy and holdall […]. Tip here, tip there, tip every-bloody-where. […] Put on the thermals and bound down the stairwell and into 44th Street and *run* to Times Square on Broadway. GUYS AND DOLLS FOR REAL. Bright, brash, busting with people and I feel about as *alive* as I think I ever *will* be.

A […] voice is coming from way back in my head saying, 'sssssSSSSSSSSEEEEEEXY!' And *yes* it is. *Sexy*. Get a grip, boy, you're talking about a *city*…

Withnails: The Film Diaries of Richard E. Grant

ACTIVITY

- How does the writer want us to see New York?
- How is the excitement of the city conveyed? Look in detail at the way he uses language: sentences, vocabulary, verbs and adjectives.

ASSESSMENT FOCUS

Compare the three travel-writing texts about New York.

Summarise the similarities and differences in their purposes in a grid like the one below.

	Guidebook	NYCVP website	Film Diaries of Richard E. Grant
Similarities in purposes			
Differences in purposes			

Write a paragraph discussing these similarities and differences, making reference to the three texts.

Remember

- **Identifying purpose will help you interpret a text.**
- **A text can have more than one simple purpose.**

Audience

Learning objective

- To understand how texts are designed to target particular audiences.

Why is it important to think about the audience of non-fiction texts?

Writers always keep their **audience** in mind, and write in a style appropriate for them. For example, an article from a broadsheet newspaper would mean nothing to a five-year-old.

An awareness of the target audience helps you read texts more effectively: you know why things are there and the effect they are intended to have.

Read this short report from *The Times*.

Birth of Asian elephant is trumpeted by zoo

Whipsnade The first Asian elephant to be born at Whipsnade Zoo in Bedfordshire makes her public debut at the age of six days under the watchful trunk of her mother Kaylee, 27. The 3ft-tall female calf, yet to be given a name by keepers at the zoo, weighs 126kg (278lb). The zoo's elephant population has declined this year after two of its animals died from a herpes virus. David Field, Whipsnade's director, said that the calf's birth was important for its endangered species programme. The calf's sire, Emmett, is the only adult male in the zoo's herd of eight elephants.

ACTIVITY

With a partner, discuss these questions.

- What about this article might appeal to a young child (aged 6 or 7)?
- Which words and phrases would not be suitable for a young child?
- If some of the language here is not suitable for children, who, do you suppose, is the target audience for the report?

Working on your own, rewrite the article using language and ideas suitable for a young child. Make sure you use words and ideas that will be understood and sentences that are simple enough for your audience.

Focus for development:
Identifying target audiences

Advertisers usually have a clear target audience in mind for a product, and design advertisements specifically for that group. So, for example, television adverts for toys are likely to feature happy children, and adverts for zit-busting face washes show teenagers' lives transformed by clearer skin.

Looking closely at the language and presentational features of an advert can provide clues about the target audience.

Look at these two adverts for holidays. The first is from a hotel chain's publicity brochure.

Escape!™ Romance package by Marriott

Rediscover each other

Secluded walks, breathtaking sunsets, crackling fires and romantic dinners. Or perhaps it's simply champagne and room service. Whatever the time of year, whatever the reason, the perfect setting awaits those treasured times together.

For Valentines, anniversaries, honeymoons or just a spontaneous weekend getaway, nothing kindles the magic quite like an Escape! Romance package by Marriott. We'll even add extra sparkle with champagne and breakfast for two included or for something extra special book a fairytale romance package at Dalmahoy, A Marriott Hotel & Country Club.

To book | Call the hotel of your choice *(see page 29)*, *call* 0800 328 3528 *or visit* MarriottEscape.co.uk   09

The second advert is from the travel section of a newspaper.

Discuss these questions with a partner.

- What sort of people might be the target audience for each advert?
- How does each advert try to appeal to its audience?
- What does each writer want the audience to think about the holiday?

Copy and complete the grid below to answer these questions.
Support your explanations with evidence from the text.

	Rediscover each other advert	Arctic Spirit advert
Target audience		
Effect of…	In each case, say what the target audience might think	
Pictures	• *Happy couple – implies holiday will provoke this reaction.* •	• •
Headings and subheadings	• • •	• *colours used make holiday seem beautiful, like the lights* • *'Greatest spectacle' sounds unmissable*
Language	• • •	• • •

Grade B responses tend to **explain** effects:

> *The advertisement is aimed at people who love to travel and have experiences: the night sky is there to show the wonders you encounter. The colours are reflected in the word 'spirit', as if this is showing the spirit of adventure and discovery. The 'experience' is made to seem amazing...*

Here is an extract from a **Grade A★** response.

> *'Search for the elusive Northern Lights' is intended to appeal to readers who like an adventure. The verb 'search' makes it seem a hard task and exciting – and, perhaps, as if you could be the first one to achieve it. The fact that the Lights are 'elusive' suggests it could be a long search, challenging and difficult, because the Lights are not easily seen. It flatters the target audience that they would be the ones to succeed in this challenge.*

ideas extended and developed

more than one
interpretation offered

ASSESSMENT FOCUS

Write an analytical response to the 'Rediscover each other' advert, explaining

- who it is appealing to
- how it appeals to its target audience.

Remember

- Focus on how the text is intended to affect the target audience.
- Be prepared to consider the presentational features and the language.
- Make connections in your analysis between different text features, to develop your points.

Focusing on language

What do we need to know about language?

In the exam, you will have to compare the use of language and its effects in two texts. Being able to identify more than one simple meaning will bring more marks. So, instead of just saying 'it makes us think…', you might say 'it makes us think… and suggests… and makes us remember…'. One explanation has now developed into three ideas.

Checklist for success

You need to compare how writers use language. This might be

- imagery: similes or metaphors
- alliteration, onomatopoeia and other language devices
- sentence length and structure
- vocabulary choices, repetition, exaggeration.

How incidents are presented gives an insight into writers' feelings, as we interpret the words used.

Here is an extract from an autobiography written by a First World War nurse about her experiences of looking after injured men close to the battlefields.

> Outside the guns roar and inside the *baracques* shake, and again and again the stretcher bearers come into the ward, carrying dying men from the high tables in the operating room. They are all that stand between us and the guns, these wrecks upon the beds. Others like them are standing between us and the guns, others like them, who will reach us before morning. Wrecks like these. They are old men, most of them. The old troops, grey and bearded.
>
> There is an attack going on. That does not mean that the Germans are advancing. It just means that the ambulances are busy, for these old troops, these old wrecks upon the beds, are holding up the Germans. Otherwise, we should be swept out of existence. Our hospital, ourselves, would be swept out of existence, were it not for these old wrecks upon the beds. These filthy, bearded, dying men upon the beds, who are holding back the Germans. More like them, in the trenches, are holding back the Germans. By tomorrow these others, too, will be with us, bleeding, dying. But there will be others like them in the trenches, to hold back the Germans. […]
>
> They seem very weak and frail and thin. How can they do it, these old men? Last summer the young boys did it. Now it is the turn of these old men.
>
> *The Backwash of War*, Ellen la Motte

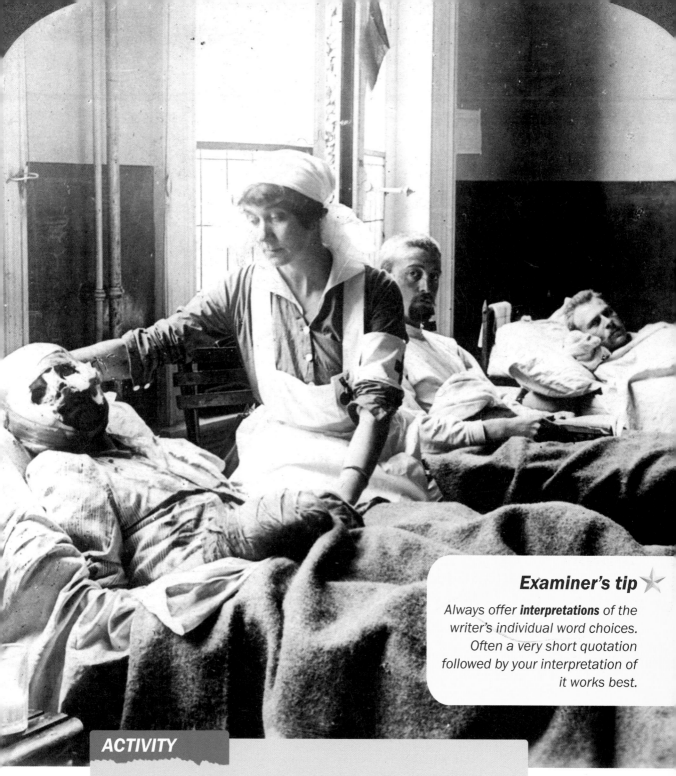

Examiner's tip ☆

Always offer **interpretations** of the writer's individual word choices. Often a very short quotation followed by your interpretation of it works best.

ACTIVITY

- How does the nurse feel about what is happening?
- What do these phrases tell us about the writer's attitude?
  - 'They are all that stand between us and the guns'
  - 'these filthy bearded men'
  - 'others, too, will be with us, bleeding, dying'
- Decide and comment on how the writer uses other linguistic features, such as repetition, emotive language, powerful adjectives and verbs.

Glossary
emotive language: language designed to affect our emotions

Here is an extract from a Grade A response to the text.

offers interpretation ⟶ *The fact that the nurse keeps repeating 'old' and mentioning the frailties of the men perhaps suggests that she is appalled that they are having to fight. At the*

extends the analysis ⟶ *same time, it suggests her amazement that they are able to perform so heroically when they are so unsuited to fight a war...*

shows engagement with the text ⟶

Focus for development:
Different view, different language

Next, notice how another nurse in the same war presents what is happening rather differently. In her diary, an American volunteer nurse is describing a typical day. In the afternoon, she changes the dressings and bandages of the injured soldiers.

what picture is she creating? ⟶ … Dressings all the afternoon until it is time for temperatures; then soup for the soldiers; and mine, which is soon finished; then the massage for those that need it, etc., after which I prepare my soothing drinks and give the injections. It is the sweetest time of the day, for then one puts off the nurse and becomes the mother; and we have such fun over the warm drinks. They are nice and sweet and hot, and the soldiers adore their 'American drinks'.

effect of these details? ⟶ When this is done, I go round and stuff cotton under weary backs and plastered limbs, bid all the children goodnight, polish my instruments, clean out the surgical dressings room, and hurry home through the frosty night.

what is suggested? ⟶ This is the rough outline of an ordinary day, and into that let your fancy weave all that is too holy or terrible, too touching or humorous to put into words: the last kiss a soldier gives you for his family he will never see; the watches with the priest when all is still and dark, but for the light of my little electric lamp and a bit of moonlight through the window; the agonies and heroisms; the wit and affection that play like varied lights and darks along the days.
Mademoiselle Miss

what is suggested? ⟶

ACTIVITY

- What is the difference in this nurse's attitude to what is happening?
- Comment on how we react to these phrases or images:
  - 'It is the sweetest time of the day'
  - 'one puts off the nurse and becomes the mother'
  - 'bid all the children goodnight'
  - 'the wit and affection that play like varied lights and darks along the days'.

Read this extract from a **Grade A★** response to the use of language in the text.

gives overview

extends comments on this, analysing the language

offers related ideas, using embedded quotations

... The nurse wants us to see her as brave, as if she is a heroine in a story. Even the horror is more romantic than brutal, so she takes time to describe 'the light of my little lamp...' rather than the soldiers' convulsions. 'Little lamp' makes us think that she is wonderful in such difficult conditions and the alliteration of 'l's seems childlike: it could even have been taken from a fairy story. It all seems unreal, so the soldiers die beautifully, with 'a last kiss' for the family and 'agonies and heroisms' are not detailed. It is all sanitised and heroic: 'polish', 'clean', 'frosty night'...

perceptive final thought to round off the idea

Presentational features

Learning objective

- To learn about the effects of layout and presentational features.

Glossary

pull-quote: a quotation lifted from the text and put in bold to stand out and alone – possibly in the middle of a column of text.

What is the difference between layout and presentation?

Layout is how a page is arranged. It is particularly important in non-fiction texts.

Presentational features are the elements that make up a non-fiction text: for example, pictures, text boxes, headlines, captions and pull-quotes.

Checklist for success

When reading any media text, you need to do the following.

- Consider **layout**. (What do I notice first and why? Where do my eyes go next? How have these features been arranged?)
- Decide if the use of **colour** is significant. (Is there more of one colour? For example: 'Does the yellow represent sunshine or…?', 'Is there red to suggest excitement or…?')
- Notice how **pictures** represent or add to what the text is saying.
- Ask yourself how any other presentational features are intended to affect the reader.

The use of pictures

Generally, pictures will be used to support the text.

ACTIVITY

Look at the article on the opposite page.

- List at least three possible reactions to this picture and explain your views.
- Working with a partner, decide how this picture reflects what the writer is saying.
- Consider why a close-up has been used.

The day of the vulture

Their feeding habits have not endowed vultures with the best public image, but conservation groups are trying to promote it anyway, declaring today International Vulture Awareness Day. This Cape vulture, which lives in a zoo in Johannesburg, is one of only 8,000 of its kind. Seven of South Africa's nine vulture species are under threat of extinction EPA

A student writes…

I just look at it and think: 'So… it's a picture …?'
That won't get me far, will it?

Answer …

You need to think about what the picture suggests to you. So, does the vulture look fierce, as if it will tear you apart? Or does it look friendly, worried, sensitive, clean or dirty? What gives you that impression?

Daily Mail, Monday, July, 2009

Er, does this thing have a reverse gear?

The only way is down: Bradt at the top of the torrent

PERCHED on the brink of a 186ft drop, this was the moment when Tyler Bradt probably felt the urge to start frantically paddling backwards.

Less than four seconds later, he was celebrating a world record for kayak descents.

The 22-year-old American touched 100mph as he plummeted over Palouse Falls, in Washington State.

To complete the dramatic picture, birds circled the torrent while behind it a rainbow appeared right on cue.

After disappearing at the base of the falls, Bradt emerged with a broken paddle. His only physical damage was a sprained wrist.

The previous record was set only weeks earlier when a rival plunged 127ft over the Salto Bello falls in Brazil.

Bradt, from Montana, has been accused of encouraging others to endanger their lives in the extreme sport of kayak free-falling.

He responds: 'I hope it encourages people not to run huge waterfalls but to understand that the only limits that exist are the ones you create, no matter what you are doing.'

ACTIVITY

Look at the layout and presentation of this news report. Using the grid below, decide how it has been designed to

- impact on the reader
- support and illustrate the text.

Feature	How it is used
Small (inset) picture	• •
Large picture	• •
Circle and arrow	• •
Headline	• •
Caption	• •

Give water
Give life
Give £2 a month

If you already support our work please pass this magazine on to friends and family who could help us reach more people without water.

Every day 5,000 children in the developing world die from water-related diseases. Yet a gift of just £2 a month from you today can help change this, bringing safe, clean water and sanitation to the world's poorest people.

Please call now on **0300 123 4341**, visit www.wateraid.org/givelife or complete the form below and return it to:
Freepost RRRZ-YRRB-ELKE, WaterAid, MELKSHAM, SN12 6YY

Registered charity numbers 288701 (England and Wales) and SC039479 (Scotland)

*WaterAid

FundRaising
Standards Board

ASSESSMENT FOCUS

Write about how layout and presentational features are used by this charity to persuade the reader to support their campaign.

In your answer, consider

- the picture and how it relates to the text
- the colours
- the use of the purple text box.

Remember

- Link your response to presentational features to the text's purpose(s).
- Consider the effects of layout, colour, pictures and any other features.

Analysing structure

: a short story
which illustrates a point

What is structure?

Structure is how a text starts, develops and ends, and how the parts contribute to the overall purpose.

Checklist for success

- You need to pay particular attention to how texts begin and end.
- You need to decide on the purpose of any text, then on how the writing is structured to meet that purpose.
- You need to notice how writers develop their points with quotations, anecdotes, facts and figures or contrasts.

ACTIVITY

- Below are details from an article about Radio 1 DJ, Chris Moyles.
- Decide what description of Chris Moyles you could create from the details. Put the information into an effective and logical order.
- Be prepared to justify your decisions.

1 Moyles' success is the consequence of professionalism for which he is rarely given credit.
2 His job appeared under threat recently but whilst other presenters were sacked, he remained to rule the airwaves.
3 He first worked at a radio station as a schoolboy doing work experience.
4 'I find his continued presence on Radio 1 unacceptable,' said Oxford University's professor of broadcast media.
5 His programmes appear spontaneous but that cleverly disguises his acute attention to detail.
6 He has been criticised for being racist, homophobic, anti-semitic and 'laddish'.
7 He is Radio 1's longest-serving breakfast DJ.
8 Comedy and film writer Richard Curtis is one of his admirers.

Focus for development: Developing ideas

A text might be structured so that the writer's viewpoint emerges right at the end, or it could be apparent throughout.

Read this newspaper report.

'It's wonderful to see you all': Winton reunited with the evacuees he saved

By Chris Green

reader is taken back in time →

SEVENTY YEARS ago, a 29-year-old stockbroker called Nicholas Winton stood nervously on a platform at Liverpool Street station in central London.

gives factual background →

The train that eventually pulled to a stop in front of him was one of eight he had arranged to carry hundreds of young children, most of whom were Jewish, on a treacherous 642-mile journey across Nazi Germany from Prague to London.

His actions were to save 669 of them from almost certain death in Hitler's concentration camps.

comes back to the present day →

Yesterday, Sir Nicholas – who was knighted in 2003 and is now 100 years old – met 22 of the people he helped to safety, after they recreated the journey to mark the 70th anniversary of their escape.

provides historical background →

The centenarian, from Maidenhead in Berkshire, masterminded their removal to Britain shortly after the outbreak of the Second World War.

summarises what happened yesterday and shows his sense of humour →

Yesterday, a steam train from Prague bearing his name arrived at Liverpool Street, and Sir Nicholas was standing on the platform once more, greeting the surviving evacuees with the words: "It's wonderful to see you all after 70 years. Don't leave it quite so long until we meet here again."

uses quotation to show his self-effacing attitude →

Surrounded by a crowd of several hundred people who had gathered to witness the reunion, he gave an emotional speech on the platform where he had stood seven decades earlier.

Describing the scene at the station in 1939, he said: "It was a question of getting a lot of little children together with the families that were going to look after them.

includes stirring and emotive detail →

It was quite difficult to get them together and, of course, every child needed to be signed for.

"Anyway, it all worked out very well and it's wonderful that it did work out so well because, after all, history could have made it very different."

Sir Nicholas Winton at Liverpool Street station yesterday with one of the 22 people he helped flee Prague during the Second World War, and her granddaughter IAN LLOYD

Sir Nicholas's grandson, Laurence Watson, 21, spoke with pride about his grandfather's actions. "It's very strange when someone you know as a relative turns out to be a hero," he said.

"There have always been bad things going on in the world and there have always been wars and conflicts. You see it everyday in the newspapers. Very occasionally you meet someone who has read those same articles but who decides to do something about it. That's what my granddad did. He said 'Something needs doing and I am going to do it.'"

← 'witness' portrays Sir Nicholas as hero

Perspective and point of view

Learning objective

- *To learn to identify and analyse the writer's perspective.*

What does perspective mean?

A text will usually have a point of view, a perspective or 'angle', on its subject. This influences how we react to the content.

Checklist for success

When reading a text, you need to ask yourself: What does the writer think about this subject and how does he or she want me to react? Does the writer

- balance the argument
- give a one-sided viewpoint, perhaps using a first-person voice
- use a range of points, building a singular effect
- make clear points into which you might read extra meaning
- add persuasive touches (rhetorical questions, emotive language, persuasive connectives, for example, 'Surely', 'What is more')
- include ambiguities, where one thing is said, but another thing suggested, for example, 'What a convincing idea that is!'?

Read this problem page from a women's magazine from the 1930s.

"Around the Editor's Tea Table"

How can I prevent my father from making a slave of mother?

I SHOULD suggest most emphatically, "Norah," that you don't do anything! You say that mother waits on your father constantly, wearing herself out in his service, and that he takes it all for granted and does not realise her self-sacrifice. But isn't it possible – I should say highly probable – that mother *loves* this service? You call it "slavery," but that is not a word which has any connection with love's work. Your parents have been happily married for twenty years and you are perhaps looking at them with romantic young eyes when you think your father should fuss more over mother and turn the tables by starting to "slave" after her. Leave them to their own way is my advice. If they have covered a score of years peacefully together it is more than likely that mother revels in her service and father appreciates it more than you can realise. I have yet to find the really good wife who does not love "wearing herself out" over her husband's welfare!

from the *Woman's Magazine Annual*, 1935

- What is the writer's point of view here? How do you know?
- Look closely at the language. What techniques does the writer use to persuade us that she is right? Find examples of
  - forceful language that allows for no alternative viewpoint
  - questions and exclamations
  - words that are emphasised, for example by the use of inverted commas
  - imperatives (where Norah is told directly what to do)
  - how the marriage is presented in positive terms.
- List the ideas the writer uses to persuade Norah.
- What is your opinion of her perspective?

An **Grade A★** student was asked what the writer thought of Norah's parents' relationship. Here is part of her response.

> The writer (the magazine's editor) is totally convinced that the marriage is fine. She believes that women are happy to slave over their husbands.
>
> She opens with an exclamation, telling Norah exactly what to do and does so very definitely: 'emphatically'. We can immediately hear that she is a strong woman with firm views who is used to telling others how to behave. In the same tone, she challenges Norah with a rhetorical question: 'isn't it possible... that mother loves this service?' She presents the role of a wife as being like a servant 'in service', suggesting that wives should wait on their husbands. The italicising of 'loves' emphasises the word, stresses the bond of marriage and implies that this kind of life represents true love...

Notice how

- a clear overview is supported by perceptive comments
- apt quotations are used
- a range of points is interpreted
- there is a convincing final point.

Continue and complete this response.

Focus for development: Examining a different perspective

Here is a more recent article.

headline includes pun

subhead includes the phrase 'might injure vandals' in speech marks, mocking the idea

first sentence stresses 'fury' and uses another pun

Daily Mirror SATURDAY 05.09.2009 M 29

BARBED IRE
Allotment fence 'might injure vandals'

BY EUAN STRETCH
euan.stretch@mirror.co.uk

GARDENERS are so furious with their council they feel like throwing in their trowels.

The growers have been banned from using barbed wire to deter allotment vandals – in case they hurt themselves.

Property at the Muddy Bottom East Allotment is being damaged up to three times a week. In one attack 15 sheds were smashed, water butts were overturned and taps were left running.

But when allotment holders asked Southampton council to put up the wire, it said no for fear of being sued.

Grandfather Mervyn Hobden, 67, who rents several spaces there, blasted the decision as "absolutely crazy". He said: The fences are easy to climb over. We asked for four lines of barbed wire to be added to the top, but the council said they have a liability towards the trespasser.

"Some of the sheds cost £500. And we have to pay to repair them. Some people have packed in because of the vandals."

Lib Dem environment spokesman Tim Farron said the decision was "ridiculous".

Bizarrely, the council has allowed the old barbed wire around the allotment's entrance to stay, because it is "historic".

A council spokesman said: "A member of the public who falls on the barbed wire can prosecute – that includes thieves."

This week, the Mirror told how angry gardeners in Torquay planned to patrol their allotment after vandals wrecked grower Tony Mason's prize pumpkins.

▲ **FURIOUS** Grower Mervyn Hobden

next paragraphs add information

quotations add subjective views to story

Adverb gives editorial comment

quotation marks show sarcasm

offers 'expert' to support view

picture personalises report: stance looks strong

What is the reporter Euan Stretch's point of view?

Here are some ideas you might include in your answer.

picture suggests Mervyn Hobson is …

tone of headline: pun and words in speech marks

imbalance in opinions

emotive language

jokey approach implies that the writer thinks …

effect of detail included

effect of quotations

'Bizarrely'

Write your own ideas in two paragraphs, in response to the article.

Remember

- The writer's perspective affects how we respond to the subject of the text.

- In the exam, you will have to answer one question on inference – what you think is being *suggested* in the text. The more you practise analysing perspective in a range of texts, the better you will be able to answer this type of question.

Grade Booster

Extended Exam Task

Choose a lead story or article from a newspaper.

Keeping in mind the text's purpose and audience and answering in detail, analyse the text by responding to these questions.

1 What is the writer's point of view?
2 How has language been used to influence, interest or inform the reader?
3 How has the text been structured?
4 What is the effect of the presentational features?

Evaluation: What have you learned?

With a partner, use the grade checklist below to evaluate your work on the Extended Exam Task.

- I can make a perceptive analysis of a writer's viewpoint and the language, structure and presentational features in a non-fiction text.
- I can use quotations and evidence which are perfect for the context.
- I can interpret the ideas in the text in a detailed and persuasive way.
- I can offer originality in what I write.

- I can make a detailed interpretation of a writers' viewpoint and the language, structure and presentational features in a non-fiction text.
- I can make points persuasively and use valid quotations and evidence which supports and clarifies them.

- I can begin to analyse viewpoint and the use of language, structure and presentational features in a non-fiction text.
- I can make effective points and show an ability to see layers of meaning in the text.
- I can use quotations and evidence to support my points.

- I can make clear and relevant comments on a writer's viewpoint and on the use of language, structure and presentational features in a non-fiction text.
- I can offer relevant quotations and evidence in support of my ideas.

- I can identify a writer's viewpoint.
- I can understand how language and presentational features are used in a non-fiction text and comment on how they have been used.
- I can use some appropriate evidence.

You may need to go back and look at the relevant pages from this section again.

Close Reading in the Exam

Introduction

This section of Chapter 1 helps you to

- focus on the reading skills you will have to demonstrate in the exam
- develop and practise the necessary skills by analysing different non-fiction texts in detail
- understand the requirements of the exam by offering advice.

What will 'close reading' mean in the exam?

You will have to select the right material to answer the **four questions** on the Higher tier paper. These will require the following skills:

Question 1: Finding information in the text

Question 2: Dealing with inference – what the text is suggesting

Question 3: Analysing presentational features

Question 4: Comparing the use of language in two texts.

A **Grade C** candidate will

- understand and demonstrate how meaning and information are conveyed in a range of texts
- make personal and critical responses, referring to specific aspects of language, grammar, structure and presentational devices to justify their views.

C

A **Grade A/A★** candidate will

- develop perceptive interpretations of texts
- respond personally and persuasively to texts
- employ apt quotations to support detailed understanding
- comment perceptively on thoughts, feelings and ideas in texts.

A **A★**

Prior learning

Before you begin this unit, think about

- what you have already learnt about language, structure and presentational features such as pictures and headlines
- the different kinds of non-fiction texts you read every day.

Consider the use of colour, font size and why a particular illustration has been used. How do these features add to the text?

How can reading these more analytically help you to prepare for the exam?

Retrieving and collating information

Learning objectives

- To understand the need for precision when selecting information.
- To learn about how to collate information.

What does retrieving and collating information mean?

To respond to questions with authority, you first need to be able to **select** and **retrieve** the details from the text that are most appropriate to answer the question. Then you analyse and **collate** (put together) information from different parts of the text so you can comment on the overall impact.

Checklist for success

Whenever you write about texts, you need to

- make sure the information you select answers the question
- ensure any reference or quotation actually supports the point you are making
- be selective when retrieving information so that you are not putting random points together.

ACTIVITY

Look at the two different adverts on pages 35 and 36.
With a partner:

- decide how each product appeals to the reader
- retrieve one piece of appropriate information from each advert.

Completing the entries in a grid format like this will help.

Harley-Davidson	Fiat
Relaxation/open road/freedom suggested by …	A car for a particular season suggested by …
Bike and rider's overall image captured in one word: …	One specific attraction of car captured in one phrase: …

BRIGHTSUN BIGSMILE
SHADESON SOUNDSUP
ROOFDOWN HAIRLOOSE
CAREFREE COOLBREEZE
ICECREAM TANNEDSKIN

500C
NOW OPEN

FIAT

fiat.co.uk

Fiat, the car brand with the lowest average CO_2 emissions in Europe.* Fuel consumption figures for the Fiat 500 C range mpg (l/100km) and CO_2 emissions: Urban 53.3 (5.3) - 36.7 (7.7) Extra Urban 78.5 (3.6) - 55.4 (5.1) Combined 67.3 (4.2) - 46.3 (6.1). CO_2 emissions 110 - 140 g/km. *Source: JATO Dynamics. Volume-weighted average CO_2 emissions g/km among European top 10 selling brands 2008.

★ Examiner's tip

When you are collating information, you need to decide on the most effective order for it. You could put the points in order of priority, perhaps starting with the most important, or you might write about related points together.

Focus for development: Putting ideas together

Here is a Grade A★ response to this question:

> **What impression of the Harley Davidson is produced in the advertisement?**

provides an overview →

selects another feature to develop the point →

This motorbike, as shown in the advertisement, seems to be offering all the freedom a young person in America could ever want. It stretches across the page, just like the country seems to stretch out all around the rider. Putting it all in black and white takes us back many decades, as if we can go back in time to when there was still some of America to be discovered. The Harley Davidson badge looks like something from an era now gone too. However, it is also saying this is a bike for the young and 'hip', as summed up in the price: 'A cool £4995'. The guy looks cool, even in the desert – just like people used to be cool in the old movies.

← selects details to support overview

← gives sensible detail to link with previous point

makes additional point but with appropriate quotation/comment as supporting evidence and linking back to a previous point at the end

36

Here is a Grade B response to this question:

> **How does the Fiat advertisement try to appeal to the reader?**

The words across the top of the advert are in different colours, making the car seem exciting and modern – this is also shown by all the words running together as they do. The car is open-topped and seems to be the sort of car that would attract young people. It might attract the ones who want – or who have – 'tanned skin'. Maybe it is suggesting it is a British version of the sort of car we imagine them cruising around in in America...

ACTIVITY

- Which details from the Fiat advert are well selected in the Grade B response?
- What further analysis might have been added and about what?

ASSESSMENT FOCUS

The analysis of the Fiat advert could be improved by giving an overview, then selecting and collating information to support that overview.

Write an improved version by

- offering a brief overview to begin with
- adding appropriate details which, together, support your overview.

Remember

- Make sure you retrieve evidence that is appropriate to the task and to the point you are making.
- Be prepared to offer a general overview, then collate your points carefully so that they work together.

Using quotations and examples effectively

Learning objective

- To understand how to use evidence to support the points you make.

What do we mean by evidence?

How you support points will depend on the question you are asked and the nature of the text, but you are likely to be using direct quotation or mentioning detail from the text to back up your ideas.

Checklist for success

You need to

- remember that any analytical points you make require proof from the text
- select brief quotations – usually no longer than two lines
- refer to detail and make your examples precise, rather than offering generalised thoughts.

ACTIVITY

In the Grade A response below, a student begins to analyse this estate agent's house advert to explain how this property is made attractive to potential buyers.

Read and then complete the response.

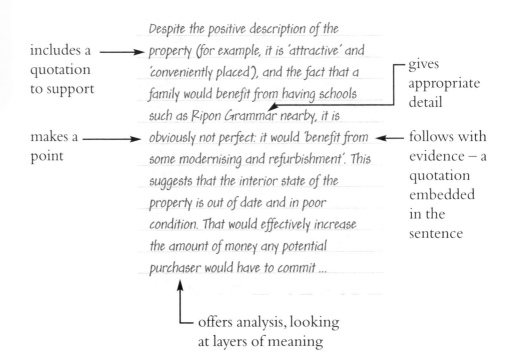

includes a quotation to support → *Despite the positive description of the property (for example, it is 'attractive' and 'conveniently placed'), and the fact that a family would benefit from having schools such as Ripon Grammar nearby, it is* — gives appropriate detail

makes a point → *obviously not perfect: it would 'benefit from* ← follows with evidence – a quotation embedded in the sentence *some modernising and refurbishment'. This suggests that the interior state of the property is out of date and in poor condition. That would effectively increase the amount of money any potential purchaser would have to commit …*

offers analysis, looking at layers of meaning

THORNTON HOUSE, RIPON, NORTH YORKSHIRE
PRICE: £500,000

This attractive home offers generous living space and is conveniently placed within walking distance from Ripon city centre. Dating from 1865, Thornton House has belonged to the same family for the past 100 years, so this is a real opportunity. The six bedrooms, family bathroom and four reception rooms would benefit from some modernising and refurbishment, while the basement, with wine cellar and four rooms, offers plenty of storage. Schools such as Ripon Grammar and Cathedral Choir School are close by, and Leeds, York and the Yorkshire Dales are within easy driving distance. Best offers need to be received in writing by 12 noon on Monday, September 14.

Call Peters and White Estate Agents on 01597 111523 or visit www.peters&white.co.uk.

Focus for development: Interpreting references and quotations

This letter was sent to a local newspaper in Oldham.

Academics are the only way forward

EDITOR – We are proud that Oldham's academy programme has this week been advertised to bidders.

This means that over the next few months we will be choosing the construction partner to build our three state-of-the-art new schools.

Considerable work remains to be done to make these projects successful, however that should not detract attention from our fundamental aspiration: to provide every student in Oldham with a new or nearly new secondary school by 2014.

This brave and ambitious aspiration is the only way forward for Oldham.

Our children are growing up in enormously challenging times - not just in terms of the credit crunch - but also the changes in the global economy. Jobs and skill requirements are transforming and so is the market of people competing for them.

The position for young people in Oldham has many positives. Greater Manchester's economy is still bigger than that of Beijing, for example, and is projected to grow, despite the current financial crises, to 2020.

This will give local children real opportunities, but they will

The Orb Mill site, which will be transformed into one of Oldham's three academies. Inset: Cllr Kay Knox

only be able to capitalise if they acquire high level skills. Education is key to helping them achieve this. Set against these aspirations, Stuart Paulley's criticisms of academy schools (Advertiser letters, September 10) seem out of touch.

He selectively uses evidence to try and sustain his case that academies are selective and failing. Yet we have made it clear that the model for Oldham means all of our academies will have the same admissions criteria as the local authority.

The picture on academies' performance nationally is, on the whole, encouraging and we

have always maintained that ours will be introduced into a local context which is favourable to their success.

Mr Paulley repeatedly criticises, but never proposes a realistic alternative to these plans.

I want the very best opportunities for all our children in order that they, their families, and this borough can prosper.

I refuse to have a two-tier system where some children have the best opportunities but others are left behind.

Cllr Kay Knox
Cabinet member for
children, young people
and families

ACTIVITY

To help examine how convincing the letter is, complete your own copy of the grid below, adding evidence and analysis for Points 2–4. Follow the example for Point 1.

Point	Evidence	Analysis
Cllr Knox says the academies will be totally up-to-date	*'our state of the art new schools'*	• *comes at the start of the letter so has immediate impact* • *suggests nothing could be more advanced* • *contrasts with what we might imagine the old schools are like*
Cllr Knox believes Greater Manchester is big enough to provide these expensive academies		• • •
Cllr Knox claims that Mr Paulley has no alternative plan		• • •
Cllr Knox claims the decision is not just brave		• • •

ASSESSMENT FOCUS

Write a response to this question.

How successful is the Councillor's attempt to convince readers that Academies are necessary?

In your answer, try to

- begin with an overview of the letter's viewpoint
- select the main points the councillor makes
- offer point, evidence and analysis for each of these.

Remember

- **Find evidence from the text, then explain or analyse it.**
- **Analysing will bring greater rewards than giving an explanation.**

Making inferences

Learning objective

- *To understand how to identify implications and 'read between the lines'.*

What does reading between the lines involve?

In the exam, you will have to interpret the writer's feelings or attitudes towards their subject.

So, if someone writes, 'This could be the most money ever spent on something so small', it might suggest the price is far too high, or that it is really precious, or that those paying are fools…

To write about what is being suggested, it helps to have a strategy.

- Identify the relevant parts of the text (underlining them in the exam).
- Open with an overview of the content.
- Write about each point in turn, saying what it suggests about the subject.

ACTIVITY

With a partner, read the article below about weather patterns and discuss these two questions.

- Why does the writer think a wet country is better? Find three reasons and explain why he suggests they are valid.
- What is the writer's opinion of British weather and what does he think of hot climates?

★ Examiner's tip

A detailed response might give an overview first, showing the writer's attitude, then work through relevant points in the text, explaining what they say and analysing what they imply. (For example: 'He uses the example of ripping out the hearts of altar maidens to show what happens when a country is hot, implying that we would all go mad and lose all civilised behaviour. This exaggeration makes us think…').

Let's rejoice in the rain

by Andrew Grimes

The suspension of global warming over Britain this summer has spared us all a lot of grief. Why some people are complaining about it is beyond my understanding.

This is not a hell-hot country, and with any luck it never will be. We are a group of islands off the northerly side of Europe. It rains a lot. The rain keeps us resourceful, resilient and glossily-wet.

No good ever comes of a country that is perpetually hot. I have just been reading about the Incas of Peru who got on perfectly well until, around AD1100, they were overcome by a cyclic heatwave that lasted 400 years.

The new-fangled sun went to their heads, causing them to build an empire, start wars and found a religion that demanded a constant flow of altar maidens to have their hearts ripped out. They also, poor devils, found tons of gold.

The Incas, who may have been half-way barmy to start with, reacted to their hot sun with manic hyperactivity, and the Spanish wanted their gold. When the conquistadores arrived to destroy them they were too worn out to fight.

Is there, in the Incan tragedy, a moral for those Brits who hanker for a permanency of hot suns?

Focus for development: Inferring from written text and presentational features

WHAT A HE ROW

Boat lad Will, 12, helps cops nab drowning fugitive

A BOY of 12 was hailed a hero yesterday for rowing two policemen out to save a drowning drugs suspect.

Will Abbotts — who uses his small boat to fish from his family's lakeside mansion — went into action after cops in riot gear raided a neighbouring home.

Officers arrested one man and found 1,000 cannabis plants. But a second men leapt from a balcony at the rented house, fracturing at least one leg, and then tried to escape by swimming the lake.

Will heard shouts as he stepped off his school bus and saw the fugitive's head bobbing in the water.

The lad — who was still in his public school uniform — said: "I shouted across that I had a boat. I was shaking a bit because I didn't know what this suspect was capable of.

"And when we picked him up there were four people on the boat and it is only meant for two adults at most. We were very pleased to get back to shore."

PC Mike Dawber — one

By BEN ASHFORD

of the officers he helped on a millionaire's row in Mere, near Knutsford, Cheshire — said: "Will's action was brilliant.

"His expert rowing got us across very quickly."

Chief Supt Mick Garrihy said: "He contributed to a police operation against organised crime and saved a man from drowning. He showed speed of thought, bravery and calmness under pressure."

Will's father Gordon, 63, said: "We're very proud, although his mother would have preferred he took the time to put on a life jacket."

Two suspects are facing trial.

b.ashford@the-sun.co.uk

Oarsome . . . Will rows his boat with PC Mike Dawber

Writing about presentational features

What does writing about presentational features involve?

The presentational features – pictures, headings, text boxes and so on – are there to create an effect: to make the reader react or think in a certain way. By focusing on why the text has been produced, you can link your ideas to its purpose and audience. This will give your writing more focus.

Checklist for success

- You need to make sure you understand and can use a range of **technical terms**: for example, headline, subhead, caption, banner.
- Rather than just describing or identifying features, you need to write about their **intended effect** on the reader.

ACTIVITY

- In groups of four, pool your knowledge and draw up a list of all the media terms linked to layout and presentation you know. (For more about presentational features see pages 24–27.)
- Produce a brief definition of each term.

Analysing presentational features and layout

ACTIVITY

- In your group of four, discuss the following questions about the leaflet above.
    - Why are two such different pictures used? How do we react in each case?
    - Are the colours used significant? How are they used?
    - Does the layout grab our attention?
    - Why have the fonts been used in this way?
    - Do the publicity quotation in white and strapline question in red work?
- Write your own response to the following question:

> **How have presentational features been used to attract the reader in this text?**

Examiner's tip ☆

*Look at the texts you are given and **be critical**. Consider purpose and audience, and weigh up how some techniques have more impact than others.*

Focus for development: Presentation and layout in web pages

Web pages often offer a range of presentational devices and the layout is carefully designed to

- appeal to readers
- help them to navigate the site easily to find what they want.

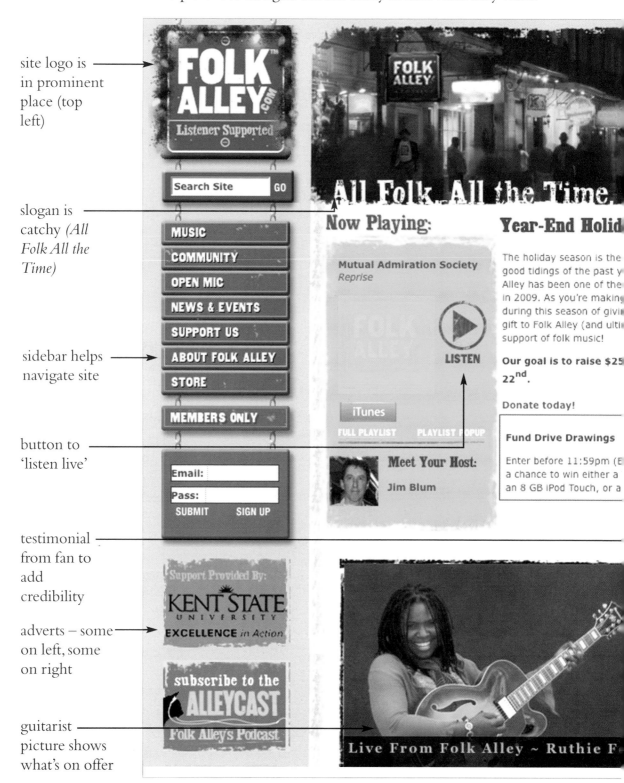

site logo is in prominent place (top left)

slogan is catchy (*All Folk All the Time*)

sidebar helps navigate site

button to 'listen live'

testimonial from fan to add credibility

adverts – some on left, some on right

guitarist picture shows what's on offer

competition
offer
highlighted

picture at top
adds atmosphere

ive

Support Provided By:

text in small
digestible bites

eflect on the
ve hope Folk
s in your life
day list
consider a
yourself) in

December

$25,000
**HELP US MEET
OUR GOAL!**

CURRENT TOTAL
$10,380

KEEP THE **MUSIC**
PLAYING.

ec 22th for
-325 guitar,
Folk CDS.

Testimonials

Lisa Meissner: Lisa
is a Folk Alley
supporter from Tupper
Lake, New York. She's
a life-long folk music
fan and a musician in
the duo the Rustic
Riders. She says she listens AND
contributes to Folk Alley because of
the quality and range of folk genres
and the mix of old and new artists
that she hears.

SAM BUSH
CIRCLES AROUND ME

THE NEW RECORD
AVAILABLE NOW

dave
rawlings
machine
a friend of a friend

Available Now

ASSESSMENT FOCUS

- In a group, decide how
  successful this text is in
  appealing to its audience.
- Then, working on your
  own, write about the
  layout and presentational
  features.

Remember

- Link your comments about
  presentational features and
  layout to your understanding
  of the text's purpose and
  audience. It makes things
  easier.
- Move beyond description to
  analysis of significant
  features.

Comparing language

Learning objective

- To understand how language comparison questions work in the exam.

⭐ Examiner's tip

It is vital to compare things that are actually comparable, for example sentence length or how particular words are used in the texts. 'Comparing' metaphors with alliteration, for example, is unlikely to bring the best marks.

Will there definitely be a comparison question in the exam?

You will always have to compare language. You will be writing about the impression created by the language in each text. You need to compare the effectiveness of the language used.

Checklist for success

- You need as much practice in comparing texts as possible. Try to find texts to compare at home. You could
  - examine two football reports of the same match, perhaps from a tabloid and a broadsheet newspaper
  - analyse how two 'Agony Aunts' respond to their correspondents in different styles.
- You need to focus on similarities, where they exist, and on differences, using examples from the text to support your ideas. That is the key to success.

ACTIVITY

Read the two extracts on the following page. They deal with the same subject but in different ways.

Complete a grid like this one to compare the extracts.

	Extract 1	Extract 2
General style or tone		
Opening sentence		
Punctuation		
Sentence length		
Similes and metaphors		
Illustrations/vocabulary		
Use of repetition		

Extract 1

Frankly, who cares about endangered species? Environmentalists rush around like demented wombats telling the rest of the known world to give money to save the lesser-spotted iguana or the Siberian toad. But why? If the world's last white rhino were to pass away tomorrow, would it make the slightest difference to my beans on toast? Would the beans be more expensive? I don't think so, because they already cost too much: and that is what worries me, not the fate of the Great White Shark. I'll be dead in fifty years, so who cares about the climate? What matters is my life now…

Extract 2

We are living in desperately difficult times. With the massive expansion of the human race, animals are the last thing on most people's minds; yet once rare species have gone, they will never come back. If we look at the situation of the wild salmon, where stocks are rapidly diminishing; if we look at the Mediterranean, which used to teem with fish but now laps emptily against so many shores; if we think about the fall in the number of sharks and the effect that has on the entire eco-system; if we think about how similar situations are happening on land too – we must see that mankind has to change…

ACTIVITY

Write a summary of how the writers use language to put their message across, taking some of the information from your grid.

You are likely to reach a higher grade if you offer more

- detail
- layers of analysis
- points of comparison.

Focus for development: Analysing how language creates a style

The viewpoint of the writer affects the approach to his or her subject. This viewpoint will be reflected in the language used.

Read these two obituaries for the writer, Keith Waterhouse.

Text 1

Farewell Keith, king of Fleet Street

by Sam Greenhill

Keith Waterhouse, acclaimed journalist, novelist, dramatist, raconteur and *Daily Mail* columnist, died in his sleep yesterday.

A legend of the golden age of Fleet Street and a man whose plays have filled theatres around the world, he was at his home in London when he passed away. He was 80.

His former wife, journalist Stella Bingham, said: 'He died peacefully at home.'

They had divorced in 1989 but remained friends and in recent times she was a crucial figure in his life, looking after him in his final weeks.

Waterhouse had been unwell since earlier this year.

The revered writer, whose extraordinary career spanned 60 years, came from humble beginnings in Leeds and rose to become a luminary in the worlds of literature, theatre and film.   *Daily Mail*

Text 2

Keith Waterhouse Daily Mirror legend, 1929–2009
Champion of the Word

by Anton Antonowicz

Keith Waterhouse, one of Britain's greatest journalists, novelists and dramatists, died before lunch yesterday.

Which would have annoyed him, given that his hobby listed in *Who's Who* was simply, 'Lunch'.

He could afford to enjoy that mid-day break because he rose early and wrote quickly, knowing that 'summat to eat' and the regular bottle of champagne beckoned at the end of that noontide full-stop.

But what he could write in those few hours before dawn and drink-time was marvellous.

In his distinctly northern way, this lad from Leeds – to whom he contritely returned library books 25 years overdue in a pantechnicon – was a constant child.

His finest work, whether writing those sparkling columns for the *Mirror* (and later the *Daily Mail*), harked back to more innocent times.

He was at his best summoning childhood memories of kids 'falling into ponds, eating poisonous berries, contracting stomach-ache from under-ripe stolen apples, getting lost, being bitten by dogs, fighting and starting fires, sitting in cow-pats and acquiring bumps the size of a duck egg on their heads'.   *Daily Mirror*

Discuss these questions with a partner.

- What is similar about the two headlines?
- What other similarities can you find in the two texts?
- What is the major difference in the way these two writers remember Keith Waterhouse?
- How does the language used reflect their attitudes towards him? For example, write about
  - 'king' and 'champion' in the headlines
  - how Text 1 uses words like 'acclaimed', 'legend' and 'luminary', whilst Text 2 also uses 'summat to eat' and 'lad'.

Here is an extract from a student's response comparing the articles.

Grade A★ response

Whilst Greenhill uses predictable praise for Waterhouse ('king' and 'revered' making him seem a hero) Antonowicz uses language to show us the real Waterhouse, behind the writing. You feel he knew the man, is able to capture his northern speech ('summat to eat' – he was a 'northern lad'), and pick out the words Waterhouse probably liked best: 'lunch' and 'champagne'. We sense Waterhouse was a man of appetite and there was fun in him: his articles were 'sparkling' – presumably funny, enjoyable and as bubbly as the champagne he loved...

Notice how this Grade A★ response

- actively makes comparisons between the texts, using appropriate evidence
- captures the tone of the obituaries
- collates or groups ideas ('summat to eat' and 'northern lad')
- offers layers of analysis
- shows an understanding of **why** and **how** the texts were written.

ASSESSMENT FOCUS

Write a full comparison of how language is used in the two obituaries to capture the memory of Keith Waterhouse.

Remember

- **Make your comparison detailed.**
- **Start from your understanding of the writer's purposes, and build your analysis of the language around that.**

WIN a weekend in Paris

Julie & Julia. At cinemas 11 September

There's always an excuse to visit Paris. Whether you're drawn there by your love of food, fashion, architecture, romance or just a well-earned weekend away, you'll always find what you're looking for.

That's why we're offering one reader and a friend a fabulous weekend in the French capital.

You'll fly to Paris where a glass of chilled champagne will await you at the Hugo Hotel – your accommodation for the next two nights. You'll have £200 spending money, plus an evening dinner for two where you can sample true French cuisine.

Julie & Julia, starring Meryl Streep and Amy Adams, will be in cinemas on 11 September. It brings together the true stories of two women, a generation apart, who find the answer to their dreams through their experiments with French cookery.

For your chance to win, complete the film title:

MERYL STREEP STARRED IN THE FILM: THE DEVIL WEARS ____?

Extended Exam Task

Write a response to this question.

How does the text attempt to interest the reader?

Comment on

- its purpose and audience
- its layout and presentational features
- the main messages in the text
- the language techniques used.

Evaluation: What have you learned?

With a partner, use the grade checklist below to evaluate your work on the Extended Exam Task.

- I can make a perceptive appreciation and analysis of the presentational features, messages and language techniques, demonstrating how they combine to create their effects.

- I can make a detailed interpretation of the presentational features, messages and language techniques, incorporating them into a unified analysis.

- I can begin to analyse how the presentational features, messages and language techniques have been used.

- I can make clear and relevant comments on the presentational features, messages and language techniques.

- I can understand how the presentational features, messages and language techniques are used but my comments are not developed.

You may need to go back and look at the relevant pages from this section again.

Exam Preparation
Unit 1A: Reading non-fiction texts

Introduction

In this section you will

- practise the reading skills you have been learning about in this chapter
- read, analyse and respond to sample answers by different candidates
- write your own answers to sample questions
- evaluate and assess your answers and the progress you have made.

Why is exam preparation like this important?

- You need to be able to work under timed conditions
- Looking at sample answers by other students will help you see what you need to do to improve your own work.

Key Information

Unit 1 is Understanding and Producing Non-Fiction Texts.

- It has an exam of **2 hours**, worth **80 marks.**
- It is worth **40%** of your overall English Language GCSE mark.
- Section A of the exam is on Reading and Section B of the exam is on Writing.

Section A Reading

- This section is **1 hour long**, and is worth **40 marks** or 20% of your English Language GCSE.
- You will be asked to read three non-fiction texts and to answer four questions on the texts:
  - **Q1**: finding information in a text (**8 marks**)
  - **Q2**: analysing presentational features (**8 marks**)
  - **Q3**: examining what is inferred (suggested) in a text (**8 marks**)
  - **Q4**: comparing the language used in two texts (**16 marks**)

Examples of the different question types can be found on pages 55–57.

The Assessment

The assessment objectives for reading state that you must be able to do the following:

- Read and understand texts, selecting material appropriate to purpose, collating from different sources and making comparisons and cross-references as appropriate.
- Develop and sustain interpretations of writers' ideas and perspectives.
- Explain and evaluate how writers use linguistic, grammatical, structural and presentational features to achieve effects and engage and influence the reader.

Targeting Grade A

Some of the key differences between Grade C and Grade A/A★ answers are as follows:

Grade C candidates	See examples on page 59.
• show clearly that the texts are understood • use appropriate evidence to support their views • offer relevant interpretations of the texts • make clear connections and comparisons.	

Grade A/A★ candidates	See examples on pages 58 and 60
• develop perceptive interpretations of texts • respond personally and persuasively to texts • employ apt quotations to support detailed understanding • comment perceptively on thoughts, feelings and ideas in texts.	

EXTENDED TASK/PRACTICE

Complete the sample exam paper on the next pages.

Item 1

Grizzly bears starve as fish stocks collapse

Calls grow to suspend hunting season in Canada after wildlife guides sound alarm at lack of cubs

by Tracy McVeigh

Chief Reporter

First it was the giant panda, then the polar bear, now it seems that the grizzly bear is the latest species to face impending disaster.

A furious row has erupted in Canada with conservationists desperately lobbying the government to suspend the annual bear-hunting season following reports of a sudden drop in the numbers of wild bears spotted on salmon streams and key coastal areas where they would normally be feeding.

The government has promised to order a count of bears, but not until after this year's autumn trophy hunts have taken place. It has enraged ecology groups which say that a dearth of salmon stocks may be responsible for many bears starving in their dens during hibernation. The female grizzlies have their cubs during winter after gorging themselves in September on the fish fats that sustain them through the following months.

"I've never seen bears hungry in the fall before, but last year they were starving," said British Columbian wildlife guide and photographer Doug Neasloss. "I noticed in the spring there weren't as many bears coming out, but I felt it was premature to jump to conclusions." But now, he said, "there just aren't any bears. It's scary."

It was the same story, he said, from other guides over 16 rivers where once they would have been encountering dozens of grizzly bears. "There has been a huge drop in numbers. I've never experienced anything this bad." Reports from stream walkers, who monitor salmon streams across the vast territories, have been consistent, according to the conservation group Pacific Wild – no bears, and more worryingly, no bear cubs.

Grizzlies once roamed across most of North America and the Great Plains until European settlers gradually pushed them back. Only 1,000 remain in the contiguous US, where they are protected, but the number is less clear in the vast wilds of Canada and Alaska, where they are prized by hunters who shoot hundreds of the 350kg giants every year, providing a lucrative income for provincial governments that license the hunts. "It's appalling wildlife management, considering the widespread concern for coastal bears at the moment," said McAllister.

A report released last week showed species numbers to have fallen dramatically in the province of Alberta, where local officials have decided to suspend the annual hunting season despite intense lobbying from hunters. "There's no question that bears are worse off now than 20 years ago – both in numbers and range," said Jim Pissot, of the group Defenders of Wildlife.

The few grizzlies spotted this year in their usual haunts are said to be starving.
Corbis

NATIONAL GEOGRAPHIC HD/NATIONAL GEOGRAPHIC (543/526)

skymag

EIGHT PAGES OF THE
BEST TV SHOWS ON
SKY THIS MONTH
this month

Siberian tigers
are under threat
from poaching

FROM RUSSIA WITH LOVE

The beauty of the Russian wilderness is revealed – in stunning high definition

HD WILD RUSSIA
Sun 4, 8pm, National Geographic Channel **HD**/
National Geographic Channel **(543/526)**

This scene of Siberian tigers sparring in the snow is breathtaking, but for the crew of National Geographic's new series *Wild Russia* it was just one of the many jaw-dropping moments captured in HD during an epic 1,200 days' filming. "From the frozen forests of Siberia to the geysers of Kamchatka, the territory where we filmed is unknown even to many Russians," explains executive producer Amanda Theunissen.

Wild Russia reveals the secrets of the world's largest wilderness – almost 70 times the size of the UK – including many animals that, sadly, may soon be extinct. "Siberian tigers are under threat from poaching," says Amanda. "There are around 40 Amur leopards left, just 440 European bison and 1,500 breeding pairs of Siberian crane – a tiny amount."

Amanda points out that *Wild Russia* isn't purely an animal behaviour show. "It's also about the area – more than 60,000 miles of land between Moscow and Vladivostok where hardly anyone

ventures. There aren't many roads or places to land a helicopter. In high definition, the scenery is gobsmacking!" However, the remoteness did cause problems... "One of the crew was bitten by a snake and had to be stretchered for two days to get to a road," says Amanda.

The harsh landscape is a backdrop to scenes of beauty, including a surprising bear ritual. "Their mating is usually rough and ready," smiles Amanda. "So it was touching when we saw a pair being tender, before ambling off into the forest together. It was like a fairy tale."

Love this?
Watch these! ↘ ● *After the Attack*, Thu 1, 9pm, Animal Planet (525) ● *Secret Life of Elephants*, Wed 7, 9pm, Eden (532) ● *Orca Killing School*, Thu 15, 9pm, Nat Geo Wild **HD**/Nat Geo Wild (544/528) ● *Hooked: Monster Fishing*, Mon 19, 8pm, National Geographic Channel (526)

october 2009 **skymag** 11

Item 3

The Deaths of Animals

In America, thirty species of large animals – some very large indeed – disappeared practically at a stroke after the arrival of modern humans on the continent between ten and twenty thousand years ago. Altogether North and South America between them lost about three-quarters of their big animals once man the hunter arrived with his flint-headed spears and keen organisational capabilities. Europe and Asia, where the animals had had longer to evolve a useful wariness of humans, lost between a third and a half of their big creatures. Australia, for exactly the opposite reasons, lost no less than 90 per cent.

Because the early hunter populations were comparatively small and the animal populations truly monumental – as many as ten million mammoth carcasses are thought to be frozen in the tundra of northern Siberia alone – some authorities think there must be other explanations, possibly involving climate change or some kind of pandemic. As Rose MacPhee of the American Museum of Natural History put it: 'There's no material benefit to hunting dangerous animals more often than you need to – there are only so many mammoth steaks you can eat.' Others believe it may have been almost criminally easy to catch and clobber prey. 'In Australia and the Americas,' says Tim Flannery, 'the animals probably didn't know enough to run away.'

Some of the creatures that were lost were singularly spectacular and would take a little managing if they were still around. Imagine giant sloths that could look into an upstairs window, tortoises nearly the size of a small Fiat, monitor lizards 6 metres long basking beside desert highways in Western Australia. Alas, they are gone, and we live on a much diminished planet. Today, across the whole world, only four types of really hefty (a tonne or more) land animals survive: elephants, rhinos, hippos and giraffes. Not for tens of millions of years has life on Earth been so diminutive and tame.

From *A Short History of Nearly Everything*, Bill Bryson

Answer these questions:

1. Read **Item 1**, the newspaper article entitled 'Grizzly bears starve as fish stocks collapse' by Tracy McVeigh

   What are the problems for bears in Canada, according to Tracy McVeigh?   **8 marks**

2. Now read **Item 2**, from a Sky television magazine, headed 'From Russia with Love'.

   How do the heading and the picture add to the effectiveness of the text?   **8 marks**

3. Now read **Item 3**, 'The Deaths of Animals' by Bill Bryson.

   What does Bryson think about the fact that so many animals disappeared?   **8 marks**

4. Now you need to refer to **Item 2**, 'From Russia with Love', and **either** Item 1 **or** Item 3. You are going to compare the two texts, one of which you have chosen.

   Compare the ways in which language is used for effect in the two texts. Give some examples and explain what the effects are.   **16 marks**

Exploring Sample Responses

Read the following response, judging how well you have done against the quality of these answers, bearing in mind the Examiner feedback.

1   What are the problems for bears in Canada, according to Tracy McVeigh?

Example 1

McVeigh shows grizzly bears in a dreadful situation. The headline sets out her basic message ('Grizzly bears starve as fish stocks collapse') and the subheading adds the idea of 'alarm'. Clearly something needs to be done, and quickly.

— first paragraph summarises

— personal interpretation

She adds weight to that impression, explaining that there has been a 'sudden drop' in the number of bears spotted on salmon streams, probably because there have been fewer fish on which they could feed. Conservationists point out that bears are likely to starve in their dens during hibernation because there are not enough fish to fatten them to survive. Cubs are usually born in winter, but will not be born to starving mothers.

— range of details used to support ideas

We learn that, unusually, bears were starving last fall and there were fewer bears in the spring. McVeigh quotes photographer Doug Neasloss to emphasise what has happened: 'Now... there just aren't any bears. It's scary.' He adds that others have found the same over 16 rivers – no bears and no bear cubs.

— selective use of quotation

We are given a brief history, to show how things have changed: bears once roamed freely across North America but now there are only 1000 in the US and no one knows how few are in Canada and Alaska. Provincial governments allow the hunting of hundreds of bears each year.

— good use of facts

There is some hope offered towards the end of the article, though, as fewer numbers of bears in Alberta has brought a hunting ban, despite hunters' complaints.

— balance: introduces hope

However, the final quotation from Defenders of Wildlife leaves us with the seriousness of the problem: 'bears are worse off now than 20 years ago.' It takes us back to the headline and the problem.

— effective quotation to conclude

Examiner feedback

It is sometimes a temptation to just copy out relevant sections of the text. In this case, the student has given the ideas a framework. There is an overview, then the different sections are introduced, before being supported by detailed analysis of what is happening. The student includes everything that is important whilst making perceptive comments on how McVeigh has structured her article. We get the impression the student knows exactly what McVeigh is telling us and how she is putting across her message.

Suggested grade: A/A★

ACTIVITY

Read this next response, judging how well you have done against the quality of this answer, bearing in mind the Examiner feedback.

2 How do the heading and the picture add to the effectiveness of 'From Russia with Love?'

Example 2

> The title makes us think of the James Bond film, which is about beautiful spies and fighting, but really it is about many of the good and beautiful things in wild Russia. The tigers in the picture might be starting to fight or to mate but they also look beautiful to attract us to the programme. Their colours look amazing to show how lovely they can be and it is as if they might hold hands soon, or paws. The text is saying these creatures are becoming rare but they are lovely and that is what the picture shows.

Examiner feedback

The candidate has dealt with both the picture and the headline and offered some interpretation of each. Importantly, they are linked to the text, to show why they have been used. The points made have been explained.

To get a higher grade, the candidate needed to write about

- the headline with more clarity – saying why it is appropriate and interpreting it more precisely, in relation to the rest of the text
- the picture in more detail – perhaps mentioning the snow and its relevance, whether they appear to be rushing together or play fighting or whatever. Again, interpretations would need to be linked directly to words and phrases from the text (for example, 'jaw-dropping moments').

Suggested grade: C

ACTIVITY

Discuss with a partner. Based on the bullet points in the examiner's comments, how would you improve this response?

Read this next response, judging how well you have done against the quality of these answers, bearing in mind the Examiner feedback.

3 In 'The Death of Animals', what does Bryson think about the fact that so many animals disappeared?

Example 3

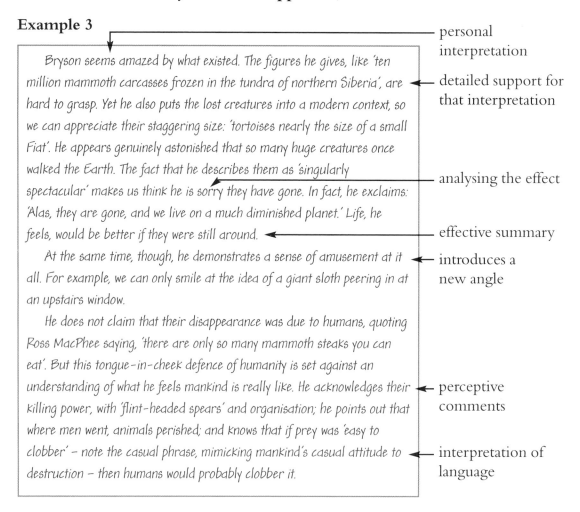

Bryson seems amazed by what existed. The figures he gives, like 'ten million mammoth carcasses frozen in the tundra of northern Siberia', are hard to grasp. Yet he also puts the lost creatures into a modern context, so we can appreciate their staggering size: 'tortoises nearly the size of a small Fiat'. He appears genuinely astonished that so many huge creatures once walked the Earth. The fact that he describes them as 'singularly spectacular' makes us think he is sorry they have gone. In fact, he exclaims: 'Alas, they are gone, and we live on a much diminished planet.' Life, he feels, would be better if they were still around.

At the same time, though, he demonstrates a sense of amusement at it all. For example, we can only smile at the idea of a giant sloth peering in at an upstairs window.

He does not claim that their disappearance was due to humans, quoting Ross MacPhee saying, 'there are only so many mammoth steaks you can eat'. But this tongue-in-cheek defence of humanity is set against an understanding of what he feels mankind is really like. He acknowledges their killing power, with 'flint-headed spears' and organisation; he points out that where men went, animals perished; and knows that if prey was 'easy to clobber' – note the casual phrase, mimicking mankind's casual attitude to destruction – then humans would probably clobber it.

Annotations:
- personal interpretation
- detailed support for that interpretation
- analysing the effect
- effective summary
- introduces a new angle
- perceptive comments
- interpretation of language

Examiner feedback

This answer shows a full understanding of what Bryson thinks and how he puts it across to the reader. There are perceptive comments about his attitudes (for example, 'tongue-in-cheek defence') and how he puts them across, and the quotations are all well chosen, supporting the interpretations being offered. The focus is always upon what Bryson says, how he says it and the thoughts behind the words.

Suggested Grade: A★

Read this final response, judging how well you have done against the quality of these answers, bearing in mind the Examiner feedback.

4 Compare the ways in which language is used for effect in 'From Russia with Love' and one of the other texts. Give some examples and explain what the effects are.

Example 4

'From Russia with Love' sets out to attract viewers, so there are many positive opinions about the programme: 'stunning', 'breathtaking' and 'gobsmacking'. It is obviously trying to attract a younger audience by using that last word. In contrast, 'Grizzly bears' is an article full of less appealing reality, which talks of 'impending disaster'. The vocabulary is depressing. In places, the bears' situation seems dreadful: 'It's scary'. The words are as if from a horror novel. We are expected to be shocked by the scale of what is happening, as reflected in the facts given. Whilst the animals in 'From Russia' are 'sparring' and 'ambling off into the forest together' sounding like playmates, the bears are starving. The language used is bleak: 'I've never experienced anything this bad...'

Examiner feedback

This response demonstrates clear understanding and analysis. The vocabulary is examined and compared and comments on the effects are included. Effective quotations support the points made and there are some quite sensitive comments (for example, 'The language used is bleak'). To gain a higher grade, the candidate needed to

- offer more detail and interpretation (for example, 'facts' are mentioned, but without any analysis)
- make further more perceptive comments (for example, the phrase 'impending disaster' is quoted but there is no significant comment on the actual words)
- extend the comparison through the remainder of the response.

Suggested Grade: B

If you only do five things...

1 Read as many different kinds of non-fiction texts as possible. Try to read at least one text each day.
2 Decide what the purpose and audience are for each text you read. Work out what the writer wants the reader to think.
3 Spot the techniques the writer uses to convince the reader: focus on how the writers use presentational features, and find elements of the language you could comment on, such as similes and metaphors.
4 Always try to analyse rather than explain, looking to interpret features in different ways, rather than making just one comment.
5 When writing about texts, always try to structure your answer so that ideas link and develop.

What's it all about?

Writing non-fiction texts means you have a chance to write a fantastic variety of texts, many of which will be really useful for life outside school. What is more, a good letter, exciting news article or snappy web text can be just as creative as a story or poem.

How will I be assessed?

You will get **20% of your English Language marks** for your ability to write non-fiction texts. You will have to complete **two** written tasks in an exam lasting **one hour**.

You will be marked on your writing of two responses – one **short**, one **long** – to two set tasks.

What is being tested?

You are being examined on your ability to

- write for specific audiences and purposes
- communicate clearly, effectively and imaginatively
- organise information in a structured way, using a range of paragraphs
- use a variety of sentence structures and styles
- use a range of linguistic features for impact and effect
- write with accuracy in punctuation, spelling and grammar.

Purposeful Writing

Introduction

This section of Chapter 2 shows you how to

- understand what a written response question is asking you to do
- understand the meaning of the words 'task', 'audience', 'purpose' and 'form'
- generate ideas and plan your writing
- explore different approaches to planning the structure of your work.

Why is planning for purpose important?

- To complete any written task – either in class or in the exam – you need to **understand what you have to do** and, once you have done that, **focus on how you get there**.
- The **plan and the structure** for your writing are like a **'road map'** to make sure you get where you want to go.
- This gives you the **big picture**, not just the details, so that you understand the overall effect of particular choices you make.

A **Grade C** candidate will

- plan so that the organisation of his/her writing is effective, for example in using clear and coherent paragraphing to sequence ideas
- successfully adapt form and style to different purposes.

C

A **Grade A/A★** candidate will

- plan so that the organisation of his / her writing is effective, skilful and coherent with a logical structure
- exploit the chosen form fully, in an assured, confident and controlled way
- where, appropriate, engage and delight the reader.

A

A★

Prior learning

Before you begin this unit, reflect on

- what you already know about **audience**, **purpose** and **form**

- previous occasions when you have had to **come up with ideas** for a written task

- how confident you are about the **structure and organisation** of your written work.

Could you jot down what you understand by these terms?

What did you do?
What techniques did you use?

Do you find others can follow your ideas easily? Why? Why not?

Do you use **paragraphs**, **headings** or other **organisational features** effectively?

Understanding task, purpose, audience and form

What do these terms mean?

The **task** is the question or problem you have been set: for example, to write a letter to an employer applying for a job, or an article for a travel magazine describing an exciting trip.

The **audience** means the reader or readers: the people who will receive your letter, or read your article.

The **purpose** is the reason for writing the letter or article: for example, to persuade or to explain and describe.

The **form** is the type and category of writing: letter, article, report, etc.

Checklist for success

- You need to identify the purpose, audience and form in the writing task you have been set.
- You need to consider how these things will shape your writing plan.

In the writing exam, **purpose, audience** and **form** are all present in the **task**.

ACTIVITY

Read these three sample questions and then, with a partner, note down for each case

- the audience
- the purpose
- the form.

The first has been done for you. Of course, the task and purpose are tied up together, so don't worry if you can't separate them.

Then, compare your answers with another pair. Did you agree? Which one of these would you consider the most difficult task? Why?

form ⟶   audience ⟶   task/purpose ⟶

Sample question 1: Write a **report** for your **headteacher advising** him or her about **whether it would be a good idea to lengthen the school day** by an hour and a half.

Sample question 2: Some people believe our country's energy needs will be solved by us taking responsibility at home. They advise us to save energy by turning off lights, unplugging phone-chargers, heating only the rooms we are in, and so on. Write a letter to your local newspaper either persuading readers to follow this advice, or arguing against it.

Sample question 3: A website called 'Classic Kids' Films' has asked users to suggest one classic film they would recommend to parents for their children. Describe the film you would choose, saying why you would recommend it.

Focus for development: Audiences and purposes

Now read this email from a student to a revision website:

> *Can't texts have lots of purposes? If I send an email to a friend about him coming to visit me, I could be giving him information, persuading him – if he's not sure – even making him laugh, cos we're good friends…*

Discuss this issue with a partner:

Can texts have more than one purpose? Think about the autobiography of a celebrity: what purposes might that text have?

CHRiS EVANS
LiTTLE BiGSHOT

Coleen

welcome to my world x x

ASSESSMENT FOCUS

Look at this extract from a student's answer in the exam. Can you work out what the task, audience, purpose and form were?

> *The production of Romeo and Juliet by Year 10 and 11 last night was one of the best performances to grace the school stage in a long, long time. With atmospheric lighting, moody music and fantastic sound effects, the whole production was a credit to the students, and I thoroughly recommend that you come along to see your sons and daughters performing. Don't miss out – tickets for the remaining nights are selling quickly.*

Remember

- Identifying task, purpose, audience and form in the exam question will help shape your answer.
- Texts can have more than one purpose and more than one audience.

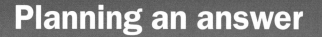

Planning an answer

Learning objectives

- *To understand how important the plan is to a successful answer.*

- *To write a basic plan for an exam-style question.*

⭐ **Examiner's tip**

You can use other ways of generating ideas – for example, a list or flowchart or whatever works for you. The main thing is to get ideas down on paper!

You don't have to use everything you write down initially: you can always leave out ideas that you later decide don't fit what you want to say.

What does it mean to plan?

When you plan an answer you are thinking ahead. Your plan is an outline of the main ideas and content you are going to include. It may also be the stage where you decide which points to analyse in greater detail.

Checklist for success

A successful plan is one that

- answers the **main purpose** of the task
- covers the **main points**
- provides **a structure**, with a **clear sequence** of steps and sharp detail
- sometimes includes **key words**, **phrases** or **sentences** you intend to use.

You will have **one hour** to answer **two questions**. Spend **five minutes** planning each answer – but before you write the plan, you need to **generate ideas**.

ACTIVITY

Generating ideas

Read **Sample question 1** on page 64 again.

A student has started to **generate ideas** for this answer using a spider diagram. Complete it by adding main points of your own. Then include detail for each main point.

REPORT – lengthening school day, good or bad?

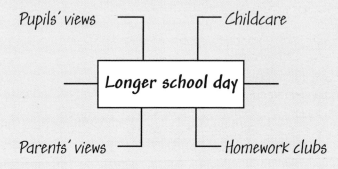

Focus for development: What makes a good plan?

The plan

Now read this plan based on the spider diagram.

Look at the plan with a friend and discuss:

- whether you would be able to write an answer to the task based on this plan

- if there is another way the answer might have been structured.

Plan

1 Intro: thank him for asking me to report for him
2 Advantages of lengthening school day:
   - less childcare for parents
   - could have tea provided
   - homework done in school so equal for everyone
3 Disadvantages:
   - pupils want to go home, may be problems
   - clubs outside school will have to change times
   - buses, trains?
4 Conclusion: good idea if problems dealt with first; parents kept informed.

ASSESSMENT FOCUS

Now look at a second sample question.

> A website called 'Classic Kids' Films' has asked users to suggest one classic film they would recommend to parents to show their children. Write a description of your suggestion, explaining why you would recommend it.

Generate ideas and then write a plan for this question. Take no more than five minutes to do so.

1 Start by reading the question and identifying the purpose, audience and form.
2 Next, generate ideas: use a spider diagram, list of points or notes.
3 Then write your plan. Use numbers or letters for each section (these could be your paragraphs in the final answer).

 Examiner's tip

When you've done your plan, jot down a variety of suitable words and phrases ready to use in your answer: for example, some good connectives ('firstly', 'however', 'moreover') or impressive phrases you might use ('spectacular experience', 'thrill-a-minute adventure').

Remember

- **A good, detailed plan will help you to write a high level response.**

- **A plan will keep you focused and give you a clear sequence to follow as you write your answer.**

Structuring your text

Learning objective

- *To understand how basic structure can change meaning and effect.*

What is structure?

The **structure** of a text is the way it is **organised**, particularly the order of the content.

Checklist for success

Successful structure is achieved by

- including the **key conventions** of a particular form of text, such as the opening to a letter
- **sequencing** the content appropriately: for example, deciding whether to state your main point at the start of a text
- **organising** content effectively (for example, deciding whether to group certain ideas together)
- making sure the reader can **follow your argument**, viewpoint or explanation.

Check the key conventions of non-fiction forms on pages 6–7.

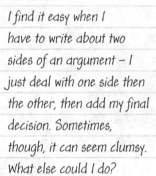

A student writes…

I find it easy when I have to write about two sides of an argument – I just deal with one side then the other, then add my final decision. Sometimes, though, it can seem clumsy. What else could I do?

Answer…

You could deal with each issue or topic in turn. It does mean, though, that you will need to use comparative language well ('on the other hand', 'in contrast').

ACTIVITY

Here is a Grade A/A★ example in which a student has written about the advantages and disadvantages of a beach holiday and a city break.

> *The weather! That's what blights beach holidays. If it's sunny – fine, but what do you do if the sand is as soggy as a marshmallow? On the other hand, bad weather in a city is actually quite welcome. No one needs an excuse to sit in some trendy café sipping a hot chocolate, do they?*
>
> *When it comes to chilling out, the beach holiday wins hands down: you can't beat the mix of fresh air and warm sea. City breaks might be relaxing, but you can never escape the traffic, the fumes and the people.*

Which structure has the student used from the two options given above in the 'A student writes…' section?

Focus for development: Sequence and organisation

Similar decisions about organisation – what you deal with and in what order – occur even in texts in which you are not comparing things. For example, what is the best way to **start** a text: to get straight to the point, or to be more subtle?

ACTIVITY

Write two plans for this task.

For each plan, jot down what you are going to include over five paragraphs.

- In the first plan, use the first paragraph for stating your point of view and then deal with all the pros and then all the cons.

- In the second plan, deal with each point in turn, looking at the pros and cons of each.

> **Task:**
> Your form teacher has asked you whether having a 'whole school litter pick' at the end of each day is a good idea. Advise him or her on what is the best course of action.

Work with a partner and give an improvised talk based on each plan. Discuss which structure worked better, and why.

ACTIVITY

Approaches to structure

You can use structure to affect tone and style, for example by having an unusual opening.

Look at these two emails students have written in response to a question about inviting an old friend to meet up. Which one do you think uses a more original and engaging opening? Why?

A *Hiya. Would you like to meet up some time? It's been ages since I've been in touch. It'd be great to hear all your news, and share a coffee. We could meet in Princes Park if you like?*

B *A sunny afternoon – Princes Park – veggie burgers, diet coke and a good laugh. Sound like fun? I haven't been in touch for ages, so it'd be great to meet up next week if you're around…*

Remember

- Changing the order or sequence of information you give changes the effect. Sometimes it is best to be direct, but don't be afraid to experiment with structure.

Grade Booster

Extended Exam Task

Generate ideas, plan a task and decide on a structure for this question:

> *Write an article for your school magazine in which you attempt to persuade your year group to volunteer to work for local charities.*

If you feel ready, write the opening two paragraphs of your article.

Remember to follow this process:

 Generate ideas ➡ Plan ➡ Decide on structure or sequence

Evaluation – What have you learned?

With a partner, use the grade checklist below to evaluate your work on the Extended Exam Task.

- I can quickly and efficiently compose a plan which shows my immediate grasp of the full potential of the task.
- I can demonstrate my creative flair by using a wide range of language choices and techniques.

- I can quickly and efficiently compose a plan which shows the most effective organisation and structure for the task, audience, purpose and form.
- I can plan how to show a wide range of ambitious language choices and techniques.

- I can write a plan which allows me to develop and organise ideas for task, purpose, audience and form, with a clear sense of the effect they will have on the reader.
- I can consider things such as alternative beginnings and endings, and variety of paragraphs.

- I can write plans with a view to interesting the reader and my organisation is clear.
- I can choose language that is appropriate, linked to the purpose and form.

- I can write plans but they are not always detailed or properly focused on purpose, audience, form and the task set.
- I can use language that is mostly appropriate.

You may need to go back and look at the relevant pages from this section again.

Communicating Clearly, Effectively and Imaginatively

Introduction

This section of Chapter 2 shows you how to

- focus on the aspects of your writing which help you communicate successfully
- explore the importance of selecting appropriate vocabulary
- craft impressive, rich sentences and structure paragraphs coherently
- improve your use of punctuation for effect and impact, as well as accuracy.

Why is it important to communicate clearly, effectively and imaginatively?

- Your ideas may be wonderful, but you need to convey what you have in your head to the reader so that they 'get' your meaning.
- Good communication, however, is not just about clarity but about engaging the reader in what you have to say.

A **Grade C** candidate will

- use a wider range of sentences
- use generally accurate punctuation and carefully chosen and varied vocabulary
- use clear and logical paragraphing.

A **Grade A/A★** candidate will

- use varied and sophisticated sentence structures
- use a wide range of punctuation for deliberate effect
- demonstrate an ambitious and varied vocabulary
- vary the style and length of paragraphs to fully support the main thrust and purpose of the text.

Prior learning

Before you begin this unit

- jot down what you already know about the four main areas addressed here: **vocabulary**, **punctuation**, **sentences** and **paragraphs**

- reflect on any particular areas which have **caused you concern** in your general written work or, more specifically, in timed or assessed pieces of work.

Do you already have ideas about how to use each of these successfully? Do you understand how to use the main punctuation points?

Paragraphing – cohesion and coherence

Learning objective

- To understand how linking ideas within and between paragraphs improves writing.

What is cohesion and coherence in paragraphs?

Coherence means that the parts of a text link together and have a logical order. For example, an opening paragraph may introduce ideas and the second paragraph may then build on them.

Connectives (such as 'and', 'so' and 'however') and **pronouns** ('he', 'she', 'it', etc.) are the words and phrases that 'glue' sentences and paragraphs together to create a flowing, **cohesive** text. For example, the first paragraph may use the name of an object or person, but subsequent paragraphs may refer back to them as 'it', 'he' or 'she' to avoid repetition.

Checklist for success

- You need to make sure that sentences in individual paragraphs link well and make sense.
- You need to compose paragraphs which are structured for a particular impact or effect: for example, a long descriptive one, followed by a short one which shows someone's startled reaction.

ACTIVITY

Read these opening paragraphs to a review of a school production.

> The school's production of West Side Story was fantastic and had everything you could wish for. It had good acting. It had good dancing. The music was great. Amy Fisher was brilliant in her role playing Maria.
>
> The wonderful set design made us all sit up and take notice. It was colourful and snazzy and really fitted the story. The art department should be thanked for all their work.

This is a C grade response because

- the paragraphs are reasonably clear and fit the purpose (to review a school performance)
- the paragraphs are organised by content (the second one is about the set design).

However, complex ideas need to be presented in a **coherent** way for higher grades. How could the **cohesion** within the two paragraphs be improved to **enhance** meaning?

Rewrite the paragraphs
- removing unnecessary repetition
- making them 'flow better' (for example, could you use connectives to join short sentences together?)
- re-organising any ideas that should perhaps be linked.

Focus for development: Making paragraphs coherent

ACTIVITY

Now look at this student's Grade A★ response to a design task on eco-friendly cars.

Make brief notes on the purpose and effect of the first short paragraph, and the reasons why the second two paragraphs are longer.

Then add another long paragraph in which you describe the interior of the car.

Finish by adding a one- or two-sentence paragraph in which you sum up the ideal car's qualities. This final paragraph could

- use a pattern of three adjectives to sum up its qualities ('the ideal car would be…, … and…')
- finish with a short sentence emphasising its importance.

ASSESSMENT FOCUS

Write four or five paragraphs describing the ideal eco-home. Make sure you

- link ideas within paragraphs by using connectives and pronouns
- use a short opening paragraph to set up your ideas
- use some longer paragraphs to develop the ideas
- end with a short, punchy paragraph to sum up your ideas.

The ideal eco-friendly car would have radical features related to outer appearance, engine and interior design. These three factors combined could revolutionise driving.

As far as external appearance is concerned, the car would blend into its environment: no gaudy colours, nor huge tyres or box-like shapes. It would be sleek, small and perfectly formed. Shifting through the air like a silent bird it would encounter little or no wind resistance, and merge almost seamlessly into the landscape.

Its engine would be capable of at least 60 mpg, use either electric power or clean fuels to ensure minimal damage to the atmosphere, and, in an ideal world, would be virtually silent, avoiding so-called 'noise pollution', thus satisfying the driver's need to save the world and save hard-earned cash.

Remember

- **Good cohesion and coherence brings clarity to your writing.**
- **Varying your paragraphs creates impact and effect.**

Using a range and variety of sentences

Learning objective

- To use a variety of different sentence structures for impact and meaning.

What does using a range and variety of sentences mean?

It is the ability to select, combine and organise simple, compound and complex sentence types in different ways, for effect.

> **Glossary**
>
> A **simple sentence** contains only one clause: *The cat miaowed loudly*.
>
> A **compound sentence** contains two clauses linked by 'and' 'or' or 'but': *The cat miaowed loudly **and** it went back to sleep.*
>
> A **complex sentence** contains two or more connected clauses: ***When I** laughed, the cat miaowed loudly **and** went back to sleep.*

Checklist for success

To write **successful sentences** you need to

- **create inventive combinations**
- select the **right sentence type** for **effect** and **impact**
- be **clear**.

ACTIVITY

Read this opening to an article in which an adult recalls her childhood.

Discuss with a partner:

- What is the effect of the two **short sentences** at the start of the article?
- How does the sentence beginning 'A little table' add to the effect created? (Is it a sentence?)
- How does the use of the **present tense** ('I **am** five years old') add to the effect?

> I am five years old. I'm being naughty about food. I am sent to eat alone at a table in the hall. A little table, a little chair, a ticking clock (I can't tell the time, but I know I must finish my food before the big hand gets to the top) and something on my plate that I don't want to eat: an omelette whose edges taste burnt.
>
> Julie Myerson, The Observer

⭐ **Examiner's tip**

Julie Myerson uses sentences to get 'inside the head' of a character (in this case imitating a child's thought-processes). A technique like this will really target Grade A/A★.

Focus for development: Making sentence choices

You need to decide on the right structure, length or combination of sentences for the task.

Consider this task.

> *Some people believe it would be better if clothing wasn't made in poorer countries and we produced more in the UK, even if that meant higher prices. Write an article for a magazine in which you argue for or against this idea.*

You probably need longer sentences to explain and develop a point here.

Discuss with a partner:

Why is the Example 1 sentence effective? Think about its length and how the different parts are linked.

To target **Grade A/A★**, you need a **variety and range of sentences**. Look at Example 2 by the same student.

Now write briefly about

- the different types of sentences used and the effect each one creates
- the effect of using this variety of sentence types.

Example 1

> *Over-population means that in many poor countries people are desperate for work, despite the low wages and the terrible conditions they often have to endure to feed their families.*

Example 2

> *The poor need work. That's a fact. Work is in short supply. That is also a fact. Within the sweatshops and the teeming factories that can be found in third-world cities, there are nameless thousands who rarely see the light of day – but if you gave them the chance to leave, would they take it? Not likely!*

Write the first two paragraphs in response to this task. Use a variety of sentence types for effect.

> **'The biggest problem young people face today is older people's attitudes towards them.'**
>
> Write an article for *SAGA Magazine* (for the over 50s) in which you argue for or against this view.

 Examiner's tip

Include some short sentences for effect, but use them sparingly.

Remember

- **Choose the right sentence type and length for the purpose.**
- **Vary sentences for impact and effect.**

Using punctuation for accuracy and impact

Learning objective

- To understand that punctuation can be creative and help to shape meaning.

What does punctuating for accuracy and impact mean?

When you punctuate **accurately**, you use the main punctuation marks – full-stops, capital letters, speech marks, commas, colons, semicolons, apostrophes – correctly.

When you punctuate for **impact** and **effect**, you are also using punctuation to convey a particular meaning, or to create a particular effect on the reader.

Checklist for success

- For Grade C you need to try and use all punctuation correctly.
- For Grade B you need to use a wide variety of punctuation accurately.
- For Grade A/A★ you need to select the right punctuation for the effect you want to create.

ACTIVITY

Read this extract. It is from a response to a task asking students to argue for or against raising the school leaving age to 19.

With a partner, consider how the use of punctuation has

- helped to organise the writer's ideas
- created specific effects and impact.

> The proposed age of 19 is clearly a bad idea for a number of reasons: firstly, everyone needs a break from education (I certainly did!); secondly, it would be very 'un-cool' to wear a uniform at that age; thirdly, teachers would certainly object.

Use the glossary below to help you.

Glossary

A **colon (:)** introduces a quotation or, following a general statement, a list.

A **semicolon (;)** is used to divide items in a long, complicated list, or to contrast or relate two ideas.

Brackets ( ) are used around extra information to highlight it or keep it separate.

An **ellipsis (...)** shows speech that trails off or shows that text or information is missing.

Focus for development: Sophisticated punctuation

Try these more sophisticated uses of punctuation to target a Grade A/A★. They are all from a piece about the perils of going out shopping.

1   Add the **bracketed text** to this sentence.

   Shopping in a crowded high street is clearly a dangerous activity if you're in a hurry (which I ....) and should be banned.

2   Add a **short rhetorical question** before this sentence.

   Go out ....?
   It's much safer just to stay at home and order what you need from the internet.

3   Use a **semicolon** to **juxtapose** two related ideas.

   Shopping or sleeping? There's a difficult one. On the one hand shopping is tiring, costs money and you have to leave your warm house on the other, sleep refreshes you, allows you to escape your boring life, and you don't even have to leave your bed!

4   Add a **colon** to introduce the list, and **semicolons** to separate the items in the list.

   So here's just a few reasons to avoid a busy shopping centre tripping over prams and buggies shops with narrow aisles and too much stock queues for fitting rooms overwrought shop assistants — to name but a few.

Share your ideas with a partner.

Write the opening two paragraphs to this exam question.

For a Grade A/A★, think how you could use a variety of sentences and punctuation for effect. For example, you could

> Write a light-hearted article for a magazine in which you argue that snowballing is *not* a fun activity.

* start with a question ('Remember when … ?')
* juxtapose two ideas with a semicolon
* make a point and add bracketed text as an aside
* use a colon to introduce a list.

Remember

■ **Accurate punctuation is vital for a Grade C (avoid using commas where there should be full-stops!).**

■ **To target Grade A/A★, use sophisticated forms of punctuation in creative ways.**

Selecting effective vocabulary

Learning objective

- To understand how the vocabulary you choose can improve your writing.

What does selecting effective vocabulary mean?

Vocabulary is your **choice** of **individual words** and **phrases**: for example, using 'thrilling' rather than 'good' to describe a book in a review.

Checklist for success

You need to **choose vocabulary** that

- fits the **subject** or **context**
- is **ambitious** and **imaginative** – but also **correct**.

ACTIVITY

Read this extract from a student's response to a request by her local council to suggest a location in her town for a new war memorial, and to describe what the memorial should look like.

> I reckon the best place would be the seafront by the old café. It is a good place because it's quiet but many people pass by taking in the view. The memorial should be big so people can see it and it will stick up or stand out and it should be made of something hard to stop the weather from getting in and ruining it.

This is a **Grade C** answer because

- the student has met the purpose – up to a point
- there is some appropriate description
- she has chosen a particular tone for her audience.

However, it could be improved, especially the vocabulary.

Look at the weaknesses and discuss the questions with a partner.

The vocabulary...	Questions
is often rather **general or vague**	What other details could she add? What word or phrase would be better than 'something hard to stop the weather'?
lacks **impact**	Is there a more effective word than 'quiet'?
lacks **detail** and terms suitable for the context or purpose.	Could she describe the memorial's appearance better?

Besides these vocabulary weaknesses, what else would you improve?

Focus for development:
Ambitious content and vocabulary

Examiner's tip ★

*For a Grade A, get the **register** right. For example, you wouldn't call a war memorial 'stunning' or 'glamorous'. These words may not actually be wrong, but they are inappropriate.*

ACTIVITY

Read this question:

> *A holiday website aimed at teenagers has asked for contributions to its section on 'The Perfect Beach' and wants to know what makes an ideal beach. Write your views on what such a beach would be like.*

Most students would probably write about a beautiful beach in summer. However, would that be an **ambitious** and **imaginative** response?

Read this Grade A★ response:

> *My perfect beach: rain lashing the concrete promenade, a scrawny terrier cocking its leg against the rotten hulk of an old dinghy, and not a person to be seen. On the horizon, grey, angry clusters of clouds would gather over breakers like mountains, and the oil-tankers would be shrouded in choking fog and mist. This is perfection for me – the cold easterly wind flattening my hair against my cheeks, red and smarting from the icy rain, clearing my mind of all worries.*

Discuss with a partner why this response is effective.

Consider

- the impact of the language (adjectives such as 'scrawny', nouns such as 'promenade', and imagery in the form of similes and metaphors)
- the general approach taken.

ASSESSMENT FOCUS

Continue the response above by adding two or three more paragraphs in a similar style. Alternatively, write your own response to the task.

Remember

- **Consider alternative approaches to the task; these can help your vocabulary stand out.**
- **Create impact and be ambitious with your vocabulary choices – use imagery to paint a picture in the reader's mind!**

Grade Booster

Extended Exam Task

Write at least three or four paragraphs in answer to the task on the right.

Make sure your focus is on communicating two or three ideas clearly and imaginatively. Use

- coherent paragraphing
- effective and meaningful punctuation
- a variety of sentences
- appropriate and well-chosen vocabulary.

> Some people believe that teenagers have only themselves to blame for the negative ways they are represented by the media. Write a letter to a national newspaper in which you respond to this statement, agreeing or disagreeing with the viewpoint expressed.

Evaluation – What have you learned?

With a partner, use the checklist below to evaluate your work on the Extended Exam Task.

- I can cleverly and clearly express my viewpoint with a real sense of organisation and development, using a wide range of sentences and paragraphs to affect the reader's response.
- I can use vocabulary which is rich, ambitious and well-chosen – yet always appropriate.

- I can state my purpose and viewpoint clearly and effectively; my ideas are very well expressed in clear sentences and a range of paragraphs which develop and sustain my argument.
- I can use vocabulary which is always appropriate and well-chosen and is often ambitious and rich.

- I can use effective paragraphs supporting each point made; my ideas are well-thought out in a range of sentences that have an impact on the reader.
- I can use vocabulary which is accurate and occasionally ambitious.

- I can use an increasing variety of sentence forms, accurately punctuated; my paragraphs are logical and I clearly present main ideas.
- I can use well-chosen, but not especially varied, vocabulary.
- I can ensure my viewpoint comes through and is supported by some good ideas.

- I can use simple sentences (and occasionally complex ones).
- I can sometimes use more varied vocabulary, but it is still rather limited.
- I can use paragraphs but they lack thought and variety and my point of view is rather undeveloped.

You may need to go back and look at the relevant pages from this section again.

Writing to Engage the Reader

Introduction

This section of Chapter 2 shows you how to

- engage the interest of your reader
- adapt form and style to meet your reader's needs
- use some particular literary devices, such as hyperbole, to create a real impact on your reader
- develop the skill of sustaining your point of view over the whole text so that the reader remains 'on track'.

Why is engaging your reader's interest important?

- Texts that work best create a relationship with the reader.
- You tend to enjoy writing more if you set out with this purpose in mind.
- You are more likely to be persuasive, appear knowledgeable and interesting, and be understood if your writing creates impact.
- The highest grades at GCSE are reserved for students whose writing is not just efficient but really makes the reader sit up and take notice.

A **Grade C** candidate will

- have a clear sense of purpose and audience, communicating ideas clearly and appropriately and with a conscious attempt to engage the reader
- use linguistic devices appropriately and make a clear attempt to sustain and develop ideas.

C

A **Grade A/A★** candidate will

- communicate in a convincing and compelling way
- engage the reader through subtle, well-judged and original language and ideas, including abstract concepts brought alive for the reader
- ensure all structure features, including varied and linked sentences and paragraphs, come together to serve the purpose of the text.

A

A★

Prior learning

Before you begin this unit, reflect on

- any particularly **impressive** texts, or parts of texts, you have written where your writing has really 'shone' and made an impact on your teacher (it could be an opening to a story or the end to a report)
- any non-fiction texts that have made an impression on you
- the **techniques** or **approaches** you already know that help your writing create an **impact** on the reader, or **sustain** their attention.

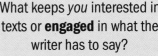

What keeps *you* interested in texts or **engaged** in what the writer has to say?

Engaging the reader

Learning objective

- To learn how to adjust your tone and language in inventive and original ways.

What does engaging the reader mean?

Engaging the reader means **capturing his or her attention**, and then **sustaining** it throughout the text.

Checklist for success

- For a Grade C you need to use the right form and style for the task.
- To target a Grade A/A★ you need to show originality to hold your reader's attention throughout. Your style and tone need to be fitting and totally engaging. Even in the most functional tasks there are choices you can make to help your writing stand out.

ACTIVITY

Read how two different students have responded to the same task: to persuade a Dragon's Den-style business man or woman to invest in their new gadget.

Student 1: Grade A

I appreciate you taking the time to read this letter. You must get a lot of crackpot inventors and slightly unhinged 'mad professor' types who want you to invest millions in some unlikely scheme or new product. I hope I am different. I have ...

- *carefully and methodically developed my idea with my own money*
- *tested it with clients, organisations and members of the public*
- *worked out exactly what I need in terms of finance.*

Student 2: Grade C

Thank you for reading this letter. I am writing to you in order to explain a really well-thought out idea which I think will appeal to you, and is worth investing in. I can assure you any money you spend will not go to waste. I have worked hard on the product and can be relied on to deliver success if you lend me what I want.

Discuss with a partner what makes the first letter more effective.

- How does the writer get on the right side of the reader?
- Look at the vocabulary and imagery used.
- Are there any structural or organisational features of writing to persuade?

Focus for development:
Being creative with form and style

ACTIVITY

Could you go even further? **Grade A★ writing** shows creative flair and style.

Student 3

Some years ago, a young man sold his house and invested his money in a secret product he was developing. In a small factory he sweated for hours at an old workbench to get the product ready for the outside world. I was that young man, and now I am ready to present it, ask for your help, and for you to place your faith in me.

Student 4

'Unique. Brilliant. Ingenious.' Three words used by renowned business guru Professor Thorpwell of Imperial College to describe my product. I hope you will feel the same way as I outline its features, capabilities and potential to change the world...

Discuss with a partner:

- What is successful about these two openings?
- What different techniques do they use to appeal to the reader?
- What do you notice about the change in tense in each?

ACTIVITY

A charity is trying to raise money to help communities in Africa build their own schools. Write the first two or three paragraphs of an email to send out to local business people. Try at least two of the more effective approaches you have seen here.

★ **Examiner's tip**

*Switching between **abstract concepts** such as 'faith' and 'hope' (things you cannot picture but which represent larger ideas) and **vivid detail** ('sweated for hours at an old workbench') will show the examiner you can control your language in a sophisticated way.*

Remember

- **Stick to the task: just because you are engaging the reader, don't forget the purpose.**
- **Try out alternative openings and original strategies to draw the reader in.**

Matching your language to the task

Learning objective

- To explore further how to develop language skills according to the form of text.

What does matching language to task mean?

Quite subtle changes of language can have a profound impact on the effect of a text. Different forms, different purposes and different audiences will require different language and approaches to writing.

Checklist for success

- Focus on the small things: types of sentence, organisation of paragraphs, simple structural features to shape the meaning of what you want to say.
- Make sure your language and tone are appropriate to the form and audience.

ACTIVITY

Read this extract from a Grade B response to the following task:

> Write an article for a magazine advising people on ways they can improve their lives through sport.

> Sport can improve all our lives. It makes us fitter so we think better; it offers us different ways of spending our leisure time; and it needn't be expensive.
> You can spend time with other people and you feel better in yourself.
> Of course, joining a club can be a good starting point. It can encourage you to be competitive...

Here are some reasons why this response does not receive a higher grade.

- The points in each paragraph are relevant but **not developed enough**.
- It lacks **facts or figures** that would help it sound convincing.
- It does not use **cause and effect language** (such as 'thus', 'consequently') that would make this clearer and more coherent.
- The **vocabulary is repetitive and uninspiring**. Using technical sports or health-related vocabulary would help.
- It could sound more authoritative by using appropriate **imperative verbs**.

Glossary
Imperative verbs tell you what to do: '**Run** up the stairs instead of walking!'

Focus for development:
Improving the language of advice

Read this extract from another response to the same task.

> The first, **and main**, benefit to **participating** in sport – at whatever level – is that it enhances and maintains your fitness. **Moreover** it allows for the intake of **oxygen** into the lungs and bloodstream, with its consequent effect on one's body, and forces you to exercise muscles and reduce the body's fat content.
>
> I recommend that you begin by initiating a full health check at your local GP surgery. In this way, you can identify which elements need attention, and develop strategies to improve your health...

Note down at least three ways in which this Grade A text improves on the Grade B text opposite.

Now write a further paragraph focusing on a new topic, for example socialising through sport. Add statistics (you can make them up if you wish) and advice as to what to do.

> A key additional benefit of sport is that it allows me to socialise with a wide range of people...

Next, read this public-health advice leaflet found in libraries and post-offices.

Discuss with a partner what subtle differences you notice in the style, tone, and organisation of this leaflet, compared with the article on the same subject on the previous page.

Consider

- the immediate impact the text needs to make
- the audience and the source of the leaflet.

THINK SPORT'S A WASTE OF TIME? THINK AGAIN!

Playing sport:
- ★ Enhances and maintains fitness
- ★ Allows for better respiration
- ★ Exercises the muscles you never use
- ★ Is fun, friendly and sociable.

You may feel you're not the sporty type. Or that sport is only for the young. Equally, you might feel it's over-competitive, aggressive and all about winning. The fact is that doctors see thousands of people every year whose best medicine would be half-an-hour throwing a tennis ball to their children. Statistics back up these findings, with nearly 1 in 3 people reporting improved well-being from exercise.

It's simple. Pop into see your GP for a quick check-up, find out what health issues you need to address, and then explore the sporting possibilities in your area. Use the Yellow Pages, the internet or visit our website...

http://www.nhs.uk/LiveWell/fitness/Pages/Fitnesshome.aspx

Many people say that there are health benefits to cooking and preparing food for yourself, rather than buying fast-food takeaways or ready-meals. Write the text for a two-sided leaflet for a doctor's surgery, which explains these benefits.

Remember

- Use professional language for informative or advisory texts that have a public readership.
- Adjust your tone and language subtly according to your audience.

Language for power and impact

Learning objective

- To understand how a range of literary devices can add power and impact to your writing.

What does power and impact mean?

Texts can convey certain information or particular messages, but the ones that affect how the reader thinks and responds have something extra. This comes from the language choices made.

Checklist for success

- For a **Grade C** you will need to use some basic literary techniques in your writing.
- To target a **Grade A/A★** you will need to use a wide range of literary techniques and select the appropriate techniques to make an impact on the reader.

ACTIVITY

Read the start of Review 1 about a wildlife documentary.

There is nothing exactly wrong with this piece.

- It is clear and gives reasons why the programme was bad.
- It gives some idea of the writer's viewpoint but is a little anonymous.
- It uses a reasonable, if not exactly rich vocabulary.

Now read Review 2 of the same programme. How does the writer engage the reader and create real impact?

You could consider the use of

- hyperbole
- repetition for effect
- adverbs to add power to adjectives (for example, 'wonderfully entertaining')
- metaphors related to the subject (for example, 'nature and the sea').

Now write your own paragraph in which you review or comment on either your football team's recent worst performance or a terrible TV programme you have seen.

Use at least two of AA Gill's techniques.

Review 1

It was clear from the start how poor the presenters were, but much worse was what they were given to say. It was full of clichés and things you had heard before. In fact, really embarrassing, even childish. It had the same old message about looking after the world, and even used really obvious pictures of Indians collecting shells.

Review 2

Worse than the empty Sea of Cortez, worse than the horrible presenters, was the utterly bereft script. A sea of intellectual plankton, an ocean of clichés, truisms, non-sequiturs and the mood music of happy-feely words, it was chronically embarrassing. The hug-a-halibut environmental message was depressingly childish; the anthropological element, showing us happy Indians collecting clams by hand then wagging a finger, telling us this was a model of sustainability for the world, was cretinously idiotic. Altogether, it was dispiriting and depressing.

AA Gill, The Times

> **Glossary**
> **Hyperbole**: deliberate exaggeration to make a point. 'He is simply the greatest, most gifted and charismatic tennis player of his or any other generation.'

Focus for development: Entertaining the reader

This sort of writing is clearly entertaining – we enjoy AA Gill's insults and criticisms. Here, Kathy Lette uses similar techniques to describe applying fake tan before a holiday.

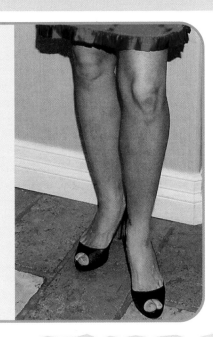

It said 'rich Mediterranean' on the bottle, but I was beginning to look more tandoori than tanning salon. My so-called 'tan' pulsated. It radiated. I looked as if I was wearing a tangerine wet suit, with darker elbow patches and kneepads. I was like a distress flare. People could employ me at the scene of a boating accident.

Good Housekeeping

Jot down two ways in which Kathy Lette has used hyperbole.

Consider her use of strong verbs to describe how the fake tan felt and her use of vivid similes (and how she develops her similes into a ridiculous idea).

Write a full account of a recent personal experience: for example, a shopping trip, a night out, a family visit or a sports event you took part in. Use as many of the techniques you have learnt here as you can.

- Use literary techniques to give your work power and impact, and to entertain and have an effect on the reader.
- These techniques are particularly useful in reviews, accounts of personal events or experiences, and discursive articles about issues of the day.

Using irony

Learning objective

- To understand how irony, used appropriately, can add to the impact of your writing.

What does irony mean?

Writers use irony to point out ridiculous or challenging ideas, or to draw attention to events, issues or situations.

For example, in a humorous text, a writer might place together two images for ironic effect:

> I had locked myself out. Through the window I could see the note I had left on the table. 'Don't forget door key,' it said.

This is **situational irony**.

Checklist for success

You need to use irony appropriately and selectively to help you get an A/A★ grade.

ACTIVITY

Discuss with a partner how this Grade A answer uses irony in at least two ways in response to the task:

> Write an article in which you describe how holidays don't always work out as they should.

> Most airports have 'meeting points' in case you get lost. The problem is that if you get lost, you usually can't find the meeting point. Or, if you're abroad, the words 'meeting point' are in a language you can't understand. In fact, it's a good idea to keep your mobile phone on at all times, although doing so will probably run down your battery so that when your friends finally get your message, you can't read their reply!

★ **Examiner's tip**

Note how the linking words and phrases ('the problem is', 'although') help set up the ironic situations. Phrases like this help link the text and ideas together coherently.

← ✈ Gates E 21 - 26

← 🛬 Ankunft Arrivals D,E

← Treffpunkt Meeting Point

Complete the contrasting 'ends' to these two ideas taken from the same response.

Often, you are told your hotel's beach is a 'short drive' away. However, in my experience, the drive may be short in distance but...

Every year when I go to a holiday destination with 'guaranteed sun all year round' I make sure I take...

Focus for development: Judging when to use irony

ACTIVITY

The same student has been asked to write a charity leaflet in which he appeals for more help for the homeless. How **appropriate** is his use of irony and sarcasm here?

Identify the uses of **irony** (where the writer has juxtaposed Tam's world and life at the Ritz), then the **sarcasm** (where the writer means the opposite of what he says).

- Which do you think is more effective?
- Is one likely to alienate the reader? Why?

Only yards from the Ritz Hotel, where tourists pay up to £100 for afternoon cream teas and cakes, a shabby figure sits in Green Park and holds a paper cup full of lukewarm coffee. A few pence are scattered on a mat next to him. Tonight, while the same tourists sleep in cotton sheets in air-conditioned hotel rooms, Tam will sleep on the streets. He'll have a wonderful night in the fresh air, enjoying the sweet smell of urine, the violence of passing strangers. Does he love his life? You bet he does! Please keep Tam on the streets by refusing to send money to us like the decent person you are. Instead, give money to any passing rich tourists you see. They deserve it!

⭐ Examiner's tip

It is easy to overuse sarcasm and irony. Whether you are using them for humorous or serious effect, include two or three examples at most, to have real impact.

ASSESSMENT FOCUS

Write your own charity text appealing for more help for the homeless. Try to use irony by juxtaposing different situations.

Remember

- Use irony to contrast or juxtapose ideas or situations for comic or serious effect.
- Use irony sparingly and, if used with sarcasm, make sure it fits the context.

Sustaining your style and tone

What does sustaining your ideas and tone mean?

Sustaining your ideas and tone means you keep to the task, follow what you have set out to say and use the same level of formality or informality throughout. Your style should be maintained, so that, for example, you do not suddenly switch from thoughtful advice to scathing sarcasm.

Checklist for success

- You need to be clear about your outcome: make clear your aim, then stick to it.
- Maintain one style throughout.

ACTIVITY

Read this response to the task:

> *Are we truly a nation of animal lovers? Write a magazine article to support or argue against this statement.*

> *Do people really love animals? In this article, I wish to explore the idea that people shouldn't be allowed to keep pets unless they have proved they can look after them. Sadly, far too many pet owners are without consideration for animals and do not deserve to have pets in their charge. My mate Tony is a perfect example. If you met him in the street, you'd say: 'Great guy! Love him.' But, oh boy, has he got a history. He's had more dead pets than some people have had hot dinners...*

1 Has the student set out clearly his aim in writing the article?

2 Is he answering the task set?

3 What effective techniques has he included so far?

4 How successful is he in maintaining his style and tone?

ACTIVITY

Rewrite the second paragraph so the style is more appropriate
and develops from the opening. You can use the same ideas, but
they need to be expressed more formally.

ACTIVITY

What might the editor want to change in this
next extract if the article were for

a) the main section of a national newspaper

b) a supplement for 14–16 year olds in the
   newspaper?

> It is amazing that some people – old ladies in
> particular – treat their pets better than they treat
> themselves. Their moggy gets the steak and they live on
> pet food. Honestly. It's happened. Staggering, eh?
> Makes you think. The fortitude and resilience of some
> hardy souls can only make you wonder.

A student writes...

*If we have to write for a younger
audience, doesn't that lead to
'dumbing down'? Will we still be able
to get good marks?*

Answer...

Remember that you are being
rewarded for the quality of your
sentences and the breadth of your
vocabulary. So, if writing for
young people, show the range of
your abilities but make the writing
appropriate for that age group.
However, don't ever use text
language and avoid slang!

Focus for development:
sustaining and extending your ideas

An effective plan will ensure you maintain your focus.

ASSESSMENT FOCUS

Produce a full and detailed plan in response to the task on page 92.
Try to include

- facts and figures supporting your view (search the
  Internet or invent any you need)
- relevant examples and, perhaps, an anecdote
- a consideration of people's different attitudes
- a conclusion suggesting what, if anything,
  should be done about the present situation.

Write the full article, for a broadsheet readership.

Remember

- **Your responses need to be consistent. Always read through to check that your
  ideas develop logically and your style has been sustained throughout.**

Writing to persuade and advise

Learning objectives

- *To learn how to persuade and advise effectively.*
- *To be aware of techniques which can be used to persuade and advise.*

What is the difference between persuading and advising?

When you **persuade**, you try to make someone accept your point of view, or do what you want.

Advising is similar, but you might offer alternatives and usually the focus will be on trying to help another person.

Checklist for success

- You need to examine persuasive writing critically: will it convince the reader?
- For advice, you need to ask yourself: is this detailed and logical enough, so someone can easily follow the advice?

ACTIVITY

Is this piece of advice persuasive?
Why/why not?
How could it be made more convincing?

> *You must be less aggressive. Sooner or later, the police will arrest you and then it will mean more than just a telling-off. You should get a therapist. That's what I'd do.*

Focus for development: Convincing the reader

Persuading

To be effective, you need to organise your ideas sensibly and use techniques to help persuade your audience that yours is the right point of view. You might

- focus on just one viewpoint
- offer both your view and the opposite point of view, as in an argument, but show that yours is the better viewpoint
- use emotive language to convince the reader
- include examples and anecdotes to illustrate your ideas
- employ rhetorical questions to hammer home what you say.

Glossary

emotive language is language which appeals to the emotions: Tiny starving babies, crying out for food...

anecdote: an extended example; a very short story

Notice how this Grade A/A★ extract uses persuasive techniques.

> There can be no doubt that Rome is ← definite, allowing no challenge
> the most beautiful of cities. It's a city ← list of three to impress
> full of life, history and love. Who can
> fail to be impressed by the Colosseum? ← rhetorical question to engage
> Who can wander through the narrow
> streets to the Trevi fountain without ← repetition to 'browbeat' the reader, plus emotive touch
> feeling the romance? It was there that ← anecdote
> once I sat beside a beautiful woman;
> we talked and fell in love, and she has
> been my wife for many years ...

 Examiner's tip

Be careful when using anecdotes. They need to be brief to be effective.

ACTIVITY

Write the opening paragraph of an article to persuade the reader that a city of your choice is the most beautiful in the world. Use persuasive techniques.

Advising

Here are the key techniques you can use to advise:

- setting out the problem, then delivering a solution
- working through different aspects of the problem and dealing with each in turn
- using imperative verbs ('**Do** this', '**Remember**')
- adopting a more sensitive approach ('Have you ever considered...?')
- using logic and evidence or experience to back up what you say.

ACTIVITY

Discuss with a friend how the advice in this **Grade C** response might be improved by

- adding detail
- adopting a more sensitive approach.

> You must find yourself a new boyfriend, it's as simple as that. It's no good just hoping things will improve, because I can assure you it's not going to happen. It's down to you now: you could tell him straight that it's all over or you could let him down more gently. In either case, you need to get on with it.

ASSESSMENT FOCUS

Write a letter to a friend to advise them to work harder in the lead-up to their exams and to persuade them it will bring rewards. Use the language techniques you have learnt to persuade and advise.

Remember

- **People generally respond better to sensitive advice and persuasion.**
- **Using suitable techniques will make your writing more convincing.**

Writing to inform and explain

Learning objectives

- To learn how to inform effectively and explain appropriately.

- To understand what is involved in each form of writing and the differences between them.

What is the difference between informing and explaining?

The difference between these two types of text is important.

Information writing involves presenting facts – and perhaps offering a personal interpretation of them.

Explanation writing involves going behind a set of facts and explaining why things have happened or how they can be improved. It demands an **interpretation of the information**.

Checklist for success

You can improve your **writing to inform** by including relevant facts and details.

When writing to explain it is best to use a logical approach, moving from information to explanation. For instance, you might choose to say

- what the situation is (information)
- how it came about (information and explanation)
- how we might resolve it (explanation).

This extract from a **Grade A★** response, both **informs** about having to move home and **explains** the problems involved.

information about the change →

personal slant on the change →

more details →

introduction to the problem →

explains how he felt about it →

> *Until you have gone from living with your father in a four-bedroom house in a country town, to living with your mother in a tiny terraced house in the roughest of areas, you can have no idea how difficult such a transition can be.*
>
> *Life with my father had been idyllic. I had my own king-size bedroom, HD television and even a quad bike for the weekends. Leaving all that was shattering. Suddenly I had no space, no spending money and no easy way of visiting the friends I had come to rely on. My life was in pieces – and the pieces were all grimy and, apparently, paid for with bank loans...*

Focus for development: Clarity and effectiveness

Informing

Writing to inform usually contains facts and an interpretation of them. Be prepared to research the facts when you can. However, in an exam you will probably have to make up any you don't know.

Explaining

When you begin to give reasons for the facts you have put forward, you might be offering explanations of

- why something happened and the effect it had
- how someone feels about something.

ACTIVITY

Write a paragraph to inform the reader about what life is like where you live. Include facts or statistics and an interpretation of them. For example: 'So, it is obvious that there needs to be more services coming in to help the pensioners…'

ACTIVITY

Focusing on your own local area, complete a table like this.

Problem with area	Explanation: how it came about	Explanation: how it could be solved
Vandalism	Not enough for youngsters to do	More youth centres or evening activities

Now look at this **Grade C** response from a student explaining what his/her area is like.

Identify both the **information** and the **explanations** that are offered in this response.

Then decide how you would improve it towards Grade A standard. Think about

- additional information that would make it better
- extra explanation that might be added.

My town is not the sort of place anyone would choose to live. There is nothing for young people to do because the council is not prepared to spend any money on what we need. At the same time, the older people have to sit indoors and just watch television because since the college closed there aren't even night classes for them to go to...

ASSESSMENT FOCUS

Write a letter to a travel company to

- inform them about what happened on the holiday you booked through them
- explain what went wrong.

Remember

- **Use detail wherever you can to make the events more credible.**
- **When you are explaining, give reasons.**

Writing to analyse and review

Learning objectives

- To learn how to analyse.
- To be familiar with the conventions of reviews.

What does it mean to analyse or review?

An **analysis** looks in detail at an object, situation, reaction or event. It looks beyond the obvious and endeavours to pick out different ideas for comment.

A **review** looks back at something and examines it critically. It offers opinions.

Checklist for success

Learn from examples in newspapers and magazines. See how they

- analyse events, from political events to football matches
- review television programmes, films and theatrical performances.

EXAMPLE

Read these **Grade A** responses.

This **analysis** considers a range of ideas in examining one situation.

> There are three important factors that have played a part in the demise of the corner shop: the fact that supermarkets carry such a range of different brands; the financial situation (small shops are often more expensive than larger stores); and, ironically, convenience – although corner shops are closer, the supermarket offers everything you need in the same place...

This **review** looks back and criticises, offering detail, not just comment.

> It is easy to see why our fund-raising day was not as successful as we hoped. First, there was the weather, which dampened everybody's spirits. If only we had taken the plunge and booked the marquee we considered and rejected! Then, our advertising was disappointing, to say the least...

ACTIVITY

Think about the last TV drama you watched. What would you say in a review analysing its strengths and weaknesses? Complete a table like this.

Strength/weakness of TV drama	Analysis: comments to be made

Focus for development:
Sustaining an approach

Any analysis or review needs to be sustained. This means **structuring your ideas** and then **using the same style** throughout.

It also means **linking your opening and ending**.

ACTIVITY

This opening and ending are from a **Grade C** TV drama review.

> I did not get excited about watching 'Dream On'. It sounded like one of those dramas my grandma used to watch on weekday afternoons. It starred John Gilbert and Francesca Prima, but since I had never heard of either of them, that was hardly a good recommendation. 'Give it a try,' said my friend Jo.
>
> [...]
>
> Jo was proved right. It had some really good episodes, like the one with the oil spillage and the hospital, but it was also about the wildest dreams of each main character, which tied in to the title, which I didn't expect. I really enjoyed it. So should you trust your friends' opinions? Yes, you should.

With a partner, identify the writer's opinions. Are they clear?

- Which parts at the end link back to the beginning?
- What techniques has the writer used to try to interest the reader?

How might you improve this opening and ending. Think about

- including more interesting vocabulary and using connectives
- extending some of the ideas using more precise detail
- making sure you maintain the same style for both parts.

ASSESSMENT FOCUS

Write the review of your chosen TV drama, using the notes you made in the activity on page 98.

- use an effective opening and ending
- analyse what happened, including relevant detail
- make your opinions clear.

Remember

- **When writing to analyse or review, you need to include details to support your opinions.**
- **Try to move beyond simple points; considering different interpretations will lead to higher marks.**
- **Sustain your style and link your opening and ending.**

Arguing with sophistication

Learning objective

- To write a high-level text which argues a particular point of view.

What does arguing with sophistication mean?

Writing to argue has some key conventions that you know already – but how can you improve to a Grade A★ level?

Checklist for success

- You need to recognise the **conventions** (typical features) of writing to argue.
- You need to use further sophisticated language and techniques to engage the reader.

ACTIVITY

Read the opening to this article.

If I were to make a list of all the rights I would be willing to fight for, it would not include the 'right to die'.

I expect the right to free speech, the right to protest, the right to freedom of movement, the right to vote. Those key rights make us free and autonomous beings, allowing us to determine the course of our lives and to carry out our daily activities without having the state peering over our shoulders.

But the right to die? The right to end it all?

The right to stop existing entirely? I don't want that right.

And yet that's the right that is being talked about and fought over most passionately these days. Elbowing aside even the ongoing battle for full freedom of speech, or the right to of migrants to travel freely to the UK, the 'right to die' has become the No.1 *cause célèbre* in contemporary Britain.

*Brendan O'Neill,
Big Issue*

Here, the writer's opinion is stated 'up front' and his viewpoint is clear. Jot down ways in which the writer uses some of the typical conventions of argument texts, such as

- repetition for effect
- rhetorical questions
- use of particular tenses
- patterns of three
- dealing with the other side of the argument
- imagery.

Focus for development: Choosing your approach

Read this opening to an article on the same topic.

> Approaching the staring glass doors of the hospital, I was struck by the faint odour of fading roses. A nurse wheeled someone past, and I caught a glimpse of a thin figure like a broken twig, staring right through me. Some would say this is a last resort for the desperate carer, others that it's a place where the old and unwanted come to die.

Note down:

- How has the writer tried to engage the reader with his/her use of language?
- What point of view emerges? Is it clear?
- How does the sequence of the sentences lead the reader into the detailed discussion?
- What might be the article's purpose (or purposes)?

A student writes...

I thought there were set ways of writing to argue, explain, etc.

Answer...

There are some typical features, but many texts have several purposes. For example, 'explain why it is a good idea to travel' is really arguing as much as it is explaining. So the key is to use a range of impressive skills.

Examiner's tip ★

Notice how the text uses literary language such as alliteration ('faint ... fading') and simile ('like a broken twig'), even though this is a text that is arguing and/or persuading.

ASSESSMENT FOCUS

Look at this task.

To get the top grades, it is important to select your approach and the skills you will use independently. For this task, consider

> *Write an article for MAX SPEED bike magazine in which you argue for the right for young people to ride their bikes on the pavement.*

- whether you will begin with a direct viewpoint which you develop through the response (as in the extract on page 100), or using a vivid account or image to set up your response (like the article opening above)
- how you can integrate the 'typical' features of writing to argue (see page 100)
- whether you need to adjust your tone in any way for the different audience the task requires.

Remember

- Texts can have a number of purposes – but will use the key conventions you know.
- Take the opportunity to show off your language skills, whatever the task or text type.

Grade Booster

Extended Exam Task

> Write an article for a cycle magazine offering advice to cyclists on how to deal with aggressive car and van drivers.

Draw on what you have learned about engaging the reader's interest to respond to this task.

Make sure you

- consider how imperatives can make your advice hit home ('Avoid …', 'Make sure …', etc.)
- use irony, if you can, to juxtapose what cyclists think their rights should be in certain situations, and the different ways in which car or van drivers see the same situation.

You could consider playing with the conventions of an advice/guidance text, perhaps using exaggerated language or ideas in the way Kathy Lette and AA Gill do on pages 88 and 89.

Evaluation – What have you learned?

With a partner, use the grade checklist below to evaluate your work on the Extended Exam Task.

- I can write with a convincing, compelling tone and use detailed ideas which engage the reader from the start.
- I can use varied and carefully selected linguistic devices such as irony to create impact on the reader.

- I can provide succinct advice supported by developed evidence.
- I can use a wide range of linguistic devices, including irony, in an effective and appropriate way.
- I can sustain tone and ideas throughout.

- I can write well thought out, detailed, reasoned ideas showing consequences and implications.
- I can use linguistic devices including exaggeration and imperatives as well as a range of more subtle ones, such as irony.

- I can use more detailed ideas and support my advice with reasons.
- I can begin to use linguistic devices such as imperatives, exaggeration and rhetorical questions.

- I can engage the reader, developing some ideas, but the tone and linguistic devices I use are not always sustained or appropriate.

You may need to go back and look at the relevant pages from this section again.

Introduction

In this section you will

- find out the exact facts about, and requirements of, the written element of Unit 1 of the exam
- read, analyse and respond to two sample answers by different candidates
- plan and write your own answer to a sample question
- evaluate and assess your answer and the progress you have made.

Why is exam preparation like this important?

- You need to know exactly what you need to do in order to feel confident when you sit the real thing.
- Looking at sample answers by other students will help you see what you need to do to improve your own work.
- Planning and writing a full sample written response after you have completed the whole chapter will give you a clear sense of what you have learned so far.

Key Information

Unit 1 is 'Understanding and Producing Non-Fiction Texts'.

- It has an exam of **2 hours**, worth **80 marks**.
- It is worth **40%** of your overall English Language GCSE mark.
- Section A of the exam is on 'Reading'.
- Section B of the exam is on 'Writing'.

Section B Writing

- The writing part of the exam is **1 hour long**, and is worth **40 marks**.
- It is worth **20%** of your overall English Language mark.
- In the exam you will be given **TWO** writing tasks.
- The first writing task is a **shorter task** worth **16 marks**. You should probably spend about **25 minutes** on this task, including reading and planning time.
- The second writing task is **slightly longer**, and worth **24 marks.** You should probably spend about **35 minutes** on this task, including reading and planning time.

The Two Writing Tasks – What's Different?

- The most obvious difference will be in how much you might write in response.
- The shorter task is likely to be more straightforward, perhaps a letter to a friend, or something in which the format is short and more easily controlled. Whatever you do, don't spend more time on this than the 'longer' second task.
- The longer task may ask you to consider different viewpoints or develop your ideas a little more.
- The tasks will change every year, but you have been working on some of the typical questions in this section so far. Here are two further examples.

Short question [16 marks]	*A family friend from abroad is coming to visit your home town or area. Write to them and describe what there is of interest to see and do.*
Longer question [24 marks]	*Some people think it is wrong that members of the public are allowed to be humiliated in talent shows by celebrity judges. Write an article for a magazine in which you argue for or against this idea.*

The Assessment

The assessment objective for Writing (AO4) states that you must be able to:

- Write to communicate clearly, effectively and imaginatively, using and adapting forms and selecting vocabulary appropriate to task and purpose in ways that engage the reader.
- Organise information and ideas into structured and sequenced sentences, paragraphs and whole texts, using a variety of linguistic and structural features to support cohesion and overall coherence.
- Use a range of sentence structures for clarity, purpose and effect, with accurate punctuation and spelling.

Targeting the top grades

Some of the key differences between a C and an A/A★ are as follows:

Grade C candidates	See example on page 106
• write with general accuracy in their sentences and punctuation and use a variety of sentence forms (short and long), although sometimes the effect has not been thought through (they just happen to be short and long) • occasionally, but not often, choose sentences and vocabulary which are bold and original • use paragraphing which is effective and helps make the meaning clear, but whereas the top candidates will skilfully change or adapt structure to create an effect on the reader, a C grade student will do this less often.	©

Grade A/A★ candidates	See example on page 108
• confidently use language for creative delight: their language is sometimes surprising and original so that it doesn't feel like the marker has read it before – but it is still under control and is appropriate to the task and purpose • produce ambitious writing – which means students don't just stick to simple or not very interesting vocabulary or sentences, but use a wide range of different types and choices for particular effects (they have consciously thought how their sentences, for example, will affect the reader) • use convincing and compelling arguments, really making the reader *want* to read.	A A★

Exploring sample responses

Read the following extract from a student's response to the second, longer question from page 104.

Consider the key elements a marker would look for:

- how clearly and effectively the writer has conveyed his/her ideas
- how appropriate and well-chosen the vocabulary is
- whether the structure and organisation fluently guide the reader through the ideas
- how much of an impact on the meaning the range of sentences and choice of language features have
- whether, overall, this text engages and interests the reader throughout.

Example one

Celebrity rudeness

We all love talent shows such as the 'X Factor' and 'Britain's Got Talent'. These shows show people making fools of themselves as well as showing off their talents, such as singing, dancing. My view is that it has all gone a bit too far and OTT. It's fine to have some criticism if you need to improve and you are not singing as well as you could, but if you are a poor person with some trashy job with no real talent, it's not fair to make you feel like a dummy.

Sometimes, what is even worse is that the person who is criticised doesn't even realise what is happening. That is terrible. It is like a private joke between the celebrities and the audience. I think it is like bullying in school behind someone's back when they don't notice. For example, calling children a horrible name but not to their face.

The thing is the shows would not work unless they had people making fools of themselves. If it was just people with talent it would be boring, and I admit that I am watching when these programmes come on. So I am as bad as the programme makers I suppose.

But you can't really stop people wanting to take part and no one really knows until someone opens their mouth whether they are going to be an idiot or a genius. I suppose you could choose not to show the really stupid ones, but probably some of them don't mind. Perhaps they would rather be on telly even if it's making themselves look stupid?

This leads me to my final point. You would need to be from a different planet not to know what goes on in these shows. Everyone knows what they are letting themselves in for – nobody is completely innocent are they? And perhaps they like being shouted at by Simon Cowell. In fact, it might be the highlight of their lives, which is pretty sad – but it's their choice. No one forced them to sing out of tune or dance clumsily!

So, as long as there are people willing to humiliate themselves, I guess it's OK. I will continue watching and may be one day I will be the daft one on stage making a fool of myself! Simon Cowell beware!

Examiner feedback

This is generally a clear, well-argued article with accurate sentences and organised paragraphs. There is a good beginning and ending, and the candidate uses some variety of sentences, sometimes to good effect. There is a sense of how the text might affect the reader but occasionally the article reads slightly informally. The language is generally clear but there is some unnecessary repetition of words, and a little more variety would be welcome.

Suggested grade: C

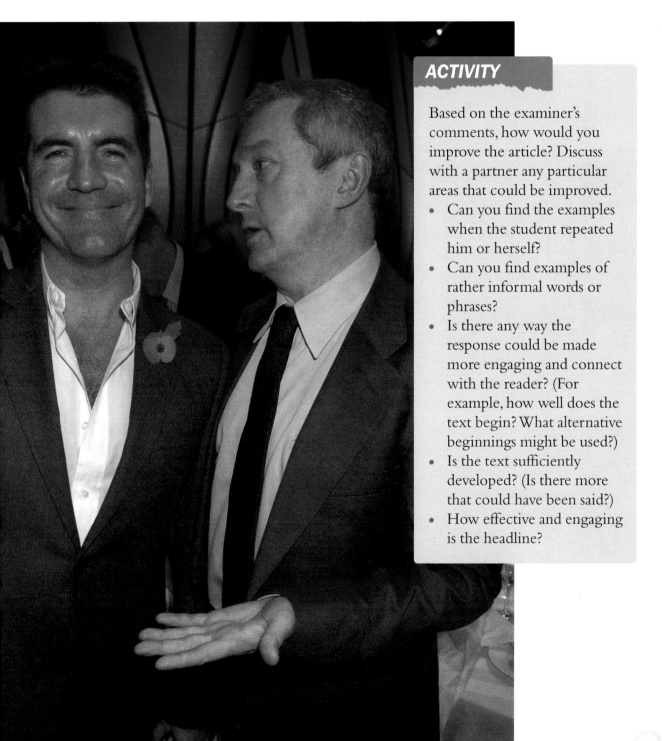

ACTIVITY

Based on the examiner's comments, how would you improve the article? Discuss with a partner any particular areas that could be improved.

- Can you find the examples when the student repeated him or herself?
- Can you find examples of rather informal words or phrases?
- Is there any way the response could be made more engaging and connect with the reader? (For example, how well does the text begin? What alternative beginnings might be used?)
- Is the text sufficiently developed? (Is there more that could have been said?)
- How effective and engaging is the headline?

Now read this response to the same question by a different candidate:

Example two

Clever headline engages reader →

Use of short, direct opening sentence speaks to reader →

Range of punctuation used to emphasise point →

New paragraph used to introduce counter argument →

Repeating questions engages reader →

Connective coherently links new paragraph and new point →

Slight shift in emphasis loses the flow of argument →

Cleverly structured ending links to title →

BRITAIN'S GOT IDIOTS
How we love humiliating ourselves and others on prime-time TV ←

Prime-time television can be so cruel. It is a talent show: on comes a poor, unemployed middle-aged man with terrible fashion sense. He tries to sing and it is awful, and the crowd laugh, the judges rip him to shreds and he leaves the stage in tears.

Is this entertainment? Is this fun? If it is, then it is more like when the Romans used to throw the gladiators to the lions. In fact, perhaps we will only be satisfied when the singers are thrown to real lions! One day, hurtful comments will not be enough – perhaps the celebrity panel could press a button and the poor singer or dancer will drop through the stage into a bottomless pit. Perhaps that is a bit far-fetched, but to me it's not as unlikely as you might think.

Some might argue that nobody forces people to audition for these shows, that no one forces them to apply, or to spend years preparing some terrible act no one wants to see. They would say, 'it's their own stupid fault'. Some might argue that these people have a right to do as they wish because it is a free country where people should be allowed to make a complete fool of themselves in front of millions. Well, I am not one of them. ←

This sort of talent (or 'lack of talent') show encourages the worst in you and me. They teach us to laugh at those who aren't naturally attractive, or who are different. Would this be allowed in my school? Of course not. The answer is 'no'. In fact, it would be seen as a form of bullying. Yes, people might lose their jobs for not being good enough, but rudeness, humiliation and spitefulness would not be acceptable.

In addition, I would like to know if there are any statistics which tell us whether people humiliated on talent shows suffer long-term problems. Imagine if you were made a complete fool of in front of millions. Imagine what it would be like walking down your street with people pointing at you and calling out, 'Hey! Look – there goes that idiot from the TV!'. Some people might be able to cope, and some (very sad) people might actually enjoy it because for them being famous for five minutes – even if it's for something humiliating – is better than not being famous at all.

No – as far as I am concerned, I'm going to press the buzzer three times on these talent shows. It's X – X – X from me – and, I hope, from you too. ←

← By-line fits the form and adds information

← Use of rhetorical questions support point

Final short sentence of paragraph creates impact →

← Pattern of three nouns in a list further support argument

Sense of personal engagement and 'voice' coming through

Before you read the examiner feedback, note down any improvements you think the student could make to his or her response. In particular, have a look at some of the literary techniques used: for example, types of imagery, sound effects, or a note of irony.

Examiner feedback

The candidate has shown a structured and well-argued response to the task. The argument is developed and sustained, and the organisation of ideas flows coherently; the beginning and end, in particular, are powerful and compelling, helping to convince the reader. The vocabulary is often ambitious, and overall the candidate engages the reader with some original ideas and expressive language.

Suggested grade: A/A★

EXAM PRACTICE TASK

You are helping to organise a charity day at school to raise money for a hostel for homeless youngsters.

> Write a letter which will be sent to all parents, persuading them to come along to the charity day. [**24 marks**]

Remember

- Read the task carefully, selecting the key information you need: what is the purpose, audience and form
- Plan very quickly what you are going to say.

If you only do 5 things...

1 Read a range of non-fiction texts and note the ways that the best writers interest and engage you. Draw on what you know about the conventions of different forms of writing, but don't let these be a straitjacket – be flexible in order to make an impact on the reader.

2 Where appropriate, plan for original ideas and different perspectives on the task set; this will make the reader sit up and take notice.

3 Develop detailed ideas so that any points you make will usually have a further stage, or other points within them can be drawn out.

4 Use a wide range of ambitious vocabulary – but keep it appropriate to the task and audience – and use powerful and original imagery – especially similes and metaphors – to make your writing come alive.

5 Use a variety of sentences, both in terms of length (short and long) and in terms of type (simple, compound and complex).

What's it all about?

We can all speak and listen, but if we develop our skills, we can communicate much better throughout our lives. Speaking and listening involves many skills that can be used elsewhere in English work and offers an immensely enjoyable change from reading and writing.

How will I be assessed?

You will get **20% of your English Language marks** for your Speaking and Listening ability.

You will have to complete three Speaking and Listening Controlled Assessments.

You will be marked on your

- presenting
- discussing and listening
- role-playing.

What is being tested?

Your teacher will be judging your ability to

- speak clearly and purposefully
- organise your talk and sustain your ideas
- speak appropriately in different situations
- use standard English and a variety of techniques when speaking
- listen and respond to what others say and how they say it
- interact with others, shaping meanings through suggestions, comments and questions and drawing ideas together
- create and sustain different roles.

Presentations

Introduction

This section of Chapter 3 shows you how to

- give a presentation to an audience
- select a topic and structure your talk
- decide what content you might include
- use a range of techniques to boost your performance.

Why is it important to develop good presentational skills?

- We can all talk generally about topics, but to get top grades you need to demonstrate a range of presentation skills.
- Planning, structuring and enlivening your presentation makes success easier to achieve.
- You will use the same skills in other parts of the English course, for example when you write in the examination.
- It is likely you will have to use these presentational skills throughout your working life. Developing these skills now will help you succeed in whatever you choose to do.

A **Grade C** candidate will

- adapt their talk to the situation, using standard English confidently
- engage the listener through their use of language, so that information, ideas and feelings are communicated clearly.

A **Grade A/A*** candidate will

- use assured standard English
- vary sentence structures to help hold the attention of the listeners
- use a broad range of vocabulary employing a style and register suitable for the task
- maintain the listeners' interest throughout.

Prior learning

Before you begin this unit, think about

- times when you have heard someone talk in a formal situation: which speakers have interested you most and why?
- how you have been taught to structure your formal essays.

When you watched someone on a news programme, listened in assembly or had an outside speaker in school, how did the speaker try to hold your attention? How did they begin and end their talk?

Which of their techniques might you be able to use?

Which essay techniques could you use when preparing and delivering a presentation?

Understanding your audience

Learning objective

- To consider what an audience expects and how to address its needs.

★ Examiner's tip

Remember – there are no marks for reading from prepared notes in Speaking and Listening assessment tasks.

What does understanding your audience mean?

Your **audience** is a vital consideration when making a presentation. You might be talking to a class, an individual, a group of people outside school or an assembly.

You need to **understand** what type of presentation is required. Should it be

- factual
- argumentative or persuasive (supporting a point of view)
- entertaining?

You also need to use an appropriate **speaking style**.

Checklist for success

- You need to be clear about who you will be addressing and what they expect.
- You need to adapt your language, content and style to suit your audience.

ACTIVITY

You are going to deliver a presentation on how your school's rules should be changed. With a partner, decide how you would vary your style and content for

- the headteacher
- your classmates
- a meeting of interested parents.

In each case, ask yourself:

- What will they already know?
- What do I need to tell them?
- How can I convince them to share my views?

Focus for development: Adapting vocabulary, content and style to audience

ACTIVITY

This **Grade A★** presentation has the right **tone** and **vocabulary** for the audience.

'In all my dreams, before my helpless sight, /
He plunges at me, guttering, choking, drowning...'
Few poems have this power: to affect our senses, to
make us feel the suffering, to plunge us into the
midst of horror and pain. Wilfred Owen's poetry still
has this power to shock, even a century on, and,
incredibly, the power to transform from a picture of
a specific time to a universal image of war...

Who do you think the student is talking to? Give reasons.

If he were talking to Year 7s, what might he say instead of

- 'affect our senses'
- 'plunge us into the midst of horror and pain'
- 'transform'?

ACTIVITY

Read this extract from a **Grade C** presentation. The student struggled at times to find interesting vocabulary. Try to improve the

- choice of words (nouns, adjectives, verbs and adverbs)
- variety of sentence lengths and types (see pages 74 and 75)
- style (making it less chatty).

> I know many of you will laugh at me for having *Sharpe* as my favourite television programme because it's what your mum and dad used to watch. Well, I've seen it on satellite and although the programmes were made quite a long time ago they are still quite good. It's about soldiers from Britain fighting against Napoleon. The sorts of things that happen are fights to win forts and there is quite a lot of falling out amongst the men. Sharpe is always the hero. He wins all the battles and all the women too.

ASSESSMENT FOCUS

Prepare the opening of a presentation to your year group, describing your favourite place and explaining why you like it. Use an appropriate style.

You might include

- your earliest memories of the place
- a precise description of what it is like
- why it is special for you
- a story about it which would be suitable for your audience.

Remember

- **Use different styles and approaches for different audiences.**
- **Focus on your choice of tone and vocabulary.**

Choosing a topic

Examiner's tip

Try to choose a subject you can talk about at length and will be confident to answer questions on.

Examiner's tip

Some speaking tasks are more difficult than others. For example, it is harder to persuade someone that your football team is the best than to describe what happened during a match. You gain more credit for completing a more complex task.

Why is choice of topic important?

If the **topic** is something you feel comfortable with because you know a good deal about it, your presentation will flow better and be richer in detail.

Checklist for success

• You need to choose your topic and approach carefully, thinking about how you can make it interesting for your audience.
• You need to know or find out as much as possible about your topic.
• When you are asked to give a presentation, you need to make sure the topic allows you to do your best. If not, negotiate a change of topic or emphasis if possible, or research enough information so that you can do yourself justice.

ACTIVITY

Which of these topics could you talk about most successfully? Why?

• Argue that knife crime is sensationalised in the press.
• Advise the parents of primary school students to send their children to your school.
• Explain why teenagers prefer technology to real life.

Focus for development: Successful topics

ACTIVITY

• If you could choose your presentation topic, what would it be? Give reasons why.
• How would you approach your topic? Would you want to describe, persuade your audience or put forward an argument, for example? Give reasons why.

Examiner's tip ★

*Your audience **will not** want to hear lists of facts, rambling stories or unconnected ideas. They **will** be interested by new ideas, touches of humour and facts that make them stop and think.*

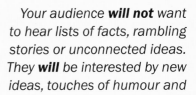

Look at these two extracts, showing how different students approached the same topic.

With a partner, decide what is good about the first one and what advanced skills are demonstrated by the second.

Grade C

> The trip was a huge success. We met at 6.45, which was really early for most of us, then the bus arrived at about seven. I rushed straight to the back, to sit with Jenny and Asma, and a whole gang of us were on the back seat. Mind you, we didn't feel like singing that early in the morning. I swear Lucy was still chewing her breakfast when she got on...

Grade A

> I know what the reaction from most of you will be when I ask this but... how can anybody justify a trip to Alton Towers in school time? And before you start, yes, I know everyone enjoys it – but what in the world does it have to do with education? Wouldn't it be better to sit in lessons during the week and go to an amusement park at the weekend? Obviously, we all love the excitement of rushing on to a coach in the early hours of the morning with our hair just washed and still wet and our latest trainers dazzling our friends, yet...

ASSESSMENT FOCUS

You must make a 5–10 minute presentation to your class on the topic of 'The Trip'.

Decide

- which trip you will talk about
- how you will approach the topic, to best show your abilities
- what details you will use to support your points and interest your audience.

Remember

- **You must know about a topic to talk about it confidently.**
- **You will be rewarded for responding well to a more complex task.**

Researching and developing Content

Learning objective

- *To understand the importance of selecting and using content wisely.*

Why is a focus on content important?

- If your **content** is not interesting and relevant, you will not engage your audience.
- Listening is a different skill from reading. What you say must be understood and each point needs to be clear and precise. If the audience misses a point, they have no second chance to hear it.
- If you confuse your audience, you are likely to lose their attention.

Checklist for success

- You need to have enough information about your topic so that you avoid making irrelevant points or unconvincing claims.
- You need details and examples to support your main points.
- You need to be very clear about the purpose of your talk when selecting your content.

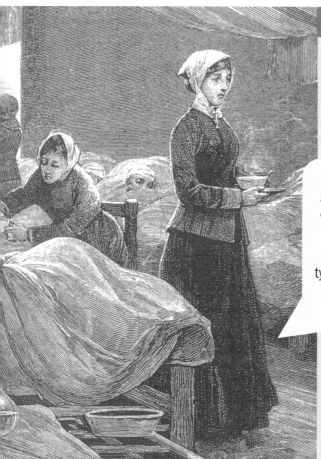

ACTIVITY

This extract is from an A★ Grade presentation. The student is clearly comfortable with her topic because she has researched it thoroughly. It is full of detail and uses a rich vocabulary and varied sentence structures.

> Florence Nightingale took a group of 38 nurses to the Scutari Barracks Hospital in October 1854, to care for wounded British soldiers in the Crimean War. Although many were in agonies because of their injuries, many more were dying of terrible diseases like typhus fever, typhoid and cholera. The nurses cared for these soldiers in a way we have come to expect nowadays, but back then it was a revolutionary move...

Discuss:

- How many facts does the student include?
- How does she use the facts?
- What is her main point?
- How does she try to make us interested in Florence Nightingale?

Focus for development: Selecting effective content

Be selective in your choice of materials. Just because you find a detail interesting does not necessarily make it appropriate to your presentation.

So, for example, the talk on Florence Nightingale

- offers facts which give a clear picture of what was happening
- indicates the problems the nurses faced
- shows the number of nurses coping with them
- moves on to talk about how the care was revolutionary for its time.

It only includes facts relevant to the main topic – nursing.

ACTIVITY

You have been asked to present to your class a review of a film you have seen recently.

Decide which of the following points you would or would not include in your review, and why.

Character details	Your range of hobbies
When you saw it	Why you watched it
Your favourite forms of entertainment	Length
Storyline	Best/worst moments
Themes	The last production you saw before this one
Others' opinions of it	Alternative ways of spending your time
Comparison with other similar productions	

Of course you don't only get marks for your main points, but also for how you comment on them.

ACTIVITY

Compare these extracts from students' reviews.

- To what extent does the first review rely on description?
- How has the second student improved her review by making her comments more critical?

Grade C response

I think 'Boys will be Boys' is a programme that would appeal to anyone. I thought about my own brothers when I was watching it. I laugh at them, and I laughed at the boys on the screen. The show made fun of Steve, Imran and Ben, but I have to say the girls seemed ridiculous too: Maeve with her hair and Sammy with her turned-up nose. She tries to be <u>so</u> superior...

Grade A response

My sister loves 'Boys will be Boys'. Mind you, she loves boys full-stop, so maybe she's not the most reliable judge of the programme. She adores Steve because 'he's cute', but she has always reacted to Bambi in much the same way, so take that as you will.

Examiner's tip

When you research, remember that finding the facts is just the start. What counts is how you use and develop your ideas around them.

The information you've found needs to be part of your central message or purpose: for example, to argue that Florence Nightingale changed nursing across the world. Your research findings need to support that message.

Effective research

Before your presentation, you can **research** the facts you need. That does not mean finding out everything you can about a subject; you need to be selective, finding information which suits your purpose.

ACTIVITY

If you were researching the talk about Florence Nightingale and how she revolutionised nursing care, which of these websites do you think might be useful? Write notes to explain why.

- Florence Nightingale Museum: www.florence-nightingale.co.uk
- Jon Baines Tours – Florence Nightingale in Istanbul: www.jonbainestours.co.uk
- Florence Nightingale quotations: www.en.thinkexist.com/quotes/Florence_Nightingale/

Use the internet to find five relevant and interesting facts about Florence Nightingale.

Having found relevant material, you need to decide how to put it across effectively to your audience. For example, you might use

- diagrams or pictures
- PowerPoint slides
- anecdotes.

A PANORAMIC VIEW OF THE SEA OF AZOF, KERTCH, YENIKALE, ARABAT, &c.
SHEWING THE POSITION RECENTLY TAKEN BY THE ALLIES, LIKEWISE COMPRISING THE WHOLE OF THE CRIMEA.

Finishing well

Organise the facts below into a conclusion for a presentation which argues that Florence Nightingale is one of the greatest women to have lived.

Try to offer a conclusion which

- summarises your argument
- includes only relevant details
- leaves the audience with a positive impression of Florence Nightingale (and of you as a presenter!)

> Died 1910, aged 90
>
> 1907: International conference of Red Cross Societies listed her as a pioneer of the Red Cross Movement
>
> Was asked by US for advice on caring for the sick during their Civil War
>
> Called 'Lady of the Lamp' because of her hours tending the sick in the Crimea
>
> First woman to receive the British Order of Merit

ASSESSMENT FOCUS

You are preparing to talk to your class on your favourite hobby. Complete a table like the one below, which is about running.

Summarise:

- the points you would select
- why you would choose them
- how you would develop them – to show their effects or go into more detail.

Point	Why	Development
Running is healthy	Health issues important at any age	How much weight I lost / How my life changed as I became healthier
15 million British people run	Pleasure / Competition / Feeling of well-being	Age no barrier: Constantina Dita became world marathon champion at 38; Buster Martin ran in the London marathon aged 101

ACTIVITY

Look at this Grade C response.

> So, Florence Nightingale was famous all over the world. She was even respected in the United States and by the Red Cross Movement by the time she died in 1910. The Lady of the Lamp, as she was called, was the first woman to receive the British Order of Merit and she certainly deserved it.

Produce a better conclusion by

- organising the material more effectively so that the ideas develop more logically
- adding more detail and commenting appropriately
- rephrasing or totally rewriting where necessary.

Remember

- **Content needs to be appropriate for your purpose and audience.**
- **Research if necessary but be selective in what you use.**
- **Ensure all your content is relevant and supports your main points.**

Structuring your presentation

What does structuring your presentation mean?

In a **well-structured** presentation, the speaker knows what they are going to say, and in what order. Planning a strong opening and a memorable ending should be part of the structuring.

Checklist for success

- You need to prepare your presentation in detail.
- You need to consider the different ways you can begin, develop and end your presentation.

ACTIVITY

You have been asked to give a presentation about your favourite school subject.

- List the points you might make.
- Put them into a logical order.
- How would you begin your presentation?
- How might it end?

A student writes...

Surely planning a presentation is just like planning an essay.

Answer...

In many ways, they are alike. However, when you are talking, you can develop ideas further on the spot and interact with your audience using different tones of voice, facial expressions and gestures.

Focus for development:
Planning, openings and endings

A **bulleted plan** can contain all the relevant information you need whilst speaking.

ACTIVITY

Complete a table like the one here, developing your ideas. The right-hand column is where you can add more detailed information.

Main idea	Points to be included
Teachers	Miss Spivey (obsessed with Crimean War) Mr Jenkin (anecdote about haunted mansion)
Lessons	dramatic reenactments
Trips	

Using your plan, run through what you would say.

Openings

Your opening **sets the tone** for what follows. It should make it clear what you intend to talk about and immediately engage your audience.

Some possible openings:

- **rhetorical questions**: 'Have you ever had the wrong tooth extracted?'
- **relevant humour**: 'Have you heard the one about the dentist, the missing tooth and the court action for damages?'
- **powerful facts**: 'Last year in Britain, 57% of children under the age of 10 had at least one tooth extracted…'

Endings

A memorable ending can leave a powerful impression upon your audience. You could try

- a summary of your argument
- one final, convincing point
- a joke
- a rhetorical question.

Which of these you choose will depend on your topic, purpose and audience.

ACTIVITY

Use these techniques to write three interesting openings for your presentation about your favourite school subject.

ACTIVITY

Look at this Grade A★ ending and decide with a partner

- what the purpose of the talk is
- how the speaker hopes to impress the audience at the end.

Grade A★ ending

Inaction and ineptitude on the part of governments across the world have led us to this state. It's not too late to save the world but it's going to have to be last-minute stuff, because midnight is approaching. And if you think you can party through the night and all will be well tomorrow, you're wrong. There won't be a tomorrow… Fight to make things better, petition parliament… If we all use our grey matter, there might still be hope.

ASSESSMENT FOCUS

Plan in detail a presentation to persuade local business leaders to donate to a charity supported by your school.

- Bullet-point your plan.
- Prepare, in advance, what you are going to say to open and close your presentation.

Remember

- **A detailed plan is essential for success.**
- **Openings and endings are vital parts of any presentation.**

Using standard english, imagery and repetition for effect

Learning objectives

- To appreciate the importance of standard English in presentations.

- To understand how imagery and repetition for effect can add to the quality of performances.

Glossary

Standard English: the form of English which is grammatically correct – not the more casual, colloquial form you might use with friends.

imagery - the use of imaginative comparisons, such as similes and metaphors (see page 18).

What does using these techniques for effect mean?

Using **standard English** creates a more formal tone, which is expected as part of your assessment.

Including **imagery** and **repeating** words or phrases will help engage or evoke a response from your listeners and emphasise your key points.

Checklist for success

You need to understand the differences in grammar and vocabulary between talking informally to friends and speaking in more formal situations. Listen to news presenters on television, as a reminder of what standard English sounds like.

Planning imagery and repetition into your presentation can create more of an impact.

ACTIVITY

Read this extract from a formal presentation.

> See, it's clear, init? There's them that's got the cash, sitting on it like some big greedy thing, and them that 'asn't. You gotta find some guy with big wads – and I'm talking major league money now – and make 'im cough up his big wads. Then yer charity's got wads of stuff to work with...

- What is inappropriate about the use of English here?
- How effective is the imagery?
- Comment on the use of repetition. Is it effective?

Presenting in standard English means using correct grammar and avoiding informal language or **slang**.

- Generally use verbs in sentences, rather than offering half-completed thoughts.
- Speak in full sentences.
- Use conventional vocabulary rather than street language.

ACTIVITY

Rewrite the example above using more formal English.

Focus for development: Imagery and repetition

This extract is from a **Grade A★** presentation. It is in perfect standard English and has been enriched by using imagery and repetition.

The years thunder on but there is no sign of a break in the darkness for so many in Africa. Darkness that oppresses. That chokes. That destroys. Support, for many, is just a gun pointing away from them rather than at them; relief is a bomb that fails to explode. Still, they are like shattered fragments in wars that know no boundaries and never seem to end, wars that rumble across the continent, wars that take lives indiscriminately, run by men who can have no heart and no soul...

ACTIVITY

Identify the imagery and repetition in the extract. Comment on the linked metaphors and the long final sentence and their effects.

Explain the effect of 'That chokes. That destroys.' These are not conventional sentences. How are they used?

Discuss with a partner:

- why each example you have found is appropriate for the purpose
- how these devices affect the listener.

ASSESSMENT FOCUS

Examiner's tip ★

Remember, using repetition because you have run out of ideas is not good. However, using it to hammer home a point is a strength and will earn you marks.

ACTIVITY

Improve this extract from a **Grade C** response by adding imagery and repetition.

And in the evening there is nothing to do at all. Just because we live in a village, no one seems to remember we exist. There's nothing here and we can't even go into town because the bus service stops at seven o'clock. It's pathetic...

ASSESSMENT FOCUS

Produce the opening of a presentation about the job you would like to have when you are older.

Use standard English, some imagery and at least one example of repetition for effect.

Remember

- **You are expected to use standard English in most presentations.**
- **By including imagery and repetition for effect, you will make your presentation more impressive.**

Using rhetorical questions, humour and exaggeration for effect

Glossary

rhetorical question: a question asked of an audience to involve them, without expecting a reply – 'How could anyone ever think that?'

exaggeration: making things seem bigger to hammer home a point – 'I've told her a million times not to exaggerate.'

What does using these techniques for effect mean?

The careful use of **humour**, **rhetorical questions** and **exaggeration** will appeal to your listeners and bring variety of tone to your presentation.

Checklist for success

- You need to used rhetorical questions, humour and exaggeration sparingly and only when suitable for a topic or an audience.
- You need to plan in advance which of these techniques you will use.

ACTIVITY

Read this extract from a presentation to a group of university lecturers.

With a partner, decide which rhetorical questions, humour and exaggeration are inappropriate.

> So, how are you guys doing? I've got to say, you look pretty bored: I suppose you always do. Anyway, I've managed to cheer up thousands and thousands of conferences like this one, so it was worth your while turning up today. Actually, it's just as well you came today, because I don't suppose many of you will be around much longer. I bet your doctors are pretty busy, aren't they?

Focus for development: Making presentations more interesting

Rhetorical questions

Rhetorical questions will challenge the audience to think more actively about an issue. For example:

'Can this ever be acceptable?' – desired reaction: 'Probably not!'

'Why, then, have these changes been introduced?' – desired reaction: 'Tell me more.'

> The royal family is an institution we should treasure. They stand above politics and give stability to our country. Without them, we might not have our current status in the world. It's not even as if they are so different from us any more: the princes are just ordinary young men, with ordinary interests and ordinary problems,

Humour

If you can add witty touches it may encourage the audience to warm to you. Try:

- a funny **anecdote** (or short story) to support your point, for example: 'I caught measles on holiday. Well, actually, measles caught me. What happened was…'
- an **aside** (a quick 'throw-away' comment) for example: 'I knew you wouldn't be interested in this photograph of a steam train. My dad said I'd do better with a picture of Lily Allen…'

Exaggeration

Be careful not to over-use exaggeration, but used sparingly it can have considerable impact.
For example:

'Crack SAS commandoes couldn't track down and bring back my father when he's out for a night on the town.'

A student writes…

I always try to use a rhetorical question to begin my presentations. It seems to get everybody listening.

Delivering your presentation

⭐ **Examiner's tip**

Make sure any props that you might choose to pass around during your talk don't distract your audience. Use PowerPoint to identify the main points you will be developing or to illustrate your ideas (with a short video or photograph, perhaps). It can help guide you through your talk as well, but never read from the screen or from notes. You get no marks for reading!

⭐ **Examiner's tip**

Making regular eye contact with your listeners shows confidence. A smile helps too.

What is needed to deliver a presentation well?

To deliver a presentation successfully you must present the material with style. If you are not prepared, you could underperform.

Checklist for success

- You need to organise your presentation so that you know what to say and in what order.
- You need to know how to handle your audience: this is crucial for success.

Speakers deal with audiences in different ways: a stand-up comedian might move around and joke with the audience; a presenter at an awards ceremony will be more serious.

ACTIVITY

In a small group, discuss what you think will be your major problems when presenting to your class, and how you might overcome them. For example:

- students not being interested
- the way the room is set-up
- your nerves.

ACTIVITY

In a group of four, improvise two scenes where young people attend job interviews at a supermarket.

- One interviewee knows about the job, is prepared and enthusiastic.
- The other knows nothing about the job and shows no interest.

Talk about the different impressions created.

Focus for development: Establishing and maintaining a good impression

First impressions

First impressions count. If you appear calm and prepared, you will impress your audience. People notice body language, so try not to look nervous.

Sustaining your role

Having created a good impression, you need to maintain your confidence throughout. Remember:

- Listeners can get bored quickly, so vary your pace to sustain their interest.
- A strong opening is wasted if it's followed by a muddle of points.
- Move through your well-planned material towards a clear ending.

Dealing with questions

You will probably have to answer questions at the end and audiences will expect direct responses. Try to foresee questions you might be asked and have the information ready.

ACTIVITY

Discuss with a partner:

Which of these will make the worst impression on your audience?

- Losing track of where you are in your notes
- Messing up a funny line
- Speaking in a monotone and not making eye contact.

What could you do to remedy each of them?

Examiner's tip ★

Not being direct in answering questions – a politician's trick – might appear a clever tactic but can also make you seem evasive.

ACTIVITY

Look at these two answers to the question:

What more can we do to help old people?

Discuss with a partner why the Grade A answer is better.

Grade B answer

I have a friend who suggests we could carry them across the road! No, seriously, we need to take time to talk to them... that sort of stuff, they're much happier if they feel wanted.

Grade A/A★ answer

Obviously, it's never easy. Age Concern gives out leaflets like this one, with advice, but we can't just wave a magic wand to transform their lives. Nevertheless, to just give up on them isn't an option. And even little things matter. Last week, for instance...

ASSESSMENT FOCUS

Deliver an impressive opening to this presentation:

My life out of school

Then take questions and ask for feedback on how you performed.

Remember

- **Prepare thoroughly and be ready for questions.**
- **Impress your audience from the start.**
- **Sustain their interest to the end.**

Grade Booster

Extended Assessment task

> Produce a detailed plan for a presentation to your class, entitled:
> **What is the best sort of day out?**
> Persuade your audience to accept your view.

Or, you could choose one of the following topics:

- Argue that there is no such thing as a good day out.
- Argue that it would be better if people concentrated on making everyday life better rather than being obsessed with holidays.
- Offer advice on how to enjoy your time and avoid problems on holiday, or on how to enjoy yourself without going away on holiday.

Make notes in your plan of the techniques you will use at various stages to interest your audience.

Pay particular attention to your opening, how you develop your ideas and your ending.

Deliver the presentation and ask for feedback.

Evaluation – What have you learned?

With a partner, use the grade checklist below to evaluate your work on the Extended Assessment Task.

- I can organise and deliver a challenging and sophisticated presentation which impresses the audience from start to finish.

- I can organise and deliver an assured presentation which uses imaginative techniques for a desired effect on the audience.

- I can organise and deliver a confident presentation using techniques which affect the audience.

- I can organise and deliver a structured presentation, using some presentational techniques.

- I can plan and deliver a presentation as required.

You may need to go back and look at the relevant pages from this section again.

Discussing and Listening

Introduction

This section of Chapter 3 shows you how to

- prepare for a discussion with one or more people
- speak and listen effectively in group situations
- improve your discussion skills.

Why is it important to spend time improving speaking and listening?

- Although we all talk and listen each day in many different situations, many people do not understand how to take part effectively in group discussions.
- Discussion is not about simply making your point of view known; it is also about listening, responding and possibly adapting previously held views.
- Listening sensitively and accepting other views is a sign of maturity.
- We spend our lives having discussions with all kinds of people on all kinds of subjects; it benefits us if we can do it skilfully.

A **Grade C** candidate will

- communicate clearly, using language that is appropriate to the situation
- listen carefully, develop their own and others' ideas and make significant contributions to discussions.

C

A **Grade A/A*** candidate will

- communicate in a suitable style, depending on the situation, using language confidently in discussion
- begin, sustain and develop discussions
- listen well so they can respond effectively and sympathetically to what others say.

A **A***

Prior learning

Before you begin this unit, think about:

- discussions you have watched on television

Who has appeared to be in control? How do they direct the conversation? Which people seem left out, and why?

- discussions you have taken part in at school

How successful have they been? Why have they sometimes ground to a halt or not produced a conclusion? What can go wrong?

- discussions with friends.

Who do you most like to talk with, and why? When do you find conversations with friends annoying?

Preparing for discussion

Learning objectives

- To appreciate how preparation can improve some types of discussion.
- To practise preparing for a discussion.

Examiner's tip

Notes are fine but you should never read directly from them.

What is there to prepare?

The type of preparation needed will depend on the topic. For example, if you are discussing teenage crime, you may **research facts, figures and opinions** from the Internet. If you are asked about what policies the government should change, you might **assess a range of options** and then **adopt a point of view**.

If you are working as a group, preparation might be done together; if you are speaking from a particular standpoint, you might prepare alone.

Checklist for success

- You need to know what you will be discussing and, if appropriate, what your role in the discussion will be.
- You need to prepare ideas and information and note them down.

ACTIVITY

What would you need to find out in advance to allow you to contribute successfully to this discussion?

> *With a group of friends, come to an agreement about who are or were the five greatest ever Britons.*

Focus for development:
Roles and research

Chairing the discussion

You might be asked to chair a discussion. As chair you need to have questions ready to ask and information ready to keep the discussion going. You will need to direct the discussion but must also be prepared to adapt to what others say.

ACTIVITY

You have been asked to chair a discussion about how £5 million should be spent to improve your school.

Draw up notes you might use. For example:

- How will you start? For example, you could offer a range of ideas to be discussed.
- Will each person speak in turn?
- Will there be summaries?
- How might you draw the group to a conclusion?

Examiner's tip ★

Make sure your notes are brief. They can be put into a possible running order but should not be developed into any form of script.

A student writes…

We did the £5 million discussion. I found some facts, figures and quotes from students and staff to use. It was the first time I've performed like a 'star' in English.

Adopting a point of view

You may be asked to take a particular point of view. If so, you need to be clear about what view you represent and prepare how you are going to support that viewpoint.

ACTIVITY

Imagine you are to be involved in the discussion about spending the £5 million.

You are supporting the view that half the money be spent on new sports facilities and half on new teachers. Prepare your notes.

Examiner's tip ★

Work as a group as you prepare, but avoid practice run-throughs. They can make your discussion sound stilted and you will not speak and listen as impressively as if it's fresh to you.

ASSESSMENT FOCUS

Your teacher has warned you that you will be involved in a group discussion about whether there is still time to save the world from climate change.

You can choose whether to agree or disagree.

Organise notes and details to support your opinion.

Remember

- **Prepare for discussions as much you can, to enrich the content of what you say.**
- **Don't over-prepare: reading from scripted notes is not acceptable.**
- **Be ready to adapt your notes as the discussion develops.**

Developing strategies for confident talk

How can anyone become more confident?

Confidence is important in all speaking and listening activities, including group discussions. You will feel more confident if you are well prepared and can use strategies to help you feel more comfortable.

Checklist for success

- You need to stay in the discussion and not allow others to dominate.
- You need to make your points clearly, including detail to support them.
- You need to engage with what others say and make sensible responses.

ACTIVITY

Look at these titles for discussions.

> *Should we should bring back hanging?*
>
> *Who should be in charge of the world: men or women?*
>
> *'Everyone should be able to go to university.' Is this a realistic target?*

- Which topic would you feel most confident to participate in? Why? How could you increase your confidence about the other topics?

Focus for development:
Demonstrating confidence

Speaking with confidence does not just mean speaking clearly. You also need to sound as if you **believe** in what you are saying.

Some hesitation is natural, because we think as we speak, but hesitating all the time indicates a lack of confidence.

ACTIVITY

In this extract from a discussion, the students are analysing advertisements. They have not prepared their ideas.

What impression do Jenny and Abi create? Give your reasons.

Abi:	So, this magazine cover balances the idea of men ruling the world – that's why he's standing on all that money – with the figure of the intelligent woman over here. It's a neat concept. But does it work for readers of this magazine?
Jenny:	Well… the picture…
Abi:	Yes. *(Raises her eyebrows to Jenny.)*
Jenny:	Erm… The colours are good. I like them… Some of them…
Abi:	Do they have any effect though? Do they make us think..?
Jenny:	Yes. No… Some… I don't know really…

Asking questions

With her confident opening comment and then her questions to Jenny, Abi seems more in control in the discussion. Asking **appropriate questions** can also show you are listening carefully.

For example, you might be

- requesting extra information: 'So, if you think Pythagoras was the greatest mathematician ever, what did he do that has improved the quality of my life?'
- encouraging more reluctant speakers: 'James – can you add to that point?'
- challenging what someone else has said: 'Surely not! Have you forgotten Van Gogh?'

ACTIVITY

Use a table like the one below to note down the different types of question that Grade A student, Steph, uses in this discussion.

Question	Type of question and use
1	Steph is encouraging Anne to be clearer and make a point more simply
2	

A student writes…

I never feel I'm saying enough in discussions. Other people say a lot more than me. But I think what I am saying is important.

Answer…

Confidence is not just about talking at length. Careful listening, followed by a pertinent comment or question, can show your confidence just as well.

Steph:	So, can you just simplify what you've just said?
Anne:	OK. Shakespeare makes no sense because the stories are utterly stupid.
Steph:	Stupid?
Anne:	Yes, stupid. Come on, they could never happen in real life. None of them.
Steph:	Which means there is no point in studying his plays?
Anne:	Exactly.
Steph:	Mm. Why has he been popular for over 400 years then?
Anne:	No idea.
Steph:	So you really can't see why he's regarded as a genius?

ASSESSMENT FOCUS

In a group of three, choose one of the topics from the first activity opposite. One of you needs to lead the discussion and

- introduce the discussion confidently
- allow others to do most of the talking, but try to use questions at different stages to prompt the discussion

Then choose another topic, with another person leading the discussion.

Remember

- A confident performance will gain you more marks.
- A confident performer knows when to speak and when to prompt or listen.

Developing and supporting ideas

Learning objectives

- To learn how to develop ideas in discussion.
- To understand how to argue effectively.

What does developing and supporting ideas mean?

In conversation, speakers often simply state an idea but then fail to **offer evidence** to support it or develop it.

Being able to **extend ideas** or **offer alternatives** to ideas put forward by others sustains the discussion and moves it on.

Checklist for success

- You need to know what you are talking about and to extend ideas in a discussion to be convincing.
- You need to listen carefully so that you can successfully challenge or support what others say.

ACTIVITY

If the points below were made in a discussion, how would you develop them (add information) and argue against them?

Statement	Development	Counter argument
'Football is a total waste of time.'		
'Nothing in life is more important than love.'		
'London gets a chance at everything. It's time for the rest of the country to be treated equally.'		

Focus for development:
Extending and opposing ideas

Extending ideas

Discussions are better if you can make your own ideas detailed and encourage others to clarify their ideas.

To improve your own ideas, you can add **supporting evidence**: for example, facts or statistics, examples, anecdotes or others' opinions.

To **encourage others to extend their ideas**, you can use phrases like

- 'True! What else?'
- 'And can you take that idea one stage further?'

To **develop an idea yourself**, you might use phrases like

- 'Yes. And that reminds me of when…'
- 'Yes, I agree. Not only that, but…'

Countering a viewpoint

To argue your point in a controlled way, you can

- support a viewpoint
- challenge an alternative viewpoint
- try to change other speakers' minds.

ACTIVITY

Discuss with a partner:

Why is Carl, the Grade A student, coming out on top in this argument with Grade C student, Amy?

Carl:	The advertisement is basically fine, but who actually buys the soup? Shouldn't they be targeting housewives?
Amy:	That's sexist!
Carl:	OK. Househusbands as well. We all know about appealing to target audiences. We did that in Year 9, didn't we? So… the target audience here is…?
Amy:	Everybody. Everybody eats soup, everybody can understand the ad and everybody's likely to buy it, aren't they?
Carl:	(smiling) Barristers? The royal family?
Amy:	Stupid! You know what I mean…

ACTIVITY

What evidence could you use to develop this point? Jot down some ideas.

> *Everyone should take more care to avoid sunburn.*

Add some **facts** and an **anecdote**. You can invent what you need.

Examiner's tip ★

*The key word when countering a viewpoint is **tact**. If you respond tactfully you just might make the other speaker reconsider their view.*

ASSESSMENT FOCUS

Write down what would you say in response to these statements made during a group discussion. How would you counter each point successfully?

> *There is only one good place to live: Australia. Australia has everything anyone could ever want. Only a fool would choose to live anywhere else.*

Remember

- **Extend your ideas to make them more convincing.**
- **Challenge other people's ideas tactfully and in detail to encourage them to change their minds.**

Responding to talk

Learning objectives

- To understand the significance of physical and linguistic responses to talk.
- To understand how you can show you are listening closely.

What does responding to talk mean?

You are assessed on your ability to **talk *and* listen**. Your **physical reactions** will indicate how well you are listening, and **linguistic responses** – what you say – will show how well you have understood the discussion.

Checklist for success

- You need to remember that both speaking and listening skills are vital in any discussion.
- You need to focus on listening carefully because what you hear affects how well you respond.

⭐ Examiner's tip

Don't force a reaction – you aren't acting! If you are listening carefully, your face will reflect this naturally.

Focus for development: Responses

Physical responses

It is easy to identify who is not listening carefully. Try to avoid

- gazing out of the window or muttering to someone else
- messing around or, perhaps, doodling.

Facial expressions are revealing too. A careful listener is likely to

- raise eyebrows or open or narrow their eyes slightly
- smile, bite a lip or take an intake of breath.

Such signs are only slight, but they show the listener is reacting.

Linguistic responses

What you say reveals how well you are listening because you respond appropriately. Poor listeners are easily identified.

Effective listening allows you to absorb others' ideas and develop new ones.

Read this extract from a group discussion about whom we should respect.

Discuss with a partner:

- How are Lucy's listening skills limiting this discussion?
- How are the others better at listening?

doesn't answer/just another idea

Shabnam:	OK. So we're putting these people into order of importance. Lucy, you start.
Lucy:	Princess Diana.
Steve:	I think she was over-rated. No one talks about her now. When did she die?
Lucy:	There's Martin Luther King too. He was good.
Steve:	They all were, weren't they?
Shabnam:	My dad never liked Margaret Thatcher. What was she like?
Steve:	First woman Prime Minister…
Lucy:	President Kennedy… I don't know anything about him…
Shabnam:	He changed America, didn't he? He fought Russia or something and got shot.
Lucy:	Mohammed Ali…

forced to respond, rather than developing original idea

Decide:

- How well do Grade B students, Jermaine and Laura, collaborate here?
- How often do they take on board and develop each other's comments?
- What more will they need to do to get A/A★ grades?

Jermaine:	Why do people love fashion so much?
Laura:	Well, it's not everybody, is it?
Jermaine:	No. There's my dad for a start. Talk about bad taste. And he doesn't care…
Laura:	It's often girls, though, isn't it? I mean, boys too – but are they as obsessed?
Jermaine:	Some are. It's to do with friendship groups and how they want to be seen, very often: hip… Kind of in vogue. All that.
Laura:	Yes. I was just thinking about how you were dressed last year for that trip we went on…

Discuss this in a group. Record the discussion, then play it back.

Is fashion really important?

How often did you

- 'disappear' from the discussion (Were you still listening?)
- argue effectively
- develop an idea?

Examiner's tip ★

It's all about focus. Pay attention to the task and you will be listening. It's simple.

Remember

- In discussions, listening is as important as speaking.
- Your listening ability will be clear in how you react and what you say.

Reacting to implications and summarising

What does reacting to implications and summarising mean?

Responding sensitively – not only to what people **say directly** but to what they **imply** – shows you are a good listener. People regularly say things which imply something else, for example: 'I love your new dress. It's so… different.'

A good listener picks out what is implied and comments on it.

Summarising briefly what has been said during a discussion proves that you have listened and understood well. It also helps to round off the discussion.

Checklist for success

- You need to listen sensitively and make perceptive responses.
- You need to show that you understand others' arguments and their implications.
- You need to be able to sum up what has been said.

Focus for development: Demonstrating listening skills

Reacting to implications

Responding to implications demonstrates good listening skills – but your response must be appropriate.

Examiner's tip

Look out for what other speakers are implying just as you try to spot things they say which are inconsistent. Challenge them if necessary

ACTIVITY

Look at this discussion.

- Which responses could have been challenged by a perceptive listener?
- What is implied in each response you have identified?

Daniel:	Geography's like RE: a total waste of time.
Jenny:	I agree. I've hated it since Year 7. I've had Mrs Bates every year and she's always had it in for me.
Daniel:	Too right. And I've had Mrs Cowen. How can she teach? She's too old to even know what's going on.
Maisie:	She said, 'An understanding of geography is vital if we are to understand the world around us.' You don't have to have a degree to know that's rubbish.
Daniel:	And she said, 'You've got to work hard to achieve anything.' That's like something my grandma would say.

What implication is B challenging here?

How might A respond?

A: I know you're right. You're always right.

B: So, are you saying I'm wrong?

Summarising

If you listen closely, you will be able to

* sum up what has been said in a discussion so far
* explain the main points of view at the end of the discussion.

Making brief notes though the discussion will help, so nothing is missed. Notes are useful to

* group members, for weighing up different opinions
* the chair, for maintaining the balance between people with different views
* the summariser, for commenting at the end.

ACTIVITY

In groups of four prepare a discussion entitled:

> **'Space exploration is a waste of time. The money could be spent on more worthwhile things.'**

Two of you should take one viewpoint and two the opposite point of view.

* Note down the points made by each speaker taking the opposite view.
* Summarise what each speaker thinks.

ASSESSMENT FOCUS

In a group of three, discuss this statement.

> ***Out of school, most teenagers waste most of their time.***

* Look out for implications and challenge them.
* Afterwards, each member of the group should summarise the discussion.

Examiner's tip ★

To summarise, use phrases like 'On one hand… Whereas on the other hand…'. This shows you are balancing the views.

Remember

* **Attentive listeners will identify implications and respond to them.**
* **If you can summarise accurately, you show you have been listening.**

Leading a group

Learning objective

- *To learn how to manage a discussion successfully.*

Why is the ability to lead important?

In assessments, high-achieving students are expected to support others in the group, responding to and showing understanding for their ideas, and to lead the group through a discussion to its conclusions.

Checklist for success

- You need to be able to employ all the discussion skills covered so far.
- You need to be prepared to direct discussions, help resolve disagreements and bring the discussion to a conclusion or outcome.

Notice the leadership qualities here:

- **initiating:** 'Right, to kick things off, why don't we like this story?'
- **prompting and supporting others:** 'Are you sure, Satish? Let's just look at…'
- **directing:** 'Well, that's a totally different point. For now, can we get back to…?'
- **summarising:** 'That's agreed, then. We think…'.

Focus for development:
Working on effective leadership skills

ACTIVITY

This extract shows the difference in performance between students working at Grade C, Sheri and Abdul, and a Grade A/A★ student, Jessica, who leads the discussion.

Discuss with a partner:

- What skills are being demonstrated by Jessica?
- How does she prompt and negotiate with Sheri and Abdul?
- How does she summarise?
- How will the others react to her suggestion at the end? Explain why.

Jessica:	So, are we in favour of single-sex education or against it? Abdul?
Abdul:	It's unnatural. Boys and girls are part of society, so why keep them apart at school?
Jessica:	Sheri?
Sheri:	We'd get more work done if the boys weren't there, messing about. Then there's the time wasted while they all explain why they've not done their homework.
Abdul:	That's a silly line to take. Often it's girls with their stupid questions who are the timewasters.
Jessica:	OK. So, if you're both saying the others waste time, could it be better if they were kept apart? Only half the time lost?
Abdul:	Maybe. But I work better with girls around…
Sheri:	We definitely don't need the boys…
Jessica:	Are we saying we need single-sex schools as an option, then? I mean, for those who want it. Or maybe single sex classes for subjects in the same school? Would that work for both of you?

Examiner's tip ⭐

Just because you are leading a discussion doesn't stop you agreeing with one point of view. However, you must make sure that all viewpoints are allowed and that all participants feel comfortable.

ACTIVITY

Here, a group is discussing where they would like to live. What might a leader in the group have said to

- make this discussion more positive?
- move the discussion forward?

Wayne:	This is the worst place to live.
Jane:	It's better than the middle of a slum.
Wayne:	This is a slum.
Jane:	It's not. Have you ever been to places with rubbish lying around and broken windows everywhere?
Wayne:	It's like that round here …

A student writes…

I like working in groups but I'm hopeless at leading the others. I always get swamped by their ideas.

Answer…

The ability to manage a group is expected from a top student. However, you can always try to guide the group through sections of the discussion. Taking brief notes might help you stay in touch.

ASSESSMENT FOCUS

In a group of three, have a discussion in which two take directly opposed viewpoints and the third is responsible for leading them to an amicable conclusion. Choose from:

- *Football is more important than anything.*
- *Exams should be banned.*

The important thing is that it must be a topic on which there is strong disagreement.

Repeat with a different topic and different roles.

Remember

- **When leading a discussion your priorities are to balance views, avoid conflict, encourage agreement and move to a resolution.**
- **Sensitive listening and the ability to encourage involvement and compromise are key leadership skills.**

Grade Booster

Extended Assessment task

Working as a group, prepare a discussion on the topic below. Then hold the discussion.
From the age of 14, young people should have much more freedom in every area of their lives.

Each member of the group should

- decide on their initial viewpoint
- produce some bulleted notes and/or other materials for discussion
- come to the discussion with an otherwise open mind.

It is likely to help if

- one member of the group chairs the discussion
- at least one person takes each side of the argument
- one member summarises the discussion for the rest of the class.

Evaluation – What have you learned?

With a partner, use the grade checklist below to evaluate your work on the Extended Assessment Task.

- I can listen sensitively, showing empathy for others' views.
- I can probe opinions through searching questions, encourage interaction in groups and resolve outcomes.

- I can initiate discussions and perform with assurance in them.
- I can listen sensitively and sustain discussion in suitable ways.

- I can reflect on what is said, challenge others and build on their ideas.
- I can help structure and manage the discussion.

- I can communicate clearly and interest other members of the group.
- I can listen carefully, ask relevant questions, develop ideas with detail and make significant contributions that move the discussion on.

- I can sustain involvement and make effective contributions.
- I can show evidence of understanding and respond appropriately to what is said.

You may need to go back and look at the relevant pages from this section again.

Adopting a Role

Introduction

This section of Chapter 3 shows you how to

- approach the task when adopting a role
- develop a role successfully
- improve performances.

Why is the ability to adopt a role important?

- It is one of the three tasks you must complete for the Speaking and Listening Controlled Assessment.
- If you can adopt a role successfully, it demonstrates empathy with the character you portray. Adopting a role also help you understand how writers create characters and how actors can portray them.
- Adopting different roles is something everyone does in different situations in life, so this is good preparation.

A **Grade C** candidate will

- develop and sustain roles through appropriate language and effective gesture and movement
- engage watchers' interest by showing understanding for characters, ideas and situations.

C

A **Grade A/A*** candidate will

- create complex characters to fulfil the demands of challenging roles
- sustain the watchers' interest through the skilful use of a range of vocabulary and non-verbal techniques.

A **A***

Prior learning

Before you begin this unit, think about

- soap operas and/or television series or films you watch

> What is distinctive about your favourite characters? How are facial expressions and gestures used? How are the most memorable lines delivered, and why?

- how the characters were portrayed in any live theatre you have seen

> How were they made convincing?

- what the acting was like in any amateur drama you may have seen.

> How might the characters have been made more realistic and engaging?

Getting into role

Learning objectives

- To learn how to explore a role and what is required when improvising it.

- To think about what can be done to improve your performances.

What does improvising a role mean?

In your Speaking and Listening assessment, you will be asked to **improvise a role** using drama techniques. You might have to play a character from literature or someone from real life such as a doctor or cleaner, or you might have to represent a viewpoint in a discussion – supporting a new leisure complex, for example.

You need to prepare in advance to create and develop a **convincing character**.

Checklist for success

In order to portray a character convincingly, you need to explore

- their **history**: what has happened to them
- their **attitudes**: what they think about different issues/people
- their **behaviour**: how they speak to and treat others
- their **relationships**: with people around them
- their **motivations**: why they behave as they do.

ACTIVITY

Choose a character from a novel/play/poem you have studied.

- Make notes about this character for each of the areas listed above.
- In a group of three, imagine your characters meet in heaven. Introduce yourselves, describing your life and what has happened to you.

Focus for development:
Planned improvisations

How well you perform can often depend on how well you work with others. Shared preparation and positive criticism will improve performances in most cases.

ACTIVITY

Look at this improvisation by two Grade C students.

Situation: a headteacher is meeting an angry parent whose child has been excluded for fighting.

Examiner's tip

Some improvisations are disappointing because they have no 'depth'. To succeed, you need to know as much as possible about your character, so that you can think and behave as they would.

Lisa:	*(sitting at her desk)* Hello, Mrs Garvey, please come in.
Katie:	Yes, well, I had to come. *(She sits down)*
Lisa:	I think I know why you're here.
Katie:	I'm not happy about what's happened to Susannah.
Lisa:	No, I thought that would be what has brought you in. Would you like a cup of tea?
Katie:	Er… No, I don't think so. I'm here to talk about Susie, not join in a tea party.
Lisa:	OK. So, what exactly would you like to happen? *(She sips a cup of tea)*
Katie:	That's obvious, isn't it? I want our little Susie back in school. She didn't do anything wrong *(hammering the desk)*. We're tired of her being held responsible for everything that happens in this place. She's a good kid.
Lisa:	Well, let's not get over-excited, Mrs Garvey…

Discuss with a partner what advice you would give these performers to help them improve their marks. Consider:

- what they say
- their movements
- who is in control of the situation.

Improvise this situation yourselves, bearing in mind the improvements you have suggested.

ASSESSMENT FOCUS

- With a partner, act out your own headteacher/parent interview. Choose your own topic.
- First, make notes to help you play your role. Try to make your character distinctive – through gesture, movement or ways of speaking. Avoid exaggerating your character as your performance could turn into a caricature.

After performing, decide which were the most successful parts of your performance, and why.

Improve any details and try again. Ask yourselves:

- Do we need to know more background about the characters or the situation?
- Can we structure how the conversation will start – develop – finish?
- Could we change the mood to increase the interest for the audience, for example by building gradually to a climax?

Remember

- **Careful planning for your characterisation is essential.**
- **Try to make your character convincing.**
- **Co-operating well with your group will help make your performance better.**

Speaking in role

What does speaking in role mean?

Sometimes, characters appear two-dimensional; the audience do not believe they could be real. Knowing your character's background will help create this credibility but, to be really convincing, you also need to pay attention to **how** your character speaks and **what** you say, so you reveal what you are thinking and feeling.

Checklist for success

Before your practise your performance, ask yourself:

- Have I prepared properly?
- Have I thought through what will happen and what I need to do at every stage?

After a practice run-through, ask yourself:

- Have I worked effectively as part of the group?
- What can I do to improve my performance?

Before the final performance, ask yourself:

- Do I know roughly what I will be saying at each stage?
- Am I secure in my character: how will I react?

A student writes…

How precise should we be about preparing our performance?

Answer…

You need to know enough before starting so that no one in the group will be surprised by the events and everyone is aware of roughly what will be said. Beyond that, you should feel free to improvise what you do and say.

ACTIVITY

In these extracts, a father, who is a single parent, is talking to his ex-wife.

Both students are convincing in this role, but the Grade A student has developed his part by adding more obvious emotion.

Write down what creates the emotional appeal of each sentence in the A Grade response.

Grade B response

They're not just my kids. They're yours too. I need you to help support them because you know I simply don't have enough money. My wages can't stretch far enough and it's hard to even feed them properly, never mind buy new clothes...

Grade A response

Look, you are going to have to help. <u>We</u> decided to have children; now <u>we</u> have the responsibility for feeding them and clothing them. I'm doing all I can – you know that – but I just can't manage. You have to understand what a mess we're in and you have to help: not for my sake – for theirs!

Focus for development: Speaking in character

Obviously you need to speak clearly, but you also need to speak in the way your character would. This means you won't always use standard English.

ACTIVITY

Look at this **Grade A★** improvisation in role as the Nurse in *Romeo and Juliet*.

Notice how the way she speaks gives the audience a clear impression of what the Nurse is like.

Discuss with a partner what features of her speech make this successful?

> Lordy, lordy, lordy. What a day I'm having! Rush here, rush there! It's been so hectic that every part about me quivers... Dust this! Shift that! I'm at everyone's beck and call and especially that Juliet... 'Course, she's a dear. Love her. Love her. But she's wanting this and needing that. Never a thought for poor old me...

The Nurse is a chatterbox who feels she has to look after the whole household.

Continue her speech, detailing what else she has had to do today and how she feels about it.

ASSESSMENT FOCUS

Work with a partner, each choosing two different characters from literature, the media or real life. One could be the character you chose on page 144.

Demonstrating clearly how they speak, make a 30-second speech by each character.

Ask a friend to criticise your performances, identifying:

- what was convincing
- what you said that was unconvincing, in terms of the characters' personalities and the words you used.

Remember

- **Focus clearly throughout your improvisation on what you say and how you say it in character.**

Developing a role through expression and movement

How can I develop a role through gesture and movement?

As well as thinking carefully about the words your character would use (see page 146), you can develop a character by adding physical actions. This might be a limp, a mannerism such as furrowed brows, or showing anger with the jab of a finger, for example.

However, to develop a role successfully though **gesture** and **movement**, you first need to understand the character's emotions. Then you can act accordingly.

Checklist for success

You need to observe people closely – their expressions, movements and peculiarities. Notice how they

- register emotions through facial expression
- stand
- move
- show feelings in their mannerisms (for example, scratch their head, play with their fingers).

Try imitating some of these mannerisms to develop your skills.

Focus for development:
Expression and movement

ACTIVITY

Your face usually shows what you are thinking. In groups of three, each produce three facial expressions your group would recognise. Decide what emotion each expression represents.

ACTIVITY

Read these statements.

- I'm happy here. There's nothing more I want from life than this.
- Things have got to change if we are going to get through this.
- Oh, yes. I'm just going from strength to strength.

Create very different characters by delivering each statement as

- an old person
- a confident business person.

Concentrate on giving your characters physical characteristics, such as a bad leg or a habit of smoothing their hair. Make your facial expressions convincing.

Gestures and movements add to the feelings you want to show. For example:

- Hugging someone shows affection.
- Hands to the mouth could show shock.
- Arms wide apart could show welcome.
- A waved fist demonstrates anger (or triumph).
- Sitting down suddenly could register dismay.
- Walking away could show a struggle to accept what has been said.

> **A student writes…**
>
> My father was an actor. When he was getting into role, he'd behave like the character around the house. He called it method acting. He said it helped him make the role convincing.

ACTIVITY

In pairs, decide what facial expressions, gestures and movements you might use when reacting to the following statements. Mime your response to each one.

- We have no money left. We will have to move away, I'm afraid.
- She simply stepped into the road without looking. It wasn't the driver's fault. He couldn't stop.
- There's news! The war is over. At last, life can go back to normal.

ASSESSMENT FOCUS

With a friend, act out the extract below, using expression and movements.

- The first time, A is drunk and B is confused.
- The second time, A is frustrated and B is happy.
- The third time, A is angry, B is relaxed.

> **A:** When the guy walks in…
> **B:** Yeah… What?
> **A:** Make sure it's safe…
> **B:** It's safe?
> **A:** Yes, safe.
> **B:** Then what?
> **A:** Get him.
> **B:** Get him?
> **A:** Yes. Are you stupid? Get him!

Remember

- **Create an impression by how you react and move – but don't overdo it.**
- **Show your feelings even if you are not speaking.**
- **Support your words with appropriate expressions and movements.**

149

Maximising the impact

Learning objective

- To learn how you can make the most of your role and gain high marks.

What does maximising the impact mean?

Maximising the **impact** of your role means making every effort to engage your audience's attention throughout your performance. This means doing more than just showing aspects of your character and sustaining your role.

Checklist for success

- Plan exactly what you will do, what you will be talking about and how you will move and behave.
- Think seriously about how you will begin, maintain your role, and finish in a memorable way.

ACTIVITY

You are auditioning for a part in *Hollyoaks*. The part is a teenager who has just moved into the area and comes from a rich family but does not get on with their parents.

You have to walk into the café for the first time. How will you set about making an impact?

- What aspects of your character will you want to show?
- How will you behave towards the owner and other customers?

Focus for development: Making an impact

The opening

Performances can **start in different ways**. However, your opening section is likely to concentrate on establishing your character.

ACTIVITY

You are 24 and have just arrived on holiday with a friend from work. You know no one else in the hotel. Your friend has gone out to look around and you go down to the pool.

In a small group, you are going to act out your first entrance. Imagine the people by the pool all go silent as you arrive. What will you do? What will be the first thing you say and to whom?

You might want to

- tell them about yourself/what kind of person you are
- tell them about your journey
- ask about the resort.

The middle

Stay focused on your role. Even if you are not playing a lead role, you can continue to impress if you

- react in a convincing way, using speech, expression and movement
- remain focused and do not become distracted by the audience
- do not allow yourself to be excluded from the main action.

Examiner's tip ★

Talk to the people around you, but remember the audience too. Sometimes, actors on stage talk directly out to the audience when they have something important to say.

ACTIVITY

On the same holiday, your friend has been bitten by a cat. Doctors fear she could have caught rabies. You go with her to the local hospital. In your groups, role play what happens. One of you will play the bitten girl, one the friend and another two, the hospital staff.

Make sure you are fully involved in what happens. Jot down some notes on

- what you will do in this section of the role-play
- the conversations you might initiate.

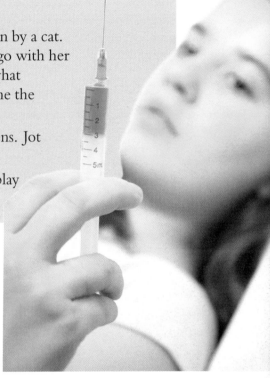

The ending

Your final appearance or your final speech will be your last chance to create an impact. It will help you if you can

- demonstrate that you have sustained and developed the role – for example, you could show how you have changed from the start or how you have been affected by the action
- end memorably, perhaps with a jokey line or a sad farewell, depending on the situation.

ASSESSMENT FOCUS

To end the improvisation, you phone your friend's mother to explain what has happened. Deliver your speech in the form of a monologue.

Ensure your performance is memorable.

Remember

- Begin and end by making a strong impression.
- Make sure you sustain your character – you will be assessed throughout your performance.

Interviews

Learning objectives

- To understand what is required in an interview situation.
- To understand how to act as an interviewer or interviewee.

When might I come across an interview situation?

You might have to take part in an interview as your presentation task – responding to questions – or when you adopt a role.

Many of the necessary skills are the same in each case.

Checklist for success

- You need to know how to be successful as an interviewer and interviewee, to ask probing questions and to give detailed answers.
- Watch interviews on television to see how it can be done.

ACTIVITY

Watch two different interviews on television, one involving a TV personality and one a politician.

Compare the two styles of interviewing:

- How do the interviewers ask questions differently?
- How and why is the style of answers different?
- What are your impressions of the interviewers and interviewees?
- What are the differences in language used, facial expressions and body language?

A student writes…

When I've been the interviewer, I've sometimes felt tied to my list of questions.

Answer…

It's fine to have a list of questions but only as a guide. You need to listen to the answers, ask for clarification, comment on what is said if appropriate and change your next question if necessary.

Focus for development:
Good questioning and good answers

Interviewing

ACTIVITY

In this extract, what does Sarah, the interviewer, do badly?

Sarah:	Tell us about your early life. ←	standard opening
Beata:	I was brought up in Warsaw, then we moved to England.	
Sarah:	What did you first think of university? ←	sudden switch
Beata:	I had a terrible time…	
Sarah:	Yes. I think we all know that story.	

Being the interviewee

Prepare fully for the interview so that you know your subject well.

If you are in role as a character from literature, research the following:

- what happens to you in the text
- how you are going to play this role and what you plan to say

Always try to extend answers with relevant details and opinions. An extended answer might even become a short monologue.

Examiner's tip ★

In a role-play interview, work though the detail as a pair before you start. Then the interviewer will know where to delve during the interview itself.

ACTIVITY

This is the start of an A★ performance where George, from the novel *Of Mice and Men,* is being interviewed.

> How do you remember Lennie, looking back over your time together?

> It was OK with Lennie. We had a lotta good times. He was a good guy. No, he really was. I remember once I was hungry an' he went an' found a chicken – don't ask me where he foun' it. He wouldn't eat none of it. He just sat there, an' he said, 'Ya do so much for me, George, an' I don't do nothin' for you, but this is for you, George.' See, he was like that, but people didn't see none of that. People didn't see none of that at all...

- short simple sentences capture character of George
- aware of audience
- anecdote appropriate to characters
- correct style of language
- effective, sad repetition

ASSESSMENT FOCUS

Imagine you are a famous person of your choice.

Prepare to answer these questions in role, inventing any necessary details:

- What are your earliest memories?
- Tell us about your time at school.
- How has fame affected your life?

A partner will ask the questions. Then analyse your performance:

- How interesting were you?
- What went well?
- What did you need to improve?

Remember

- **Interviewers must listen and respond appropriately and interviewees must engage the audience.**
- **You are assessed on your speaking and listening skills, so show both.**

Grade Booster

Extended Assessment Task

In a group of three or four, plan an improvisation set in a workplace. A valuable item has gone missing and one person is accused.

Work though these stages:
- Plan what will happen.
- Divide the improvisation into scenes and decide what will happen in each one (or, decide what will happen in one scene, if that is all there is).
- Make detailed notes on your own character.
- Decide how you will play your role.
- Practise as a group.
- Discuss improvements.
- Have a run-through.
- Perform for the rest of the teaching group.

Take feedback on the performance. Discuss it with your group, then improve your performance in the light of what you have learned.

Evaluation – What have you learned?

With a partner, use the grade checklist below to evaluate your work on the Extended Assessment Task.

- I can perform persuasively, sustaining the audience's interest and emotional investment throughout and fulfilling the demands of a challenging role.

- I can create a complex character skilfully, using verbal and non-verbal techniques to intensify the impact on the audience.

- I can create a complex and convincing character, shaping the audience's response through the use of different techniques.

- I can sustain and develop a role.
- I can use effective language, gestures and movement to show I understand how the character thinks and feels.

- I can prepare a performance, perform in role and use some appropriate language, gestures and movement.

You may need to go back and look at the relevant pages from this section again.

Controlled Assessment Preparation
Unit 2: Speaking and Listening

Introduction

In this section you will

- consider what is required of you in Speaking and Listening
- examine candidates' responses and see how well they have performed
- undertake activities and an extended practice task.

Why is preparation of this kind important?

- The example responses in this section allow you to take time to think about how well others speak and listen.
- Taking the opportunity to consider and discuss how activities can be approached and how others have performed will help you to improve the quality of your own performances.

Key Information

Unit 2 is the Speaking and Listening assessment.

- It has three parts: Presentation, Discussing and Listening, and Role-Play.
- The three activities are worth **20%** of your overall English Language GCSE mark.

What will the assessments involve?

The essential requirements are that you

- make an individual presentation
- perform in a group, discussing and listening
- play a role.

You are likely to complete more than one assessment in each of the three areas, with your best mark in each case being used.

It is crucial that you avoid reading from notes in any of the activities. You are allowed to use notes if they are appropriate (for example, in the presentation), but you are expected to refer to them as you talk, not simply read them.

The Assessment

The assessment objectives for Speaking and Listening (AO1) state that you must be able to do the following:

- Speak to communicate clearly and purposefully; structure and sustain talk, adapting it to different situations and audiences; use standard English and a variety of techniques as appropriate.
- Listen and respond to speakers' ideas and perspectives, and how they construct and express meanings.
- Interact with others, shaping meanings through suggestions, comments and questions and drawing ideas together.
- Create and sustain different roles.

Targeting Grade A

Some of the key features of Grade C and Grade A responses are as follows:

Grade C candidates	
<ul><li>adapt their talk to the situation</li><li>use standard English confidently</li><li>clearly present information, ideas and feelings</li><li>interest the listener through their use of language</li><li>listen carefully and develop their own and others' ideas</li><li>make significant contributions to discussions</li><li>develop and sustain roles through appropriate language and effective gesture and movement</li><li>interest the audience by showing understanding of characters, ideas and situations.</li></ul>	*See example on page 158–159*

Grade A/A★ candidates	
<ul><li>select suitable styles of English for a range of situations</li><li>show assured use of standard English when it is required</li><li>demonstrate a sophisticated vocabulary and vary sentence structures confidently</li><li>express information, ideas and feelings in an engaging way</li><li>initiate conversations and listen sensitively</li><li>make contributions which sustain and develop discussion</li><li>can fulfil the demands of challenging roles and can perform formally and imaginatively</li><li>listen sensitively, showing empathy for others' views.</li></ul>	*See example on pages 157, 158–159 and 160*

Exploring Sample Responses

Individual presentation

ACTIVITY

Read the following extract from a student's presentation, in which she talks to her class about looking after a grandmother with Alzheimer's Disease.

Consider these key elements an examiner would look for:

- speaking appropriately in the situation
- using Standard English
- using a broad vocabulary and varied sentences
- being interesting.

Example

introductory complex sentence to begin/introduction to subject

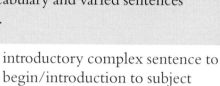

precise vocabulary →

broken sentences, making it seem disturbing and emphasising 'Until'

personalised

I imagine most of you will have some idea of what Alzheimer's Disease is: it progressively takes away the memory, so that sufferers lose touch with reality more and more, until they eventually can't even recognise their wife, their husband, or their children... They jumble the past and present. Until there is no past or present for them. They can't even recognise night or day. And my grandmother has Alzheimer's. We noticed it starting when her memory suddenly got worse. She struggled to cook our special meal on Friday night, which had always been her treat for us at the end of the week. Then she wasn't sure what day it was. She didn't know what she had done earlier in the day. People's names were forgotten even more easily than they had been before. She needed help.

We actually thought that we needed help too, but as time goes on, you discover that the early stages were nothing. It is a degenerative disease which can only get worse. She takes tablets and somehow manages to still live alone, but now it is as if she is in a different kind of world altogether. Conversations are always the same:

'What day is it?'

'Wednesday.'

'Do I have meals on wheels tomorrow?'

'Yes, they'll be here.'

'Do I have to pay for them?'

'No, they are all paid for'

'What day is it?'

'Wednesday.'

'Do I have meals on wheels tomorrow...'

possible pause before this word, for effect

sense of climax for the paragraph

examples, to shock/ emphasise the seriousness

short sentences hammering like nails

sophisticated vocabulary

reality of conversation makes situation clear and tragic

Examiner feedback

This is a candidate who engages the audience and offers a variety of information, presented in interesting ways. Sentences are varied, there is some excellent vocabulary and the grandmother's situation is brought to life with the examples and conversation. The candidate can use standard English with great confidence.

Suggested grade: A★

With a partner, decide how the audience is likely to respond to each section and which language techniques will provoke that reaction.

Discussing and listening

The example below is a transcript from part of a discussion between two boys about the national anthem.

Consider these key elements an examiner would look for:

- speaking appropriately in the situation
- using vocabulary and sentences effectively
- initiating ideas and sustaining them
- listening carefully.

Example

Luke:	I love it. We sing it before international matches and things. ← *simple opening*
	(He hums the tune)
Sam:	I know lots of people do love it, but have you ever stopped ← *rhetorical questions to challenge and offer more ideas*
	to think about the words? It's not about the nation at all really, is it? We're all expected to stand up and sing about the Queen. I might prefer to sing about the Prime Minister or, better still, the people here. After all, we are supposed to be ← *moving the discussion on, and using logic*
	equal, aren't we? Why sing about the Queen, then?
Luke:	Because the tune represents the country. You know that. It ← makes everybody proud of where they come from. When you hear the tune, it stands for England, doesn't it?

listening and responding; slight development of idea

Sam: Ah, yes, England. But there is Wales and Scotland and Ireland too… *(He looks questioning, tongue-in-cheek)* ← more challenge; ellipsis to leave the idea hanging; facial expression expects response

Luke: You know what I mean. It includes them as well. ← only brief retort

Sam: Well, we did something on this in history, and it hasn't always been like that. There's one verse that goes:

> May he sedition hush and like a torrent rush,
>
> Rebellious Scots to crush

← moving the discussion on using fresh idea/evidence

Not much fun if you're Scottish, eh? ← sarcasm

Examiner feedback

Sam is clearly offering more to the conversation and challenges Luke throughout. Even when he uses sarcasm, he is giving reasons for consideration. He includes questions, directs the debate, offers some evidence and fresh ideas. He is demonstrating high-level skills. Luke is listening carefully but only develops one idea in this extract. He uses a rhetorical question and language appropriately and contributes some ideas to the discussion.

Suggested grades: Sam A, Luke C

ACTIVITY

With a friend, discuss the national anthem, deciding whether we should retain it or choose another hymn or song to replace it – and if so, what you would choose.

Adopting a role

This example is an extract from two students delivering a modern-day version of part of *Romeo and Juliet*.

Consider these key elements an examiner would look for:
- speaking appropriately in the situation
- being interesting and being able to be creative and convincing in a complex role.

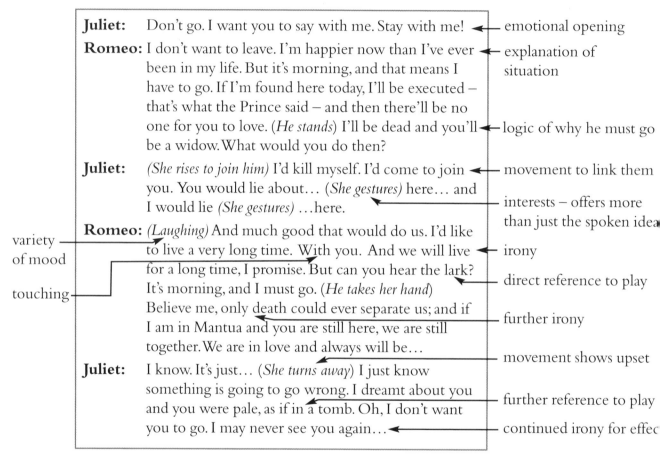

Juliet: Don't go. I want you to say with me. Stay with me! ← emotional opening

Romeo: I don't want to leave. I'm happier now than I've ever ← explanation of situation
been in my life. But it's morning, and that means I
have to go. If I'm found here today, I'll be executed –
that's what the Prince said – and then there'll be no
one for you to love. (*He stands*) I'll be dead and you'll ← logic of why he must go
be a widow. What would you do then?

Juliet: (*She rises to join him*) I'd kill myself. I'd come to join ← movement to link them
you. You would lie about… (*She gestures*) here… and
I would lie (*She gestures*) …here. ← interests – offers more than just the spoken idea

variety of mood ——
Romeo: (*Laughing*) And much good that would do us. I'd like
to live a very long time. With you. And we will live ← irony
for a long time, I promise. But can you hear the lark?
It's morning, and I must go. (*He takes her hand*) ← direct reference to play
touching —— Believe me, only death could ever separate us; and if
I am in Mantua and you are still here, we are still ← further irony
together. We are in love and always will be…

movement shows upset
Juliet: I know. It's just… (*She turns away*) I just know
something is going to go wrong. I dreamt about you
and you were pale, as if in a tomb. Oh, I don't want ← further reference to play
you to go. I may never see you again… ← continued irony for effect

Examiner feedback

The candidates approach a difficult scene seriously; both use irony and make their situation credible. The characters seem complex, emotional and realistic. Movements and gestures add to the effect and the candidates work well together to move the scene along. Although this is only the beginning of the activity, there is clear evidence that the candidates are likely to reach a high grade.

Suggested grade for both students: A

Working with a partner or partners, take characters from a literary text you have studied, and either produce a modern version of part of a scene or produce an extra scene.

After you have rehearsed, perform for the group and ask for feedback on how you have done.

EXAM PRACTICE TASK

Prepare and deliver a presentation from one of the options below:

- argue in favour of Britain being closer to Europe and try to persuade your class to think of themselves as European rather than British
- argue that Britain should not be a part of the European Union and is better off as a totally independent country
- persuade your class to be more interested in current affairs
- argue that the world would be a better place if only young people could be put in charge
- argue that we are very lucky to be living in this country at this time in history.

Whichever topic you choose, remember to

- plan carefully
- aim to interest your audience
- use the techniques and approaches you have practised in this chapter.

If you only do five things...

1 Observe and take note of people using Standard English so you can use it confidently when you need to. Try to speak appropriately in any given situation: formally, perhaps,
for a presentation; much less formally, perhaps, if you are playing a character from a literary text.

2 When you are undertaking assessment tasks, avoid the temptation to use only simple words and short sentences – remember that you will be rewarded for variety.

3 If you are given the opportunity to plan, grasp it with both hands, because it will prove to be time well spent when you have to perform.

4 Try to be confident when giving a presentation – if people respond positively to you, you will perform better and gain more marks.

5 Take Speaking and Listening seriously. The 20% of marks awarded to it can be the difference between success and failure in your GCSE.

What's it all about?

Exploring longer texts in detail means you can read, discuss and write thoughtfully about really interesting ideas and characters.

How will I be assessed?

You will get **15% of your English Language marks** for your ability to respond to a range of texts. These might include plays, novels, poems and works of non-fiction. You will complete a Controlled Assessment task on **one extended text** (such as a novel) over the course of **3–4 hours**. The recommended word limit is **1200 words**.

You will be marked on your writing of one response. This will be based on a choice between two task areas (**Characterisation and voice** or **Themes and ideas**).

What is being tested?

You are being examined on your ability to

- read and understand texts, selecting material appropriately to support what you want to say
- develop and sustain interpretations of writers' ideas and perspectives
- explain and evaluate how writers create particular grammatical or linguistic effects (for example, imagery) to influence or engage the reader
- explain and evaluate how writers use structural or presentational features (such as rhyme patterns in poetry) to influence or engage the reader.

Characterisation and Voice

Introduction

This section of Chapter 4 shows you how to

- understand what a 'Characterisation and Voice' Controlled Assessment task requires you to do
- develop responses to different forms of texts.

Why is it important to learn about characterisation and voice?

- Texts can be looked at in a range of ways, and focusing on characterisation and voice sometimes requires a different approach from a focus on themes and ideas.
- Characters are at the centre of most of the texts we read. Your understanding and enjoyment of a text can be enhanced by exploring how a writer constructs characters or presents ideas through a specific voice.
- Looking at how writers create character and voice will provide a model for your own creative writing.

A **Grade C** candidate will

- show clear evidence of understanding the main ways in which a character has been presented and explain writers' presentation of character clearly
- demonstrate understanding of various features of language and structure used by writers to create characters
- support points they make with relevant and appropriate quotations.

C

A **Grade A/A*** candidate will

- sustain their interpretation of how characters are presented (in other words, develop and write about these ideas at length, not just in small pieces of writing)
- imaginatively select quotations and detail to support their ideas
- analyse in a sophisticated way how character is presented through language and structure (going beyond the obvious to consider different interpretations and explore layers of meaning)
- make their own original interpretations.

A

A*

Prior learning

Before you begin this unit, think about

- what you already know about analysing character and voice
- any recent text you have read in which a particular character made an impression on you.

What do you understand these terms to mean?

What was it about the *way* the character was presented that made him or her memorable and kept you interested?

What do you remember about the character? Did you empathise or engage with the character's feelings, actions or viewpoint on life?

Characterisation

Learning objectives

- To understand the ways in which writers depict character.

- To consider the features of a good response on character.

What does characterisation mean?

Characterisation is the way in which a writer creates and develops a character.

Checklist for success

- You need to comment on **how** a character is created by the writer.
- You need to consider the **development** of characters (if and how they change over the course of a text).

Judging character

As readers, we make judgements about characters by looking at

- what they say and what they do
- how others (the writer or other characters) speak about them
- how others behave towards them
- in particular, their first and last appearances in a text.

EXAMPLE

Here is the opening of a response on the character of Inspector Goole in J.B. Priestley's play, *An Inspector Calls*. Which features of characterisation from the list above has the student commented on?

> Our first glimpse of Inspector Goole is when he appears in Act 1 Scene 1 and is described by the playwright as giving an 'impression of massiveness, solidity and purposefulness'. From this we already have in mind that he is large and imposing, and unlikely to be moved or shifted from the goal he is pursuing. Priestley's use of three nouns lends weight to the description: the words themselves seem heavy and unmovable. They are abstract concepts which, ironically, make him a considerable physical presence. Over the course of the play, this impression will not be lessened but strengthened by what we learn of the inspector.

This would fulfil many of the A/A★ criteria in

- choosing an **apt and original** quotation (selecting something from a stage direction might not be the obvious thing to do but is totally appropriate here)
- **analysing what this quotation suggests in detail**
- and, if we were to read on, probably **sustaining this interpretation** by explaining how Inspector Goole's character is developed **over the whole play**.

★ Examiner's tip

Notice how the student has also successfully woven the quotation into the response. You will need to do this in your Controlled Assessment response.

Focus for development: Revealing a character

Often we learn about character by what they wear, what they do and say and how others view them. For example, read these extracts from John Steinbeck's *Of Mice and Men*.

one person's view

The old man stood up. 'Know what I think? Well, I think Curley's married a tart.'

pretty? but what does 'sausages' suggest?

A girl was standing there looking in. She had full, rouged lips and wide-spaced eyes, heavily made up. Her finger nails were red. Her hair hung in little rolled clusters, like sausages…
'I'm looking for Curley,' she said. Her voice had a nasal, brittle quality. She put her hands behind her back and leaned against the door-frame so that her body was thrown forward…

could be seen to be supporting the old man's opinion

maybe she has frailties

sexual approach?

'Jesus, what a tramp,' George said.
'She's purty,' said Lennie, defensively.

another opinion

she is certainly pretty and attractive to Lennie

ACTIVITY

Write a brief character study of Curley's wife, based on these extracts. Analyse the language used, interpreting it and saying what the reader is supposed to think of her.

ASSESSMENT FOCUS

Choose a character who interests you from a novel or play you have studied. Write an analysis of how he or she has been characterised through their dress, actions, speech and opinions.

Examiner's tip ★

*Remember that if you can interpret the language used in **more than one way**, you are beginning to analyse in detail, which will bring higher marks.*

Remember

- **Don't just produce a character study, explain *how* the impressions are created.**
- **Writing about layers of meaning brings extra marks.**
- **Details and well-chosen quotations are always vital to a good analysis.**

Voice and perspective

Learning objective

- To understand how writers create a voice that is distinctive and individual.

What does voice mean?

Voice is the specific way in which a character tells their story, or in which a writer conveys their perspective on events.

A writer usually chooses to write either in the **third person** (he/she) or in the **first person** (I).

Checklist for success

- You need to explore **why** a text is written in the first or third person (or, indeed, from a more unusual perspective).
- You need to go beyond the obvious by considering **how** a specific voice is created.

From whose perspective?

It is important – especially with prose and poetry – to think about how characters speak and from whose perspective the story is told.

Writers can choose to write in the **first person** as if they were the **character**.

> Did I hate him? He was a drunken slob and he treated me like dirt. What do *you* think? Of course I hated him. You would have hated him, too, if you'd ever met him. God knows why Mum ever married him.
>
> Kevin Brooks, *Martyn Pig*

Equally, they can choose to write in the **third person**. This allows them to see inside the head of each character, not just one.

> Sitting, Ralph was aware of the heat for the first time that day. He pulled distastefully at his grey shirt and wondered whether he might undertake the adventure of washing it.
>
> William Golding, *Lord of the Flies*

Sometimes, a writer may adopt a particularly **unusual or original** persona, as if they were someone or something unexpected. For example, in this poem a river is talking!

Once there was a lady who was too bold
She bathed in me by the tall black cliff where the water runs cold,
Stevie Smith, 'The River God'

The best writers convince us that this is what the person, creature or being would actually say or do.

ACTIVITY

- Write a short paragraph in the first person, describing what you can see from your classroom window.
- Then rewrite the same paragraph in the third person (so that 'I' becomes 'he/she'). You may feel you need to change other details, too.
- How are the two paragraphs different in the effect they create?

ACTIVITY

Read this extract from *Martyn Pig*.

> It wasn't that I was jealous. Well, I suppose I was a bit jealous. But not in a namby kind of way, you know, not in a snotty, pouty kind of way. No, that wasn't it. Not really. That wasn't the reason I was glum. All right, it was *partly* the reason. But the main thing was – it was just *wrong*. All of it. Alex and Dean. It stank. It was wrong for her to spend time with him. It was a waste. He was nothing. It was wrong. Wrong. Wrong. *Wrong*. She was too good for him.
>
> The rain was turning to sleet as I pushed open the back gate and shuffled down the alleyway that led to the back of our house, stepping over dog turds and squashed cigarette ends and bin-liners full of empty beer cans.
>
> What's it got to do with you, anyway, I was thinking to myself. She can see who she wants. *What's it got to do with you what it's got to do with me?*
>
> What?
>
> I paused for a moment, wondering who the hell I was arguing with, then shrugged and went in through the kitchen door.

With a partner, discuss what we learn about Martyn from the way the author has depicted him. Think about:

- what we are told about his environment
- what we are told about the way he moves and acts – and what this suggests about his character
- what you notice about his 'voice' (What is the effect of the short sentences? How formal or informal is the language?)
- any other distinctive features about his 'voice' (Does he talk to himself? What is the effect of this on you as a reader?)

You will now have quite a lot of ideas about Martyn's character, but how would you begin an essay about him?

Look at this opening to a **Grade C** response to a characterisation question on Martyn.

> *Martyn is a boy in a novel by Kevin Brooks. He has this friend called Alex but it's clear from early in the book that he's jealous of her relationship with her boyfriend Dean. He says, 'it was wrong'.*

Evaluate this response, considering these points:

- Has the opening sentence grabbed your attention as well as being relevant?
- Has the student really captured Martyn's 'character'? (Why/Why not?)
- How well chosen is the quotation to give a sense of Martyn's 'voice'? (Would different quotations, or more of them, have helped?)

ASSESSMENT FOCUS

Write the opening paragraph of a response to this task.

> **In what ways does the first person narrator in any text you have studied change or develop as the text progresses? Focus on how the character is presented and how you react to any apparent changes in him or her.**

If you have not studied a text with a first-person narrator, write about Robert Browning's poem 'My Last Duchess' in the AQA Anthology, *Moon on the Tides*.

ACTIVITY

Write an improved opening paragraph on Martyn's character and voice. Use this as a starting point, if it helps.

> *Anxious, fed-up and partly in denial, Martyn declares that Alex and Dean's relationship... '...' and that...*

Remember

- Consider how the writer is creating the character's voice and from what perspective:
  - in a third-person narrative, the reader relies heavily on what others say about a character
  - in a first-person narrative, the reader reacts to what the narrator is thinking as well as to their speech and actions.
- Begin your response with an impressive opening paragraph.
- Choose and use quotations effectively to support your analysis.

Learning objective

- To understand how writers create a voice that is distinctive and individual.

Why might it be good to analyse an unusual voice?

If you explore texts where a writer adopts a more unusual voice, you can write in more sophisticated ways about voice and characterisation.

Checklist for success

You need to look **beneath the surface** at the techniques a writer uses to create this voice.

ACTIVITY

Read these annotations made by a student about the opening verses of the poem 'Medusa' by Carol Ann Duffy.

Persona is a Greek monster who turned people to stone with her looks. She was killed by Perseus.

Poet speaks Medusa's thoughts as if she is a jealous woman.

Strong metaphors support image of a violent monster made of stone, yet sad too. She's crying!

Sounds as if she is talking directly to the man who will betray her.

Better to destroy the person you love – if they don't love you?

MEDUSA

A suspicion, a doubt, a jealousy
grew in my mind,
which turned the hairs on my
   head to filthy snakes
as though my thoughts
hissed and spat on my scalp.

My bride's breath soured, stank
in the grey bags of my lungs.
I'm foul mouthed now, foul tongued,
   yellow fanged.
There are bullet tears in my eyes.
Are you terrified?

Be terrified.
It's you I love,
perfect man, Greek God, my own;
but I know you'll go, betray me, stray
   from home.
So better by far for me if you were stone.

Discuss with a partner what analytical skills the student has used.

What has she chosen to focus on?

What has she made notes about?

- language (for example, imagery or poetic devices)
- the background to the poem (the Greek myth and how it is retold here)
- voice and character.

Does she offer her own interpretation of the poem?

What might she have missed?

EXAMPLE

Look at this **Grade A/A★** response to one aspect of 'Medusa'.

> Duffy creates a terrifying, yet human vision of a mythical monster who has 'bullet tears' in her eyes. The phrase 'bullet tears' suggests both her unexpectedly human emotions, but also her violence: that she will turn them into weapons. Literally, the tears are hardening and turning to stone under her gaze as they fall from her eyes.

The response

- describes the character in two, almost contrasting ways using 'yet' ('terrifying yet human') and chooses an excellent quotation which sums up both things ('bullet' – violence/terror; 'tears' – very human)
- embeds the quotation into the sentence ('…has 'bullet tears' in her eyes')
- goes on to analyse the implications of the individual words picked out in a sophisticated way.

ACTIVITY

Choose any two poems from the Anthology which use local dialect or a distinctive accent. Write 150-200 words on how the different voice of each poem (or speaker in the poem) is conveyed. You could comment on

- how the language of the speaker conveys a sense of place or the speaker's background
- how the language of the speaker conveys a sense of character or a particular viewpoint
- how the language conveys a particular atmosphere, tone or style (reflection, aggression or stressing certain ideas.

For example, in 'The Ruined Maid' you could comment on how Melia's vocabulary has changed now she is 'in town' or how the rhythm of the repeated accented words 'Dem tell me / Dem tell me' in John Agard's 'Checking out me history' reflects an oral, musical culture.

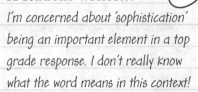

A student writes…

I'm concerned about 'sophistication' being an important element in a top grade response. I don't really know what the word means in this context!

Answer…

You show sophistication when you really engage with the text **in depth**. You follow your own pathways in thinking, and try out your own ideas. You explore the implications of individual words or images, and find layers of meaning.

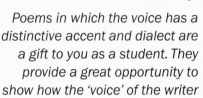

Examiner's tip

Poems in which the voice has a distinctive accent and dialect are a gift to you as a student. They provide a great opportunity to show how the 'voice' of the writer or narrator is different to that in other texts you might have read.

ACTIVITY

Write your own paragraph in response to 'Medusa'.

- Make a point.
- Support it with evidence from the poem.
- Explore the implications of the language.

Consider what impression of Medusa we get from what she says and how she says it.

Try to interpret her words in different ways to demonstrate sophistication in your answer.

ACTIVITY

A student has added some notes on character and voice to the poem below. Using a copy of the poem, can you add to the annotations?

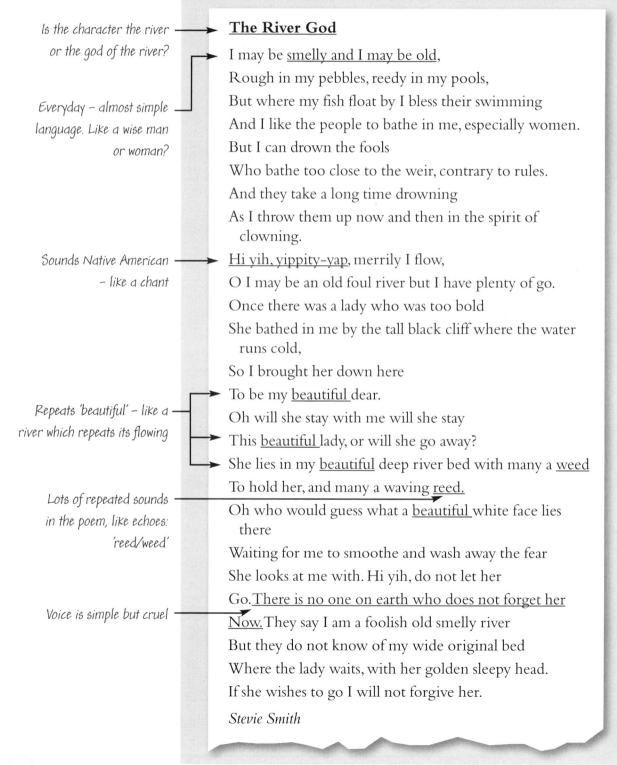

Is the character the river or the god of the river?

Everyday – almost simple language. Like a wise man or woman?

Sounds Native American – like a chant

Repeats 'beautiful' – like a river which repeats its flowing

Lots of repeated sounds in the poem, like echoes: 'reed/weed'

Voice is simple but cruel

The River God

I may be <u>smelly and I may be old,</u>
Rough in my pebbles, reedy in my pools,
But where my fish float by I bless their swimming
And I like the people to bathe in me, especially women.
But I can drown the fools
Who bathe too close to the weir, contrary to rules.
And they take a long time drowning
As I throw them up now and then in the spirit of clowning.
<u>Hi yih, yippity-yap</u>, merrily I flow,
O I may be an old foul river but I have plenty of go.
Once there was a lady who was too bold
She bathed in me by the tall black cliff where the water runs cold,
So I brought her down here
To be my <u>beautiful</u> dear.
Oh will she stay with me will she stay
This <u>beautiful</u> lady, or will she go away?
She lies in my <u>beautiful</u> deep river bed with many a <u>weed</u>
To hold her, and many a waving <u>reed.</u>
Oh who would guess what a <u>beautiful</u> white face lies there
Waiting for me to smoothe and wash away the fear
She looks at me with. Hi yih, do not let her
Go. <u>There is no one on earth who does not forget her</u>
<u>Now.</u> They say I am a foolish old smelly river
But they do not know of my wide original bed
Where the lady waits, with her golden sleepy head.
If she wishes to go I will not forgive her.

Stevie Smith

ASSESSMENT FOCUS

Read this first paragraph of a **Grade A** response:

> In 'The River God' the poet adopts the voice of the river – or of the being who controls it. The voice of the god feels like that of a wise old tribal shaman or woman who, on the one hand, does not care what they look like, commenting in simple language, 'I may be smelly and I may be old'. Yet, on the other, she is not pleasant at all, and 'will not forgive' the drowned lady.

This might well turn into a top-level response. The student presents the different aspects of the voice in the poem, which will certainly be developed later, and the subtle idea that it might not actually be the river who speaks: it could be a being controlling it. The quotations are apt and well embedded.

Picking up on this idea of the contradictions in 'The River God', add at least two further paragraphs in which you develop this point, or make your own analysis of the river god's 'voice'.

Use this structure if it helps.

Paragraph 1:	The idea of the river god as a wise old tribal leader and how she speaks The (contrasting) idea that she sounds cruel and childish and holds grudges
Paragraph 2:	The idea of giving a blessing versus clowning about or being playful

Remember

- A detailed focus on key words and phrases is likely to help you be 'sophisticated'.
- It's not a problem if your ideas about a character or voice sometimes seem to contradict each other, as long as you analyse them in your response.

Sustained writing on character

Learning objective

- *To learn techniques for writing in detail about a character's development.*

What does sustained writing on character mean?

To write in a sustained way about character, which is required in your Controlled Assessment task, you need to explain how characters develop or change over the course of a text. This might be based on

- how a character **reveals something** about their life or situation over the course of a text – for example, the river god has drowned a young woman and won't release her
- how a character **grows up** – for example how Pip changes from a small boy to a grown man in *Great Expectations*
- how a **significant incident or event affects a person** or group of people – for example, the cutting of the rope that holds the main character's friend and sends him to his 'death' in *Touching the Void*
- how a character **changes from good to bad**, from hero to villain (or vice versa) – for example, Macbeth murdering his king and taking the crown.

Checklist for success

You need to refer in detail to the character's development, using specific quotations to support the points you make.

ACTIVITY

A student has jotted down the following summary of the short story 'The Darkness Out There' by Penelope Lively. The story is seen through the eyes of the main character, Sandra.

Look closely at the student's notes.

- Why do you think the student selected these parts of the story?
- How do they suggest the development in Sandra's character through the story?

Background: Sandra and Kerry are part of a 'Good Neighbours' club. They do odd jobs for older people. They visit Mrs Rutter who lives on the edge of some woods at a place called Packer's End.

Sandra...

> remembers going to the woods as a younger child and the fears she and other friends had about the woods

> recalls stories about incidents which were rumoured to have happened, including how a plane crashed there in the war, killing the crew; thinks about herself and her hopes for the future

> is told a new – and clearly true – story by the old woman, Mrs Rutter, about the plane crash: how she had left a young German crew-man to die of his injuries in the woods over two nights after the plane had crashed

> returns home with Kerry, reflecting on what she has just heard.

ACTIVITY

Here are three extracts from 'The Darkness Out There', in the order they occur. They include the final paragraphs of the story. Read them, and **trace the development of Sandra's character throughout**. Make notes on each extract as you go along.

Consider:

- Sandra's views about 'old people' and Kerry at the start and end of the story
- how the writer selects significant details or descriptions to convey Sandra's **character**
- how the writer conveys her **voice** (that of a teenage girl).

1 On the way to Mrs Rutter's house

It was all right out here in the sunshine. Fine. She stopped to pick grass stems out of her sandal; she saw the neat print of the strap-marks against her sunburn, pink-white on brown. Somebody had said she had pretty feet, once; she looked at them, clean and plump and neat on the grass. A ladybird crawled across a toe.

When they were small, six and seven and eight, they'd been scared stiff of Packer's End. Then, they hadn't known about the German plane. It was different things then; witches and wolves and tigers. Sometimes they'd go there for a dare, several of them, skittering over the field and into the edge of the trees, giggling and shrieking, not too far in, just far enough for it to be scary, for the branch shapes to look like faces and clawed hands, for the wolves to rustle and creep in the greyness you couldn't quite see into, the clotted shifting depths of the place.

But after, lying on your stomach at home on the hearth rug watching telly with the curtains drawn and the dark shut out, it was cosy to think of Packer's End, where you weren't.

After they were twelve or so the witches and wolves went away.

2 Meeting Kerry on the way

He grinned. 'I seen you coming. Thought I might as well wait.'

Not Susie. Not Liz either. Kerry Stevens from Richmond Way. Kerry Stevens that none of her lot reckoned much on, with his black licked-down hair and slitty eyes. Some people you only have to look at to know they're not up to much.

'Didn't know you were in the Good Neighbours.'

He shrugged. They walked in silence. He took out an Aero bar, broke off a bit, offered it. She said oh, thanks. They went chewing towards the cottage, the cottage where old Mrs Rutter with her wonky leg would be ever so pleased to see them because they were really sweet, lots of the old people. Ever so grateful, the old poppets, was what Pat said, not that you'd put it quite like that yourself.

3 Leaving the cottage, after Mrs Rutter's story

The boy said, 'I'm not going near that old bitch again.' He leaned against the gate, clenching his fists on an iron rung; he shook slightly. 'I won't ever forget him, that poor sod.'

She nodded.

'Two bloody nights. Christ!'

And she would hear, she thought, always, for a long time anyway, that voice trickling on, that soft old woman's voice: would see a tin painted with cornflowers, pretty china ornaments.

'It makes you want to throw up,' he said. 'Someone like that.'

She couldn't think of anything to say. He had grown; he had got older and larger. His anger eclipsed his acne, the patches of grease on his jeans, his lardy midriff. You could get people all wrong, she realised with alarm. You could get people wrong and there was a darkness that was not the darkness of tree shadows and murky undergrowth and you could not draw the curtains and keep it out because it was in your head, once known, in your head for ever like lines from a song. One moment you were walking in long grass with the sun on your hair and birds singing and the next you glimpsed darkness, an inescapable darkness. The darkness was out there and it was a part of you and you would never be without it, ever.

She walked behind him, through a world grown unreliable, in which flowers sparkle and birds sing but everything is not as it appears, oh no.

Now look at how these two students have commented on the final two paragraphs in the story. With a partner, discuss how the second response is better at conveying the change in Sandra.

Grade C response

Sandra has changed her view of Kerry and Mrs Rutter from the start. To begin with she thought Mrs Rutter was 'really sweet' but in fact she's a 'bitch' as Kerry says. She has also changed her attitude to Kerry because she objected to him coming at the start and wanted to be with her girlfriends. He understands what they have gone through and she likes how he reacts. The writer emphasises the shifts in Sandra's understanding of how the world has now changed by ending with the idea that 'everything is not as it appears'.

Grade A response

Sandra has entered a 'world grown unreliable' by the end of the story, but in fact it is the adult world she has entered, in which the things which seemed simple, clear and superficial at the start now have shades of meaning. Kerry hasn't literally changed in appearance but Sandra's view of him has. She now looks beneath the surface. The change in her character is reflected by the symbol of the 'darkness' of the woods, which represents reality, not the fears of childhood. Sandra is both a child, yet now grown-up.

Stories like this which are told from a child's point of view and involve the change from childhood to adulthood are often referred to as 'rites of passage'.

ASSESSMENT FOCUS

Now look over the notes you have made. In a written response, how would you describe Sandra's development in 'The Darkness Out There' in detail?

Plan your ideas, ensuring you have

- a strong introduction that shows the direction your analysis will take
- detailed and analytical development of your main points
- a conclusion which sums up the development.

Be ready to adjust your conclusion, if necessary, once you have drafted the rest of your analysis.

Remember

- **Focus on detail and how it is used, as you chart the character's development.**
- **The storyteller's techniques are important elements in your analysis.**
- **Structure your response appropriately, so it extends logically and is framed by the opening and ending.**

Planning your controlled assessment task

Learning objective

- *To explore ways of planning and structuring a response on 'characterisation and voice'.*

Checklist for success

For the Controlled Assessment task you will need a clear idea of the focus of the task. This might be about

- how a character develops or changes
- how a character makes an impression in some way or other
- how a character who undergoes some sort of life-changing experience is presented
- the way a character's voice conveys what they are like, and how they behave.

Look at this task.

> *Explore how the first-person narrative voice presents the character in any text you have studied.*

A possible structure, using *Martyn Pig* as the text, might be:

START: Impress with an imaginative opening. [para 1]

You could use a quotation (or any of the other beginnings in the table on page 179): *'That's how I felt. I felt glum. Glum as a... whatever.'* This is Martyn, talking to us, confiding in us, letting us into his world.

DEVELOP: Pick up on the main point – the 'voice' – and look to explore further. [para 2]

*Why is confiding so important to Martyn, and what language does he use? Sometimes the language is **informal and chatty**, sometimes **it's vivid and full of images** of his world, **other times** it's...*

FOCUS: POINT 1 about LANGUAGE [para 3] Informal language examples from Martyn	**FOCUS: POINT 2 about LANGUAGE** [para 4] Vivid imagery	**FOCUS: POINT 3 about LANGUAGE** [para 5] Another way Martyn speaks about his world

---

DEVELOP AGAIN: Further work on the main point [para 6]

*Martyn uses the first-person voice to allow us into his world, but even this is not straightforward. Because we also hear his other voices – the one for his **dad**, the one for **Alex**, and for people **he doesn't know well**...*

FOCUS: POINT 1 about talking to his DAD [para 7]	**FOCUS: POINT 2 about talking to ALEX** [para 8]	**FOCUS: POINT 3 about talking to people in authority** [para 9]

CONCLUSION [para 10]: **End by summarising, but not in a dull or boring way; find a nice, flowing phrase to end with, or a question or a good quotation.**

Once you get the structure of your response right, concentrate on getting the detailed language of the content right too.

Examiner's tip ★

It is often wise to begin with an overview, then move on to prove your ideas using specific detail.

Make clear what the writer's perspective or voice is:	*In 'The Darkness Out There',* **we follow Sandra's perspective** *as she* **experiences the moment, but also remembers the past**…
Sum up the character's **role** with well-chosen words:	*Martyn, the* **central figure** *in the novel, is a* **teenager with a drunkard for a father**…
Tackle difficulties and contradictions in a reflective way:	*Mrs Rutter,* **sweet and gentle, yet in her own quiet way able to deliver a hammer blow** *to Sandra's innocent visions*…
Use **character adjectives** in a succinct way to describe the character or persona:	**Unloved, bitter and vengeful***, Medusa speaks directly to the reader*…
End impressively by using some of the same language techniques you used for the beginning. For example:	*By the end of the novel, Ralph is* **beaten, desperate and defeated**… *Who, then, is 'Medusa'? Is she all women – all betrayed wives?* **Or, most frightening of all, is she a girl like me who has grown old and grey and remembers her youth?** *As the Prince states as the play ends, staring at the bodies of the dead Romeo and Juliet 'All are punished', but, in fact, it is our two young lovers who are 'punished' most of all for daring to profess a love as* **'boundless as the sea'***.*

ASSESSMENT FOCUS

Write your own plan for the same question.

> *Explore how the first-person narrative voice presents the character in any text you have studied.*

If you have not focused on a text with a first person narrator previously, read and respond to either 'The Darkness Out There' or 'My Last Duchess' from the AQA Anthology.

Remember

- **Build from general ideas to specific, focused ideas.**
- **Be ambitious and original: ask questions and explore ideas, use and embed appropriate quotations fluently.**
- **Develop and sustain your response.**

Grade Booster

Extended Assessment Task

Write a response of around 1200 words to this task.

Explore how the first-person narrative voice is used to present the main character in any text you have studied.

Draw on what you have learned about detailed analysis and response:

- How can you make general comments about the character, linked to detailed specific examples, evidence and exploration?
- Consider alternative or personal interpretations of the character.
- Write a sustained, developed response that goes beyond basic points.

Evaluation – What have you learned?

With a partner, use the grade checklist below to evaluate your work on the Extended Assessment Task.

- I can sustain sophisticated and original interpretations of the character's perspective and voice, engaging fully with writers' ideas and attitudes as reflected through their characters.
- I can imaginatively select detail and evidence, and make subtle links and connections between ideas.
- I can refer to a wide range and variety of linguistic techniques used by writers.

- I can sustain my interpretation of the character(s) I have discussed.
- I can engage with writers' ideas and attitudes as reflected through their characters.
- I can use precisely selected supporting evidence and textual detail.
- I can analyse language and structure in convincing detail.

- I can develop ideas, and show engagement with many key aspects of the character's portrayal.
- I can select relevant evidence and quotations and analyse language and structure, sometimes in detail, sometimes in quite broad ways.

- I can clearly understand the way character is portrayed and presented.
- I can explain these main ideas in clear and logical ways.
- I can understand how language features and structure work.
- I can support comment on character with relevant quotations.

- I can show some understanding of how character is presented by the writer.
- I can support these ideas with quotations and evidence but these are not always well chosen or appropriate.
- I can make my own points but these are not developed in as much detail as they could be.

You may need to go back and look at the relevant pages from this section again.

Themes and Ideas

Introduction

This section of Chapter 4 shows you how to

- understand what a 'Themes and ideas' Controlled Assessment task requires you to do
- develop responses to different forms of text.

Why is learning about themes and ideas important?

- Understanding and considering a text's themes and ideas will add to your enjoyment of reading it.
- Texts can be looked at in a range of ways, and a focus on themes and ideas will sometimes need a different approach from a focus on characterisation and voice.
- The ways in which writers convey their ideas or explore particular themes that interest them will provide a model for your own creative writing.
- Themes are usually at the core of the text: they deliver the message that the writer wants to put across.

A **Grade C** candidate will

- show clear evidence of understanding the main ways in which themes or ideas have been presented and be able to explain writers' presentation of ideas clearly
- display understanding of various features of language and structure used by writers to convey ideas and themes
- support points with relevant and appropriate quotations.

C

A **Grade A/A*** candidate will

- sustain their response to key themes and ideas (by developing and writing about these ideas at length)
- imaginatively select quotations and detail to support their views
- analyse in a sophisticated way how a particular idea or theme is presented through language and structure, examining layers of meaning
- make their own original interpretations.

A **A***

Prior learning

Before you begin this unit, reflect on

- what you already know about analysing a writer's ideas and themes
- any recent text you have read in which a particular idea or thematic focus made an impression on you.

Decide what you understand by these terms.

What do you remember about the theme of the text? Did you agree with the writer's viewpoint or enjoy the way ideas were presented? What made it interesting?

Tracing the development of themes and ideas

Learning objectives

- *To learn how to trace and record your thoughts on the themes and ideas in a text.*
- *To practise key techniques in preparing a response on theme and ideas.*

Why are themes and ideas important?

The themes and ideas that emerge from a text reflect the particular concerns or interests of the writer – for example, the theme of 'growing up' in a poem about childhood or the part a 'journey' plays in a novel. Understanding these is central to developing your personal interpretation of the text.

Checklist for success

- You need to show you can trace the development of an idea or theme through a text.
- You need to focus on how a writer's language choices and decisions about structure and form develop a theme or idea.
- You need to make well-supported judgements about a writer's own attitude to the themes or ideas presented (answering questions such as 'Why has the writer drawn them to our attention?' and 'What would he or she like us to think?').

How themes arise from plot

Here is some background to John Steinbeck's *Of Mice and Men*.

The novel is set in 1930s California during a time of job shortages and economic depression. Lennie and George are two itinerant workers moving from ranch to ranch looking for work. Lennie is rather backward and slow and George tries to keep him out of trouble, usually failing to do so and feeling both responsible for him and irritated by his child-like simplicity which causes them problems.

Here are some student notes about a series of events in the novel.

Lennie and George discuss their dream of buying their own little farm when they have raised enough money.

At the ranch, they reveal their plans to an old ranch-hand, Candy. He offers to come with them – he sees himself as 'useless'.

Candy and Lennie tell the black stable-hand Crooks, who lives separately on the ranch, and he wants to join them, being mistreated too.

Curley's wife tells some of the workers that she could have been an actress; now she is bored and hates her life, as her husband ignores her most of the time, or is 'mean' to her.

From the notes above we can identify that the theme of 'dreams and escape' is probably central to the novel, as all the characters mentioned dreams of leaving the hard lifestyle of the ranch.

ACTIVITY

Here are two further possible themes in *Of Mice and Men*:

- friendship and responsibility
- personal isolation.

Write down any evidence of these from the student's notes on page 178 or from your own knowledge of the novel.

Focus for development: Gathering ideas

ACTIVITY

Read this extract from *Of Mice and Men*. Curley, the boss's son, has come into the bunk house where all the workers sleep.

> *His eyes passed over the new men and he stopped. He glanced coldly at George and then at Lennie. His arms gradually bent at the elbows and his hands closed into fists. He stiffened and went into a slight crouch. His glance was at once calculating and pugnacious. Lennie squirmed under the look and shifted his feet nervously. Curley stepped gingerly close to him. 'You the new guys the old man was waitin' for?'*
>
> *'We just come in,' said George.*
>
> *'Let the big guy talk.'*
>
> *Lennie twisted with embarrassment.*
>
> *George said, 'S'pose he don't want to talk?'*
>
> *Curley lashed his body around. 'By Christ, he's gotta talk when he's spoke to. What the hell are you gettin' into it for?'*
>
> *'We travel together,' said George coldly.*
>
> *'Oh, so it's that way.'*
>
> *George was tense and motionless. 'Yeah, it's that way.'*

Complete a table like the one below. Note down in the relevant column what you discover from the extract about Lennie, George and Curley. Include a supporting quotation for each of your points.

Lennie	George	Curley
Seems uncomfortable – 'squirmed…and shifted his feet nervously'		

Examiner's tip

Use synonyms and related words or phrases to expand your ideas and avoid repetition. For example, terms related to friendship could be 'companionship', 'responsibility', 'dependence', 'dominance', 'admiration' or 'sharing'.

ACTIVITY

Focusing more closely on the theme of friendship and responsibility, use the information in your table and refer back to the extract to answer these questions.

- What do we find out about the relationships between these characters?
- What is the writer trying to show us here about friendship and responsibility and the tensions this creates?
- How is he presenting the ideas to us?
- Why do you think he chooses to write about this theme? What might interest him here, as an observer of human nature?

Having decided there is an idea worth exploring, one student began their response like this.

> John Steinbeck is interested in ideas of the tension and friendships that emerge when men live and work together, as seen in Chapter 2 of the novel when we first meet Curley, the boss's son.
>
> The tension between the men is apparent in the way Curley...

A student writes…

I find writing about themes difficult, because you have to start with these big statements or ideas which aren't always obvious in the story.

Answer…

Don't worry too much about coming up with single words or terms that cover the theme or idea, like 'conflict'. It's often helpful to start by saying, 'The author is interested in how…' or 'The author is interested in why…'.

ACTIVITY

If you had to develop and write the rest of the student's response about 'friendship and tension' in the extract on page 183, what would you say, and in what order?

Produce a detailed plan, including your main points and the quotations you would use to support them.

Developing the theme

If you wanted to write further about this theme, however, focusing on one single event wouldn't be enough. You would need to look for

- **further examples** in which **Lennie and George's** friendship is demonstrated, especially George 'looking out' for Lennie
- **examples** of friendship between the **other men** in the novel
- **examples** of moments when **tension and difficulties** emerge
- **how** the tensions and friendships are presented.

Here is a further extract from the novel that highlights the theme of friendship and tension.

> *Suddenly Lennie's eyes centred and grew quiet and mad. He stood up and walked dangerously toward Crooks. 'Who hurt George?' he demanded.*
>
> *Crooks saw danger as it approached him. He edged back on his bunk to get out of the way. 'I was just supposin',' he said. 'George ain't hurt. He's all right. He'll be back all right.'*
>
> *Lennie stood over him. 'What you supposin' for? Ain't nobody goin' to suppose no hurt to George.'*
>
> *Crooks removed his glasses and wiped his eyes with his fingers. 'Jus' sit down,' he said. 'George ain't hurt.'*
>
> *Lennie growled back to his seat on the nail-keg. 'Ain't nobody goin' to talk no hurt to George,' he grumbled.*

ACTIVITY

Discuss with a partner.

To practise analysing detail that will enhance your response, offer your interpretations of

- why Crooks removes his glasses
- the effect of 'Lennie growled'.

ASSESSMENT FOCUS

If you were showing how the themes of tension and friendship are developed through the novel, you could use the extract above for part of your response.

Write at least a paragraph saying

- what we learn about the friendship between Lennie and George here
- how tension arises because of their friendship
- how the reader is affected by the scene.

Remember

- **Use the events that occur in the text to help you identify and trace a central theme or idea.**
- **Look at how the writer's language choices and structure develop the themes.**
- **Make your own interpretations or judgements, based on evidence from the text, about why the writer presents his or her chosen themes and ideas in the way he does.**
- **Ensure your interpretations link effectively.**

How themes and ideas are presented

What does presenting themes and ideas mean?

Writers convey ideas in different and sometimes subtle ways that don't state the idea obviously. For example, how characters move or use gestures can tell the reader more than what they say **directly**.

In the first *Of Mice and Men* extract on page 183:

- George's protectiveness towards Lennie is **implied** by the way he speaks. (He never directly states he is protecting Lennie, but he says defensively, 'We travel together'.)
- The tension between the men is shown through the language used to describe their movements (for example, verbs such as 'lashed' or 'stiffened').

Another key way in which writers present their ideas is through descriptions of landscape, surroundings and situation.

Checklist for success

- You need to interpret themes and ideas not only based on events but through setting and subtleties of characterisation.

ACTIVITY

In this description from *Lord of the Flies* by William Golding, a group of school–boys have been stranded on a tropical island for several days. Two of them have seen something in the night which they think is a 'beast'. (In fact, it's a dead parachutist who has crash landed in the trees.)

> They lay there listening, at first with doubt but then with terror, to the description the twins breathed at them between bouts of extreme silence. Soon the darkness was full of claws, full of the awful unknown and menace. An interminable dawn faded the stars out, and at last light, sad and grey, filtered into the shelter. They began to stir though still the world outside the shelter was impossibly dangerous. The maze of the darkness sorted into near and far, and at the high point of the sky the cloudlets were warmed with colour. A single sea bird flapped upwards with a hoarse cry that was echoed presently, and something squawked in the forest. Now streaks of cloud near the horizon began to glow rosily, and the feathery tops of the palms were green.

With a partner, discuss how this short passage brings out the following themes or ideas:

- the power of imagination
- the island as a place of beauty but also of unknown threats.

Now look at this later description. Some of the boys have placed the remains of a killed pig on a stick.

> *Suggests something is about to happen – good or bad?*

Over the island the **build-up** of clouds continued. A steady current of heated air rose all day from the mountain and was thrust to ten thousand feet; revolving masses of gas piled up the static until the air was **ready to explode**. By early evening the sun had gone and a brassy glare had taken the place of clear daylight. Even the air that pushed in from the sea was hot and held no refreshment. **Colours drained** from water and trees and pink surfaces of rock, and the white and brown clouds brooded. Nothing prospered but the flies who blackened their lord and made the spilt guts look like a heap of glistening coal.

> *Violent language; the island really is dangerous*

> *It's like death – life draining away*

ACTIVITY

A student has annotated the passage with her thoughts. What has she focused on?

What else could she annotate to show how the idea of threat is presented in this passage? Think about

- sentence structure (the arrangement of clauses in sentences) and its effect
- images used (what particular features has she commented or not commented on)?
- powerful word choices.

Make notes on how the idea of danger and threat, which was largely in the minds of the boys in the earlier extract, is now more apparent.

ASSESSMENT FOCUS

Write about the two extracts from *Of Mice and Men* and *Lord of the Flies* on these pages. Explain how the writers in each have presented their ideas in different ways.

Or

Choose two extracts from a text of your choice and show how a theme or idea has been developed by the writer. Explain how the theme is presented in each extract.

A student writes…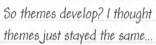

So themes develop? I thought themes just stayed the same…

Answer…

Themes, like characters, can be developed over the course of a text. So, in *Lord of the Flies* the island – as an idea – is initially a paradise-like playground; then it becomes a place of conflict and fear, and, ultimately death and despair.

Remember

- **Make your point, provide evidence, explain further and develop with detail.**
- **Focus on what is implied, not just what is stated directly.**
- **Consider the whole range of ways in which writers can present themes (through the events, the setting or the characters' speech and movements).**
- **Follow the development of themes through texts.**

How writers suggest ideas and themes

Learning objective

- To recognise the devices writers use to suggest themes that will emerge as the text progresses.

What does suggesting themes mean?

Writers use a range of techniques, such as creating recurring motifs or providing clues, to suggest larger ideas. For example, a fallen apple tree in the opening of a play may imply the loss of young people's lives in war.

Checklist for success

- You need to read a text very closely, looking for these references and hints, and exploring what they might imply.
- You need to focus on the potential meanings of particular words and phrases and how these might relate to the larger themes of a text.

The play *Kindertransport,* by Diane Samuels, takes its name from the organised movement that helped thousands of Jewish children to escape from Germany, Austria, Czechoslovakia and Poland in 1938-9, just before the start of World War Two. Around 10,000 children were sent to safety in Britain on these Kindertransport trains; most of them never saw the families they left behind again.

Kindertransport tells the story of one survivor, Eva, who is forced to confront her past when her own daughter discovers the truth about what happened to her.

ACTIVITY

Use the internet to find out as much as you can about the Kindertransport.

188

Read the opening page of the play, keeping in mind these ideas:

- the Kindertransport
- the Holocaust (which followed the outbreak of war)
- mother and daughter relationships – and the difficulty of communication
- separation.

In what ways are these particular ideas **implied** or **foreshadowed** by the scene and the conversation between Eva and her mother?

Scene One

Ratcatcher music.

Dusty storage room filled with crates, bags, boxes and old furniture.

EVA, *dressed in clothes of the late thirties, is sitting on the floor, reading. The book is a large, hard-backed children's story book entitled 'Der Rattenfänger'.*

HELGA, *holding a coat, button, needle and thread, is nearby. She is well-turned out in clothes of the late thirties.*

EVA	What's an abyss, Mutti?
HELGA	(*sitting down and ushering* EVA *to sit next to her*) An abyss is a deep and terrible chasm.
EVA	What's a chasm?
HELGA	A huge gash in the rocks.
EVA	What's a …

EVA *puts down the book. Music stops.*

HELGA	Eva, sew on your buttons now. Show me that you can do it.
EVA	I can't get the thread through the needle. It's too thick. You do it.
HELGA	Lick the thread…
EVA	Do I have to?
HELGA	Yes, lick the thread.
EVA	I don't want to sew.
HELGA	How else will the buttons get onto the coat?
EVA	The coat's too big for me.
HELGA	It's to last next winter too.
EVA	Please.
HELGA	No.
EVA	Why won't you help me?
HELGA	You have to be able to manage on your own.
EVA	Why?
HELGA	Because you do. Now, lick the thread.

Having read the opening, write two paragraphs in which you explain how the first scene sets up or suggests what the main themes of the play will be.

Here is the beginning of a **Grade C** student's response. Finding the themes was not difficult, but how well did he or she write about them?

> The play is obviously set in the past ('clothes of the late thirties') and we sense from the start that this might lead to problems. The mother is worried about whether her daughter can look after herself because she makes her daughter do the sewing herself and we suspect that the two might end up being separated. The title of the play itself will give us that idea, and then Eva mentions the 'chasm'...

This student could have developed the ideas more fully and could have examined the language more closely through more specific quotations.

Now compare it with an extract from a **Grade A/A★** response:

> There are several themes which emerge in this early scene. For example, the play establishes the idea of history and the past with the design reference to the 'clothes of the late thirties'.
>
> In addition, the writer draws the audience's attention to the violent and terrible events of the time with the seemingly innocent question about the meaning of the word 'chasm' by the little girl. We, like the mother, recognise that this implies something much more – perhaps the terrible hole that was made in the Jewish people by the Holocaust, or indeed the impending separation between mother and daughter. 'Chasm' suggests a deep divide: a parting that is, perhaps, unlikely to be bridged. As a word, it sounds catastrophic and harsh, just like the situation to come.

Discuss with a partner what the second response does better than the first.

Consider:

- the clarity of what is said
- the more sophisticated analysis of the word 'chasm'.

A different kind of transport: Holocaust victims being taken to a concentration camp in Poland

ASSESSMENT FOCUS

Write a paragraph in which you comment on the theme of survival in the extract on page 189. Consider the conversation about the sewing, the coat and the winter ahead.

You could begin…

A further theme to emerge from this scene is one of survival, as shown when…

Remember

- Recognise that particular ideas or themes can be hinted at in subtle ways.
- Look at the openings of texts to see how these ideas are sometimes 'set up' or suggested.
- Track how these ideas are then developed later in the text.
- Expand on ideas by linking them together and going beyond the obvious with your analysis.

Grade Booster

Extended Assessment Task

For any novel or play you have studied, consider one of the key themes or ideas. It could be 'family relationships that break down' or 'how people become isolated', or whatever you choose. Jot down notes under these headings:

- how the idea or theme is presented at the start of the text (including subtle hints and suggestions)
- how the theme or idea is developed or changed through the text by significant incidents, moments or situations
- how the theme is presented through choice of language, setting, movement, key detail and imagery.

Write a response on this theme or idea of not more than 1200 words, using direct evidence from your chosen text.

Evaluation – What have you learned?

With a partner, use the grade checklist below to evaluate your work on the Extended Assessment Task.

- I can sustain sophisticated and original interpretations of texts, engaging fully with writers' ideas and attitudes.
- I can imaginatively select detail and evidence, and make subtle links and connections between ideas.
- I can refer to a wide range and variety of linguistic techniques used by writers.

- I can sustain my interpretation of the texts.
- I can engage with writers' ideas and attitudes.
- I can use precisely-selected supporting evidence and textual detail.
- I can analyse language and structure in convincing detail.

- I can develop ideas, and show engagement with many ideas and themes.
- I can select relevant evidence and quotations.
- I can analyse language and structure, sometimes in detail, sometimes in quite broad ways.

- I can show I clearly understand main ideas and themes.
- I can explain these main ideas and themes in clear and logical ways.
- I can understand how language features and structure work.
- I can support main ideas with relevant quotations and explanations.

- I can show some understanding of main themes and ideas.
- I can support these ideas with quotations and evidence but they are not always well chosen or appropriate.
- I can make my own points but these are not developed in as much detail as they could be.

You may need to go back and look at the relevant pages from this section again.

Controlled Assessment Preparation: Extended Reading

Introduction

In this section you will

- find out what is required of you in the Extended Reading Controlled Assessment task
- read, analyse and respond to two sample answers by different candidates
- plan and write your own answer to a sample question
- evaluate and assess your answer and the progress you have made.

Why is preparation of this kind important?

- If you know exactly what you need to do, you will feel more confident when you produce your own assessed response.
- Looking at sample answers by other students will help you see what you need to do to improve your own work.
- Planning and writing a full written response after you have completed the whole chapter will give you a clear sense of what you have learned so far.

Key information

Unit 3 Section A is 'Understanding Written Texts: Extended Reading'.

- The controlled part of the task will last **3–4 hours**, and is worth **30 marks**.
- It is worth **15%** of your overall English Language GCSE mark.

What will the task involve?

- The task will be based on **one extended text** you have studied (fiction or non-fiction).
- This text can be the same as one you have studied for English Literature but **the task must be different**.
- If you wish, you can use the **AQA Anthology** of poetry and short stories, *Moon on the Tides*.

What does the task consist of?

You will be asked to respond to **one task**. You will have to write about either **themes and ideas** or **characterisation and voice**.

The task will be done under 'controlled conditions' – in silence, in an exam room or in your own classroom.

The recommended word limit is 1200 and you will be allowed up to **four hours** to complete the task.

Here are some example questions based on the general task areas set by the exam board.

Character	How is a central character presented in a text you have studied? *Consider how Shakespeare presents the development of Macbeth's character once he has killed the king.*
Theme	Family relationships: *Consider the methods used by Shakespeare to dramatise family conflicts in* Romeo and Juliet. *Explore how the conflict between Martyn and his father in* Martyn Pig *is a key factor in what happens in the story.*

The Assessment

The assessment objective for this unit (AO3) states that you must:
- Read and understand texts, selecting material appropriate to purpose.
- Develop and sustain interpretations of writers' ideas and perspectives.
- Explain and evaluate how writers use linguistic, grammatical, structural and presentational features to achieve effects and engage and influence the reader.

Targeting Grade A

Some of the key features of Grade C and Grade A/A★ responses are as follows:

Grade C candidates	See
<ul><li>show clear evidence of understanding key meanings in the text, with some ability to look for more significant or deeper interpretations</li><li>write clearly about writers' ideas supported by relevant and appropriate evidence/quotation</li><li>display understanding of language features used and support points with relevant quotations.</li></ul>	*example on page 195*

Grade A/A★ candidates	See
<ul><li>sustain sophisticated ideas and interpretations so they are fully developed and explored</li><li>demonstrate thorough engagement with the writers' ideas, selecting not just relevant quotations but also very carefully selected evidence, viewed in an original way</li><li>analyse writers' use of language in focused detail, understanding the sometimes complex ways in which language operates and the subtle layers of meaning.</li></ul>	*example on page 197–8*

Exploring Sample Responses

ACTIVITY

Read the following extract from a student's response to this question.

> *How is a central character presented in a text you have studied? Consider how Shakespeare presents the development of Macbeth once he has killed the king.*

As you read it, think about whether it is closer to a Grade C or a Grade A/A★, and why.

Consider the key elements a marker would look for:

- How clearly and effectively has the writer conveyed his/her ideas?
- Are the author's and the student's ideas shown?
- How well has the student commented on the language used?
- How well does the student support the point he/she makes?
- Is there any original or more 'sophisticated' interpretation of ideas?

Example 1: Characterisation

It is clear to me that Macbeth changes as a character once he has killed the king. Up until then there was the possibility that it was all talk.

He starts as a hero ('brave Macbeth'), but after listening to the witches and his wife and killing King Duncan when he was asleep, all that changes.

He clearly realises what he has done in moving himself beyond what is acceptable because he can no longer pray:

'Amen' stuck in my throat.

He also feels he has murdered 'innocent sleep' and that word is important – he himself is no longer innocent.

He is able to put up a front with his guests when the king's body is discovered but the horror of his action eventually plays on his mind. When he decides to have Banquo and Fleance killed, he keeps the deed secret from his wife. The audience is tempted to think he is now in control. He says, 'full of scorpions is my mind, dear wife'. We react to the idea of scorpions by thinking he is dangerous, but in fact he is suggesting that he is being tortured in his head. Also, the idea of 'dear wife' sounds loving but the two are drifting apart as Macbeth at first – and Lady Macbeth later – both seem to be going mad.

In no time, he is seeing visions and Lady Macbeth has to make excuses for him. There could not be a bigger change from the hero at the start of the play to the man who trembles when he thinks he can see the dead Banquo sitting in his seat at the feast...

Examiner feedback

This is generally a clear response to the task. There is a focus on the question of characterisation and development. The ideas are clear and quotations are used to support the points made, although some could be woven into the sentences more effectively. There is an examination of some of the language used to reveal Macbeth's state of mind, though in the form of explanation rather than more sophisticated and extended analysis. The response deals with the changes in Macbeth's character but also reveals some of the ways the character is presented.

Suggested grade: C

ACTIVITY

- Re-read the first three paragraphs of the response on the previous page. What extra details might have been included to make this a better response?
- Earlier in the play, Lady Macbeth says to Macbeth:
  'Look like the innocent flower but be the serpent under't'.

  If you have studied the whole play, create a paragraph in which you talk about the way animal imagery is used to describe Macbeth's character in the early scenes.

ACTIVITY

Read the extract on the page opposite from a response to this task.

> *To what extent is love an important factor in the relationships in* **An Inspector Calls?**

Look carefully at the annotations. How many of these qualities or techniques would a marker find in your own response?

Example 2: Themes and Ideas

The essay focus is mentioned straight away →

'An Inspector Calls' is not just a play about a young girl's death and the effect it has on the living; it is about love too. But, what is 'love' in this context? Are we talking about 'romantic love' or other sorts of love? This essay will explore these different forms of love in the play – and who, if anyone, shows real love for others.

← The question is a good way of showing how the essay will be structured

Sensible organisation →

The first form of love we meet is the idea of romantic love. The play seems to begin with a celebration of romance, as it starts with a party to celebrate the engagement of Gerald and Sheila. However, when Birling states that it is a marriage which has everything going for it:

'When you marry, you'll be marrying at a very good time', ←

← Good quotation to support point

he makes it very clear that as far as he is concerned, marriage is as much about money and timing as about love. In fact, Birling has already stated earlier in the same scene that the marriage between Gerald and his daughter, Sheila, has 'brought us together', not in the sense of uniting families through love, but meaning Gerald's father's

Extended point →

company is coming together with his own. It is a very old-fashioned view of marriage, and seems to be more to do with building a business empire than building a family. Of course, Sheila and Gerald certainly appear, at this stage in the play, to love each other. Sheila calls him 'darling' and almost cries when he gives her the engagement ring. But

← Fluent link to show that there is another point of view

Excellent rhetorical question engages reader's attention →

how deep – and how real – is this love? Her reactions, whilst they might be seen as typical of the time, seem artificial now. Her breathless, hyphenated exclamations seem over-stated to a modern audience.

← Detailed linguistic analysis

Even at this early point we get clues to problems that are going to return later, for example when Sheila complains that Gerald hadn't come near her during the summer and she'd 'wondered what had happened'. And when it is revealed that Gerald had been with Eva in Act 2, it seems as if Priestley is raising the question of whether real

Good to mention the author and what he might be thinking →

love can exist between people if they do not trust each other. What is really interesting is that in some ways, Gerald knew more about Eva than he does about Sheila. There is a revealing conversation in Act 2 when they find out about Gerald's affair which focuses on whether he loved Eva:

Nothing wrong with a longer quotation if it is fully analysed →

Sheila:... I'm supposed to be engaged to Gerald. And I'm not a child, don't forget. I've a right to know. Were you in love with her, Gerald?

Gerald: (hesitantly) It's hard to say. I didn't feel about her as she felt about me.

Sheila: (with sharp sarcasm) Of course not! You were the wonderful fairy prince. You must have adored it, Gerald.

This makes us wonder what Priestley has to say about their love. Sheila is claiming to be grown up, yet is in the dark, as a child might be, and Gerald does not seem to really understand his own situation or emotions either. Then Sheila sounds much more adult as her scorn erupts in sarcasm. When she describes him as 'the wonderful fairy prince', the phrase is bitter and she is clearly hurt. We know she has broken from any belief in fairy tales forever. There is nothing but scorn in her 'You must have adored it, Gerald': scorn but not love. Their love, we suspect, was a convenience, not genuine.

In the play, though, we find that Eva was the one who really loved Gerald...

More on Priestley's viewpoint

Analysis of situation

Moving on to extend the analysis

This will be an important section as there is more to say about romantic love – Eva's love for Gerald – that needs to be analysed and contrasted with the other forms of love in the play

Examiner feedback

This opening is tightly focused on the theme of love and begins sensibly with the relationship between Gerald and Sheila. Their love is identified and examined, and Sheila's feelings in particular are analysed. Quotation is used effectively. We always have a sense of the playwright and what he is trying to tell us about their emotions: technique is implicit in what is written. Obviously, there is much more to say about love in the play, but the next section will doubtless contrast the much more genuine love of Eva with what we have already considered.

Suggested grade: A

ACTIVITY

Gerald had an affair with Eva, also known as Daisy. This is his explanation of how it ended:

Gerald:	[The affair ended] in the first week of September. I had to go away for several weeks then – on business – and by that time Daisy knew it was coming to an end. So I broke it off definitely before I went.
Inspector:	How did she take it?
Gerald:	Better than I'd hoped. She was – very gallant – about it.
Sheila:	*(with irony)* That was nice for you.
Gerald:	No, it wasn't. *(He waits a moment, then in low, troubled tone.)* She told me she been happier than she'd ever been before – but that she knew it couldn't last – hadn't expected it to last. She didn't blame me at all…

Write the section of the response that deals with the picture of love between Gerald and Daisy as presented in this extract.

EXAM PRACTICE TASK

Explore the way in which conflict is presented in a text you have studied.

You could write about how a writer explores conflict as a theme in a novel you have studied, in short stories or in several poems from the AQA Anthology *Moon on the Tides*.

If you only do five things...

1 Read your texts in the particular light of 'character' and 'themes', making clear, well-organised notes on these aspects in particular.

2 Once you know your task, conduct clear research into the task set, making notes and finding appropriate quotations. Don't forget that your personal response matters; have you thought about the text on your own, or just simply noted down what you are told?

3 Set out how you will answer the task; consider what you think in general, and how and when you will tell the examiner this – at the start, the end...? Plan in detail the major points you wish to make, and make sure you make a Point, provide Evidence, and Explain. Then add a further layer of exploration. This is where you can show original thinking. Plan to use some professional language in your response, trying out phrases such as 'the writer conveys...', 'this idea reflects...', 'the central action is...', to impress the examiner.

4 Write in clear, organised paragraphs, but think of your essay as creative; use techniques such as a variety of sentences, a wide vocabulary – even similes and metaphors – to get your points across.

5 Stick to the task set. If it's about a theme, by all means mention characters, but keep on returning to the central question. Don't get distracted.

What's it all about?

Writing creatively really enables you to show off your most imaginative ideas, original thinking and the very best writing techniques.

How will I be assessed?

- You will get **15% of your English Language marks** for your ability to write creative texts.
- You will have to complete **two** written pieces in a Controlled Assessment task over the course of **3–4 hours**.
- You will be marked on your writing of **two** written responses taken **from a choice of three**.

- These two creative texts will together be **1200 words in total**.

What is being tested?

You are being examined on your ability to

- write for specific creative purposes
- communicate clearly, effectively and imaginatively
- organise information in a structured and inventive way, using a range of paragraphs
- use a variety of sentence structures and styles
- use a range of linguistic features for impact and effect
- write with accuracy in punctuation, spelling and grammar.

Re-creations

Introduction

This section of Chapter 5 helps you to

- explore the creative writing area of 're-creations', in which you take a text and transform it into another form or genre
- understand what a Controlled Assessment task in this area is asking you to do
- develop creative writing responses to a range of texts
- practise and develop extended responses.

Why is it important to learn about re-creating texts?

- The best writers know how to adapt, transform and re-work ideas and texts to create impact.
- Being 'creative' in writing does not just mean writing fictional stories or poetry; creative approaches to non-fiction can have real impact on readers too.
- Approaching written tasks in a creative way is enjoyable, and it feeds back into your understanding of reading.

A **Grade C** candidate will

- understand how the basic conventions of texts can be adapted and engage the reader's interest with a variety of sentences and vocabulary
- write in a structured and coherent way, using paragraphs, so that ideas are clear to the reader, and spell and punctuate accurately.

C

A **Grade A/A★** candidate will

- exploit the chosen form with flair and originality, clearly engaging the reader
- sustain and develop ideas fully
- use language artfully and self-consciously, with all structural features (such as paragraphing and sentence structure) contributing to the overall effect on the reader
- use punctuation not only accurately, but to create effects
- spell accurately, even unusual words.
- produce sophisticated responses, demonstrating flair and originality.

A **A★**

Prior learning

Before you begin this unit, think about

- any texts you know in which conventions or features of texts get mixed or adapted, such as a fairy tale used for advertising
- what makes a piece of writing 'creative'
- different types of text that have been inspired by a recent event, for example 9/11 or the war in Afghanistan
- how you would be able to turn the first verse or two of a poem into another form of text.

> Can you come up with five ideas?

> Take a poem you know and try turning the first verse into a story, report or diary entry.

Re-creations – from poem to letter, radio play or report

Learning objective

- *To explore ways of transforming one text into a different form, still drawing on the same ideas or context.*

What does re-creating a text involve?

When you re-create a text, or transform it, you take one of its essential elements (perhaps the story it tells, its setting or its main theme) and you shape it into something new. For example, a poem about a long-distance runner's thoughts might become a newspaper report.

Checklist for success

- You need to consider a range of inventive and original possibilities for your re-creation.
- You need to demonstrate the typical conventions of the form you choose to write in.
- You need to enrich your writing with a new perspective – maybe a change in language or structure – not merely repeat information from the original.
- You need to decide how a different audience or form will affect the approach you take.

Texts are transformed all the time

Books are turned into screen-plays and then into films, for example *Twilight*.

Letters between figures from history are transformed into stage plays, for example those between Sir Thomas More and his contemporaries inspired Robert Bolt's *A Man for all Seasons*.

Newspaper reports inspire poems about the same events (for instance, Tennyson's 'The Charge of the Light Brigade').

> **Glossary**
> **Futility** means 'pointlessness'

Focus for development: From poem to letter

Wilfred Owen's poem 'Futility' is a response to the events he witnessed while fighting in the First World War.

Futility

Move him into the sun –
Gently its touch awoke him once,
At home, whispering of fields unsown.
Always it woke him, even in France,
Until this morning and this snow.
If anything might rouse him now
The kind old sun will know.

Think how it wakes the seeds, –
Woke, once, the clays of a cold star.
Are limbs, so dear-achieved, are sides
Full-nerved, still warm, too hard to stir?
Was it for this the clay grew tall?
– O what made fatuous sunbeams toil
To break earth's sleep at all?

Discuss with a partner:

- What is the basic 'story' of the poem?
- How much are we told directly? (Is there anything that is **implied**?)
- Who – if anyone – appears to be the audience for the poem?
- What is the purpose of the poem, and what effect does it have on the reader?
- Why does Owen keep returning to the strength of the sun? (How is personification, in particular, used to create the sun's character?)

Owen also wrote letters home, especially to his mother. Here is an example in which he describes some recent events.

Immediately after I sent my last letter, more than a fortnight ago, we were rushed up into the Line. Twice in one day we went over the top, gaining both our objectives. Our A Company led the Attack, and of course lost a certain number of men. I had some extraordinary escapes from shells & bullets. Fortunately there was no bayonet work, since the Hun ran before we got up to his trench. You will find mention of our fight in the Communiqué; the place happens to be the very village which Father named in his last letter! [...] For twelve days I did not wash my face, nor take off my boots, nor sleep a deep sleep. For twelve days we lay in holes, where at any moment a shell might put us out. I think the worst incident was one wet night when we lay up against a railway embankment. A big shell lit on the top of the bank, just 2 yards from my head. Before I awoke, I was blown in the air right away from the bank! I passed most of the following days in a railway Cutting, in a hole just big enough to lie in, and covered with corrugated iron.

(To Susan Owen, 25 April 1917)

Discuss with a partner:

- Who is the audience here? How can you tell? How has the account been shaped for this audience?
- How is the letter different from the poem? (Think about its form.)
- In what ways does this text link to other texts? (Is it part of a sequence?)
- What is the intended effect on the reader?

One of the things you will notice is very little is **implied** here as it is in the poem. Most of it the events are retold directly.

How might Owen have written about the incident in 'Futility' in a letter to his mother? Here is the start of a **Grade A/A★** response.

> Dearest Mother,
>
> Thank you for your last letter; it was a great comfort to me in difficult times.
> As I write, we have just passed a night of appalling cold in a collapsed trench,
> unable to sleep due to the constant whine and clatter of shells in the near
> distance. This dawn brought the sun, though it has had little impact on the
> snow which has now compacted with the mud into a deadly rock-hard coat.
> Those who had been able to sleep found themselves in the sub-zero shade as
> they woke since the sun was so low.

With a partner, decide how the student

- draws on information from the original poem
- adds details of his own
- makes it more directly personal
- uses different line or sentence structures
- shows that a letter is often part of a sequence, almost like a kind of conversation
- begins in a different way
- makes the writing vivid and powerful for the reader.

Write another 100–150 words of the letter, describing

- the discovery of the letter writer's dead – or dying – comrade
- their attempts to 'move him into the sun'
- the writer's feelings of futility when they found there was nothing they could do to save him
- the writer's reflections and thoughts about the war and its impact.

Focus for development:
From poem to radio drama

The same poem, 'Futility', could equally have been re-created as a scene from a radio play. For example:

> **FADE UP the sound of birdsong.**
>
> **FRED:** Birds! Who'd have believed it, sir? In this bleedin' cold. It ain't natural.
>
> **OWEN:** (*coughing*) Wake the men, corporal. Peters didn't look too good last night.
>
> **FRED:** Righto, sir.
>
> *Heavy sounds from trench.*
>
> (*more distant*) Blimey. Sun's shining, sir. After all that snow 'n' all.
>
> **OWEN:** Sun? Maybe it'll do Peters good. See if he's awake, corporal.
>
> **FRED:** Will do, sir.

ACTIVITY

Read the dialogue aloud with a partner. Then discuss:

- Who is the audience now?
- How does this text retain elements of the original poem?
- What new elements have been added?
- What changes in form and layout are there?
- How has the voice or perspective subtly changed?

ASSESSMENT FOCUS

Choose one of the two tasks below, based on the poem or the letter:

- Write further scenes from the **radio drama**.

Radio drama allows you to include a range of voices (for example, Owen's private thoughts) and different text types (for example, quotation from his letters). Make use of these possibilities.

- Write a **report** from Owen or a fellow-officer to your superior on the damaging effects of cold on your men and requesting further supplies. You will need to consider carefully
  - your audience (what your commander would want or need to read)
  - the details you would include (the condition of the men?)
  - how you would be persuasive without appearing over-emotional or cowardly
  - how you can draw on what happened after the attack. (You can read more of the letter at **http://www.oucs.ox.ac.uk/ww1lit/education/tutorials/intro/owen/letters.html**)

Remember

- If you are writing a more formal non-fiction text, adapt the material to the new audience.
- Use the appropriate conventions if you choose a non-fiction prose form for your re-creation (see pages 4–9 and pages 64–69).
- Use subtle changes of tone and vocabulary to affect the reader.

Re-creations – from short story to web page

Learning objectives

- To understand how the conventions of fiction texts can be used or adapted for non-fiction purposes.

- To transform an extract from a short story into a non-fiction text.

Checklist for success

- You need to use the typical conventions of the form you choose to write in.
- You need to enrich your writing with a new perspective – maybe a change in language or structure – not merely repeat information from the original.

Read this extract from the short story 'Something Old, Something New', by Leila Aboulela, which describes a British man's drive from the airport with his Sudanese bride-to-be.

> She sat in the front next to her brother. He sat in the back with the rucksack that wouldn't fit in the boot. The car seats were shabby, a thin film of dust covered everything. I will get used to the dust, he told himself, but not the heat. He could do with a breath of fresh air, that tang of rain he was accustomed to. He wanted her to be next to him. And it suddenly seemed to him, in a peevish sort of way, unfair that they should be separated like that. She turned her head back and looked at him, smiled as if she knew. He wanted to say, 'you have no idea how much I ache for you, you have no idea'. But he could not say that, not least because the brother understood English.
>
> It was like a ride in a fun-fair. The windows wide open; voices, noises, car-horns, people crossing the road at random, pausing in the middle, touching the cars with their fingers as if the cars were benign cattle. Anyone of these passers-by could easily punch him through the

> window, yank off his watch, his sun-glasses, snatch his wallet from the pocket of his shirt. He tried to roll up the window but couldn't. She turned and said, 'It's broken, I'm sorry.' Her calmness made him feel that he needn't be so nervous. A group of school-boys walked on the pavement, one of them stared at him, grinned and waved. He became aware that everyone looked like her, shared her colour, the women were dressed like her and they walked with the same slowness which had seemed to him exotic when he had seen her walking in Edinburgh. 'Everything is new for you.' She turned and looked at him gently.

The brother said something in Arabic.

The car moved away from the crowded market to a wide shady road.

'Look,' she said, 'take off your sun-glasses and look. There's the Nile.' And there was the Nile, a blue he had never seen before, a child's blue, a dream's blue.

'Do you like it?' she asked. She was proud of her Nile.

'Yes, it's beautiful,' he replied. But as he spoke he noticed that the river's flow was forceful, not innocent, not playful. Crocodiles no doubt lurked beneath the surface, hungry and ruthless. He could picture an accident; blood, death, bones.

ACTIVITY

Discuss with a partner:

- What are the main subjects or themes of this extract?
- What different perspectives on Sudan do the man and his wife-to-be have?
- How does the writer convey these differences and the very vivid experience of the car journey?
- How can you tell this is from a fictional text? What 'story' features are present, and what effect do they have – for example, a strong plot, the inner thoughts or lives of characters, dialogue, use of imagery?

'Sudan – the country' is one of the main subjects of the story, but information on Sudan appears in many texts – tourist-board websites, and so on. A travel guide, however, might have a more neutral, impersonal style.

Note:

- the use of the present tense
- the more formal style. There is no mention of the first person, or 'inner thoughts'.

Travel in the Sudan can be a fascinating, if sometimes uncomfortable experience. If you are not accustomed to the heat and dust, it can take some getting used to.

Now look at this extract from a website for another country, Tanzania. Note down any ways in which the text is both factual or informative *and* persuasive, using the sort of vivid language you might see in a story.

TANZANIA TODAY

Lying just south of the equator, Tanzania is East Africa's largest country, and an immensely rewarding place to visit. Tanzania has the world-famous attractions; the plains of the Serengeti, Ngorongoro Crater, snow-capped Mount Kilimanjaro (Africa's highest mountain) and Zanzibar, with its idyllic palm-fringed beaches and historic Stone Town. Yet there's a whole lot more to Tanzania than these obvious highlights.

Almost everywhere you go you'll find interesting wildlife and inspiring landscapes (over forty percent of the country is protected in some form or other) ranging from forest-covered volcanic peaks to dusty savanna populated by elephants, antelopes, lions, leopards and cheetahs. Tanzania is one of the four most naturally diverse nations on earth: it contains Africa's second-largest number of bird species (around 1500), the continent's biggest mammal population and three-quarters of East Africa's plant species (over ten thousand). Add to this the country's rich ethnic diversity, some superb hiking and other activities like snorkelling and diving, and you have the makings of a holiday of a lifetime.

For all its natural diversity, Tanzania's best asset is its people: friendly, welcoming, unassumingly proud and yet reserved – you'll be treated with uncommon warmth and courtesy wherever you go, and genuine friendships are easily made.

ASSESSMENT FOCUS

You are going to prepare for a Controlled Assessment-style task in which you will write two screens for a travel website giving guidance and advice for people from the UK going to the Sudan.

Stage 1

Re-read the story extract on pages 206–7 and note down

- which of the aspects or areas of the story might be covered **in some way** on the website? (Think about first impressions, tourist attractions, and so on.)
- what you **wouldn't** include from the story.

Stage 2

Do some detailed research on the Sudan, or the city of Khartoum if you prefer to keep it simple. You will need

- basic facts, figures and information, such as geographical location, tourist sites, distances
- useful guidance about how and what to see, how to behave and what UK visitors can expect.

Stage 3

Practise the style you will need, by writing practice paragraphs:

- Welcome the website user/visitor to the Sudan.
- Describe a key tourist attraction.
- Refer to the Tanzania Home page on page 208.

Remember

- Make sure the tenses and other conventions of the form are correct.
- Use some of the constructions of language common to websites about places, for example 'from ... to ...': '*From* the fascinating Nile, *to* the refreshing Red Sea'.
- Write using imagery and powerful language in your description.

Grade Booster

Extended Assessment Task

Write a response of around 600 words to this task.

> *Take any story or text which describes a location vividly and transform it into a travel-guidance text, such as pages from a tourist website or the opening pages of a guide book.*

Make sure you

- demonstrate real understanding of the content and conventions of a tourism website or guide book in terms of what is described and the language used
- 'show off' your creativity in your use of the original story text and in your approach to the factual text you have chosen. Use imagery, persuasive techniques and detailed description as appropriate.

Evaluation – What have you learned?

With a partner, use the grade checklist below to evaluate your work on the Extended Assessment Task.

- I can take a fictional text and, with creativity and originality, transform it into an appropriate non-fiction form with sophisticated usage of key features, conventions and techniques that are convincing and engage the reader.

- I can take a fictional text and, with creativity, transform it into an appropriate non-fiction form with wide-ranging usage of most key features, conventions and techniques, which engage the reader.
- I can produce an effective and technically correct response.

- I can transform a fictional text into a non-fiction one, using a selection of features needed.
- I can engage the reader with my new text.
- I can use more advanced paragraphing, punctuation and spelling.

- I can write a non-fiction text based on a fictional one and use most of the features required.
- I try consciously to engage the reader, and my response is accurately presented.

- I can write a non-fiction text based on a fictional one, using some of the appropriate features.

You may need to go back and look at the relevant pages from this section again.

Moving Images

Introduction

This section of Chapter 5 helps you to

- explore the creative writing area of 'moving images' in which you respond to films, television and internet image sequences
- understand what a Controlled Assessment task in this area is asking you to do
- develop creative writing responses to a range of moving image texts
- practise and develop extended responses.

Why is working on moving images important?

- Moving image 'texts', such as films, documentaries and TV adverts, have their own conventions and features, as does any writing about them.
- Commentary about moving images is widespread, in the form of film reviews or blogs.
- Writing about visual texts requires many of the same techniques as commenting on printed texts.

A **Grade C** candidate will

- comment clearly on how a moving image text is constructed
- back points up with evidence
- use some appropriate technical language
- use mostly accurate paragraphs, sentences and punctuation.

C

A **Grade A/A★** candidate will

- comment on, and analyse, a moving image text in well-judged detail, supporting points with the most appropriate evidence
- use professional language and terminology related to image production
- analyse the effect of moving images and text together using sophisticated, precise vocabulary and technical terms, and effective paragraphs and sentences.

A A★

Prior learning

Before you begin this unit

- watch a range of short news items and a selection of advertisements and consider how they are constructed, who they are aimed at and whether, in your opinion, they are successful
- look over any previous reviewing or media studies work you have done and highlight what you did well, and what you needed to improve.

Writing about film

Learning objective

- To explore the different ways you can write about films and use appropriately creative language.

Checklist for success

- You need to be able to write analytically and precisely, using the technical language of moving image texts.
- You need to engage the reader by writing creatively and professionally.

Each moving-image form has its own **conventions**. For example, blockbuster films have special effects, more action, less dialogue and often quick cutting between shots or scenes.

Increasingly, however, their 'content' (the key story, concept or idea) is developed for a **range of platforms** and **media**. Take a James Bond film.

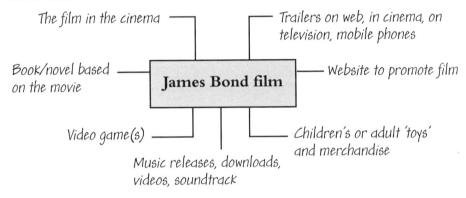

- The film in the cinema
- Trailers on web, in cinema, on television, mobile phones
- Book/novel based on the movie
- **James Bond film**
- Website to promote film
- Video game(s)
- Children's or adult 'toys' and merchandise
- Music releases, downloads, videos, soundtrack

Knowledge of these platforms and media is important when discussing or writing about moving images.

Focus for development: Writing with creative flair

ACTIVITY

On the opposite page, there are three extracts from texts about an imaginary blockbuster film called *Fangman*. With a partner, identify the extract which is from

- a free magazine handed out in the cinema
- a review of a game based on the film
- a film review in a national paper.

As you read, consider how the writer of each text

- matches style and language to the **audience**
- presents a particular **perspective** or opinion which is shared with the reader
- takes a **form and approach** which **suits the subject**.

Most reviews will follow these guidelines:

Content and ideas (**what** is reviewed)	Language and form (**how** it is reviewed)
• the basic storyline • reference to the main cast, possibly previous films, current careers, their role in the film • special effects or musical score • the style/genre of the film • the opinion of the reviewer.	• length of review – will vary • structure – does it have a 'headline'? Where is the information about the cast, director, audience? • description of events – summarised in concise, but sometimes quite complex, sentences • humour, exaggeration and language with impact (why would you read it otherwise?) • description of settings, situations in visual ways • verb tense – usually the present tense.

ACTIVITY

Look again at texts 2 and 3 and discuss

- the **facts** you find out about the story of the film and who is in it
- the **specific language features** from the list on the left you can identify
- the **attitude or perspective** on the film each reviewer seems to have.

Remember

Show flair and originality in your review by using techniques such as

- adding humorous asides to the reader (for example, 'oh sorry that was me')
- playing with film review language
- rhetorical devices like lists of three ideas.

ASSESSMENT FOCUS

Now write the first 50–75 words of a review of a film you know well but with a deliberately critical viewpoint (see text 3 above). You might like it, but the review should show your view is not just blind praise, but well-judged.

What is involved in writing about moving images?

Images are combined in many ways with either written or spoken text. This may be as commentary or as an integral part of a media text, for example, a voiceover in a TV advert. Writing in, or about, these forms requires precise skills.

Analysing advertisements

Read this task. The students have just watched a dog-food advertisement.

You work for a dog-food company. Your boss has asked you to write a commentary on the advertisement for a new product.

Here are one student's rather basic comments on shots from the advertisement.

> *First, there was like this longish shot of the field, then they go to this next shot which is a dog close up looking healthy and panting. Then he runs off, and it's back to the first scene but this time with a man throwing a stick…*

The student

- describes each shot but without using precise, professional language – and so loses clarity
- does not describe in any detail how one shot moves into the next
- offers little analysis on the effectiveness of the shot sequence.

Now read this extract from a **Grade B** commentary on the same advertisement.

> *The sequence begins with a long shot of a field in a rural environment. This shows a man walking his dog in the background with hedges in the middle distance, and hills further beyond, establishing the location and suggesting the subject matter. The idea of a healthy outdoor lifestyle is portrayed immediately. This is followed by a cut to a close-up of the dog. He is panting, and because of the angle and shot selection, appears to be grinning. His teeth look white and his tongue suitably pink, conveying how healthy he is. The next shot positions the dog in the centre of the screen as he runs away. It's a point-of-view style shot in which we, the viewer, see the dog as if we were his owner, thus drawing us into a connection with the lifestyle and care for the dog…*

ACTIVITY

Discuss with a partner what makes this commentary better than the first one. Identify

- the **precise, professional language** used
- where the student explains **the effect of the shots**
- **varied vocabulary**
- the wider points about **how the viewer is drawn into the advertisement.**

ACTIVITY

Read this examiner's comment on the Grade B response.

> The response analyses the advert in a predictable if efficient way, but could be expanded further with separate paragraphs dealing with different aspects of the advertisement.

Discuss how this could be done. Each paragraph should begin with a topic sentence that leads the reader into the next main focus. For example:

Paragraph 1: how the advert begins and establishes the initial subject matter.

The sequence begins with a long shot of the field …

Paragraph 2: how the framing and selection of content convey a particular lifestyle or atmosphere.

The selection of content – the objects, people, location – is key to conveying the sort of lifestyle the buyers of this dog food might aspire to.

And so on in subsequent paragraphs, commenting on

- the positioning of the camera (for example, assuming the man's point-of-view)
- the use of music and/or voiceover
- the use of on-screen text, logos, design features and their effects
- the overall effectiveness of the moving images and related text in persuading the target audience to buy the product.

Glossary

long shot: a distant shot of scene or people, possibly showing landscape or background

close-up: a shot close to the viewer, for example showing a person's face

cut: a new shot that suddenly replaces the previous one

Glossary

Point of view (POV): the shot appears to be seen as if by someone/ something in the scene

panning: the camera moves slowly up or down, or from side to side

fade: the shot slowly disappears from screen

ASSESSMENT FOCUS

- Freeze the opening shot of any advert.
- Make notes on what is in the frame (foreground, background, and so on), what the POV is, and the overall effect.
- Write these notes up explaining how the opening shot(s) conveys a particular message.

Remember

- **Use a topic sentence to introduce your first paragraph.**
- **Use appropriate professional language**
- **Explain the effect of each shot or frame.**

215

Adding voiceover to moving image texts

Learning objective

- To understand how the way you combine text with moving images can have a profound effect on the meaning.

Look at these three stills from a moving image sequence taken from a documentary about the effects of climate change.

Read aloud these two voiceovers in turn.

Voiceover 1
'The world is warming up.' (Still 1)
'And wherever you are, whatever you are.' (Still 2)
'The effect will be felt.' (Still 3)

Voiceover 2
'Light is finally being shed on climate change.' (Still 1)
'Wildlife and nature aren't under threat, say some scientists.' (Still 2)
'Damage to the ozone layer has been exaggerated.' (Still 3)

The images are the same but with the two voiceovers send quite different messages.

Discuss in small groups:

- How does each voiceover link to the images shown? Are the links direct, implied or both?
- What are the contrasting messages in each case?

ACTIVITY

Does the text have to be linked to climate change, or could the images be used in a completely different way?

Read this third version.

'Is there a God?' (Still 1)

'In today's programme we will look at creation.' (Still 2)

'And how Darwin's work shattered what the Victorians believed.' (Still 3)

Now write your own voiceover for the same three images to promote a bank or banking product, for example a personal loan, mortgage, savings account. Write one sentence or statement per still.

Focus for development: Professional voiceovers

Here is some advice from professional voiceover artist, Peter Drew, about writing voiceovers for commercial organisations.

As you read it, jot down up to five key points of advice the writer gives.

Writing copy for voiceovers

As with any of the performing arts, an effective voiceover begins with a well-crafted script. You don't have to have many years of writing experience to create copy that is both effective and a pleasure for the voice actor to perform. Here are some ideas to consider before you put your pen to paper or fingers to keyboard. […]

Narrations (also called 'Industrials')
For a video script, use the storyboard, if you have one, to guide the development of the script. This will help you time the voiceover to the video's scenes.

For audio only, where no storyboard exists, do a rough outline. This will help you create a basic logical structure before you start writing. The result will be a script that flows much better for the narrator and the intended listener.

All scripts
Leave room for 'verbal white space'. Just as a large block of densely printed copy is intimidating and difficult to read, a voiceover script that's crammed with copy is difficult to follow and understand. A good rule of thumb for 30-second radio or TV copy is eight lines down (double-spaced), 10 words across the page. For a slower, more intimate read, go with seven lines, 10 words across. The same idea applies for a briskly paced 60-second ad: 16 lines down, 10 words across. For a slower pace, 14 lines, 10 words across. This 60-second guideline is helpful in timing long-form scripts, too. Just count the pages and you have the total number of minutes.
[…]
Write for the ear, not the eye. Construct short, conversational sentences, with natural breaks for taking a breath. This is especially helpful to narrators when they voice technical or medical copy, which contains large, complicated, and difficult-to-pronounce terms.

Read your copy out loud, just as you intend the voice talent to read it, and time it. Then adjust your copy accordingly for timing.

Try to write in the active voice, not passive voice. […] Active voice is more conversational and easier for the ear and mind to follow.

ACTIVITY

Look at this storyboard that is part of a company's presentation of their new chocolate product to a major retail chain, to persuade them to adopt it in their stores. Note down

- who you think the target market is, according to the planned advert
- what sort of lifestyle and image the advert is trying to create.

Write the voiceover copy for this storyboard using the advice given by
Peter Drew on page 217. Make sure you

- write enough copy for each of the chunks of video represented by the
  storyboard
- have got the appropriate language.

Each image from the storyboard represents about 10 seconds of video, so
you will need to time each voiceover to go with the film. For example:

> **Image 1 (background image of chocolates)**
> *The chocolate industry in the UK is worth over two billion pounds
> a year and is a major revenue stream for large stores and shops.*

Compose the voiceover text to suit your audience and purpose. In this case,
it is a professional presentation to a major supermarket chain, so you should
aim for the following.

Include professional terms and vocabulary.	'major revenue stream'
Be suitably impersonal.	Don't use 'I'. 'We' is fine if from the chocolate brand itself, otherwise avoid personal pronouns.
It's an ongoing presentation, so check the tense.	Likely to be present tense mostly, but might feature future tenses as well ('it will generate profit').
Keep it succinct and active, as Peter Drew suggests.	You could vary sentences: short and simple ones ('We all like treats. And chocolate is top of the list.') as well as longer sentences like the one for image 1 above.
Stick to a structure that builds to a forceful conclusion.	The opening images set the scene; they establish the background on the market and product area. The final image(s) on the storyboard could focus on the product, its name and emphasise its qualities.

Remember

- Match your text to the images – but don't simply repeat what you see.
- Match the text to the context, task and purpose (sound professional).

Extended Assessment Task

Produce a response of around 600 words in answer to this task:

Write an analysis of an advertisement you know well, commenting on how the images and any text (spoken or written) combine to create effect and meaning.

Use the following grid to help you make notes and prepare. It is not necessary to list every shot; instead, break down your analysis into three parts and then jot down observations around the digital image areas already mentioned.

TV advert for analysis:	Content (what's in the frame)	Camera (positioning of viewer)	Shots (how one shot moves to another)	Music (or other sound, such as voiceover)	Effect?	Text (spoken or on screen)
How it opens						
How it develops						
How it ends						

Evaluation – What have you learned?

With a partner, use the grade checklist below to evaluate your work on the Extended Assessment Task.

- I can analyse, comment on, explain and interpret the advertisement's effectiveness in depth, making apt and appropriate reference to the techniques used.
- I can use professional language and sophisticated, wide-ranging and precise vocabulary.

- I can analyse, comment on, explain and interpret the advertisement's effectiveness, making apt references to the techniques used.
- I can use professional language and precise vocabulary.

- I can analyse, comment on and explain the advertisement's effectiveness, making generally apt references to the techniques used.
- I can generally use professional language and well-chosen vocabulary.

- I can describe an advertisement, explaining clearly how it is constructed and some of the effects created.
- I can use appropriate language but do not always develop my ideas or interpret the effect of particular choices.

- I can write about an advertisement and its features, and mention some effects.
- I can come up with generally valid ideas, if somewhat random.
- I can offer only limited explanation and technical language.

You may need to go back and look at the relevant pages from this section again.

Commissions

Introduction

This section of Chapter 5 helps you to

- explore the area of 'commissions', in which you respond to a given brief or set of guidelines
- understand what a Controlled Assessment task in this area is asking you to do
- develop creative-writing responses to a range of clearly defined tasks
- practise and develop extended responses.

Why is learning about writing to a creative brief important?

- Being able to write to a set brief, with clear limits and a defined purpose and audience, is a core skill for learning and working life.
- The best writers can adapt and turn their hand to most tasks they are set by others, such as employers, publishers and programme-makers.
- Learning how to shape your writing for very clearly defined purposes will help with a lot of your other written work.

A **Grade C** candidate will

- understand clearly the task set and write an appropriate response, engaging the reader's interest with a variety of sentences and vocabulary
- write in a structured and coherent way, using paragraphs, so that ideas are clear to the reader
- spell and punctuate accurately.

C

A **Grade A/A*** candidate will

- exploit the chosen form with flair and originality, clearly engaging the reader
- sustain and develop ideas fully, structuring them coherently
- use language artfully and self-consciously so that all structural features (such as paragraphing and sentence structure) contribute to the overall effect and impact on the reader
- use punctuation not only accurately, but to create effects
- spell accurately, even highly irregular forms
- produce sophisticated responses, demonstrating flair and originality.

A **A***

Prior learning

Before you begin this unit

- read a range of texts that have been professionally commissioned – for example, brochures for products, poems or speeches written for special occasions
- look at fiction, magazine publishers' or BBC commissioning websites, to see what advice or guidance they provide for submitting stories, articles or other ideas.

Exploring non-fiction commissions

Learning objective

- To be able to write to a very specific brief, with a clear purpose and audience.

What does writing to commission involve?

A commission is when a writer is given a clear brief to fulfil for a piece of writing. It will have defined features, usually a specific audience and content and sometimes a particular length.

Checklist for success

- You need to understand exactly what the commission or brief requires.
- You need to use appropriate language matched to the form and style of the text.
- You need to keep your reader fully engaged and interested throughout.

ACTIVITY

With a partner, look at these two examples of commissions and discuss:

- Which of these would you prefer to write? Why?
- What are the challenges you would face? Think particularly about form, audience and tone.
- How would you make the article of the webpage interesting and engaging for readers?

Commission 1

Your local paper runs a section called 'Leisure Today', which has a section for teenagers.

Write an article of between 500 and 700 words in which you recommend some positive ways of spending the summer holidays in your area. It should have a personal tone, with your own voice and ideas coming through.

Commission 2

The web host of a sports website approaches you to submit some writing for it. They are doing a series of pages devoted to 'Sporting Icons' about sportsmen or women who have had a major impact on their sport and the world beyond it. You can choose to write about any sports figure you wish, but the text should not be longer than 500 words.

Focus for development: Writing to the brief

Generally, when you write to a specific brief you need to be very clear about these points.

Elements in the brief	What this means for me
Title, theme or topic	Focus on **the title**, if there is one – for example, an article about recent fashion trends.
Form or genre of the text	Identify the form. It may be a **well-known form** which has **specific features and conventions**, such as a personal letter.
Format and extent requested	Focus on details like the **maximum number of words**, number of chapters, space allocated.
Location or context of the text	Check where the text will appear: for example, is it for a magazine, a website, a children's book? What does this reveal about audience and style?
Approach, style and content	Make decisions about what the text must include and about the style. For example, is it chatty or formal, humorous or more serious?

Once you have established these things, it comes down to the **quality** of the writing. Ask yourself these questions as you plan your work:

- How many of these features do I need to follow? How many can I adapt or develop to make my writing stand out?
- How can I make my reader really engage with what I want to say?

ACTIVITY

Here are some real commissioning guidelines from *fRoots* – an online magazine dedicated to 'roots music'.

With a partner, summarise what guidelines *fRoots* gives for the submission of reviews. In particular, note what it doesn't want from reviewers.

LIVE EVENTS: The majority of our live gig reviews are now contributed by readers in the Gig Reviews section of our interactive **fRoots Forum**. We do not generally have a lot of space for routine live reviews in the printed magazine, preferring the unique or out-of-the-way. Always check first to find out whether we want a live review for the print version – somebody else might already be reviewing the same event or a similar one, or we might feel the artist is inappropriate or over-covered. For a single artist/band at a concert or club, around 350 words maximum. Please, no song-by-song accounts; overall flavour and highlights are the most important. Remember you are reviewing that gig: we don't want biographies, history of the venue, details of floor singers or support acts, or what funny things happened to the reviewer on the way to the gig, unless very relevant (and brief!).

Here is an extract from a real review taken from the website. With your partner, decide whether it meets the brief from *fRoots*. You might wish to consider

- how the reviewer gives a strong impression of the singer
- how specific details enliven the overall description
- the precise use of the language and vocabulary of a live music review, for example 'solo' and 'delivery'
- the tense used and the effect it produces.

Tonight's show marks the end of a short tour which you might be forgiven for thinking would be treated as an extended rehearsal for the coming festival season. Wood is having none of this: in his quiet, charming way he puts in a performance of intense power and not inconsiderable daring, peppering his set full of old favourites and recent classics with a number of re-worked or brand new songs – at least one of which is getting its genuine live debut tonight. Even with the most forgiving of audiences this is a tactic that can sometimes fail spectacularly, but Wood's natural warmth and friendly charm win over his northern audience from the moment of his first "Oroight then?" to the final, heartfelt "Goodnight".

He kicks off with You Must Unload, something of an oldie in the Wood canon but tonight apparently performed solo for the first time. Chris and his mates have a regular Thursday night appointment in their local Country & Western club where they'd performed this very song the night before and there's a definite hint of the "Yee haws" in his delivery here.

Posted: Sat May 16, 2009 2:40 am
Post subject: Chris Wood: The Met Theatre, Bury, 15 May 2009

http://froots.net/phpBB2/viewtopic.php?t=4444

A student writes…

How does the writer make this sound so fluent and easy?

Answer…

It's that verb 'peppering'! By using it to link the main clause about the performance to the second clause about the song, the writer makes the whole description flow. Try using an '….ing' link yourself in your writing.

Focus for development:
Looking in detail at the skills

Look again at the music review. In the extract from it below, see how what could be quite dull 'song-by-song' information is replaced by an overall sense of the show and its effect:

Succinct summing up of the singer's manner with adjectives

Re-focus on the music itself

in his **quiet, charming** way he puts in a performance of **intense power** and not inconsiderable daring, **peppering** his set full of **old favourites and recent classics** with a number of **re-worked or brand new songs**

Great verb – suggesting added 'spice' and variety to the music!

Typical language of a live music review

ACTIVITY

Now imagine you were answering the 'Sporting Icons' commission on page 220. Complete these two sentences about a sporting legend to make them flow.

In his own, individual way, Usain Bolt put his mark on athletics in the World Championships, [add verb............+ ing] ....[complete rest of sentence]

It was a performance of [adjective + noun] and [adjective + noun], which left everyone who watched amazed and [verb ending in –ed].

Compare your sentences with a partner's. Comment on whether they

- read fluently
- include the right references to athletics, running, and so on.

ASSESSMENT FOCUS

You have been commissioned to write the introductory text of 125–150 words for a fan website for a sport or music icon.

- Highlight what makes the band, singer or sports person special.
- Introduce the particular features the fansite offers.
- Address the website fans directly and be lively and informative.

Remember

- **Follow the commission brief exactly.**
- **Choose appropriate language matched to the form and style of the text.**
- **Engage your reader and keep them interested throughout.**

Exploring fiction commissions

Learning objective

- To understand what a fiction commission is asking for and respond appropriately.

Checklist for success

- You need to match your response to the task set.
- You need to choose the most engaging content and ideas.
- You need to draw your reader in through a wide range of language devices, sustaining your tone and style and structuring your work effectively.

ACTIVITY

Read this story brief. Quickly note down the key elements of the task, and what you must do.

> A website called All-people-together.com has asked for contributions from young people about friendships or experiences of people or places from a different culture.
>
> *We would like a short story in which two people from different cultures meet. It cannot be longer than 800 words. It can be based on a real experience or be entirely fictional. We don't want worthy but boring. Make it interesting to read.*
>
> The content – where it takes place and who the characters are – is entirely up to you.

The most important thing initially is to come up with a genuinely interesting, perhaps unusual idea. Below are four possibilities.

With a partner rank them from 1 to 4 (1= most potential; 4 = least potential).

> A girl on an exchange visit to another country finds herself lost in a major city and is helped by an old taxi driver who kindly takes her to stay the night with his family.

> A teenage boy in London discovers a young refugee mother and her baby hiding in a barge on the Thames.

> A French penfriend meets his or her British penfriend at the airport for the first time. They get on really well and it shows how friendship between cultures can work.

> An American businessman/woman is trying to track down his/her ancestors in a remote village in the UK and meets an old farmer.

Once you have chosen your idea, think about the key ingredients that contribute to a compelling short story. Beginning the story engagingly will be one. Look at these openings based on the first story idea:

Grade C response

> Joey had decided to bunk school. He was being bullied and was fed up. He was small and shy and didn't have many friends, so he often went for walks by the Thames. He liked watching the boats go by and wished he could get on one and escape. So, when he saw the barge it seemed like the ideal place to spend the rest of the day until it was time to go home and face his mum.

Grade A/A★ response

> The old barge lay half on its side in the grey-brown mud, like a beached whale. The window frames were rotten, and no glass remained where the panes had once been. Joey picked his way gingerly across the gang-plank that led to the barge's side. The nameplate hung loose, rusty and bent, and the name was no longer visible. Perhaps he would sit inside the barge for a while, kill the hours until it was time to go home and lie to his mum about where he had been. Perhaps he would sit on the deck in the rain and watch the passing tankers, dreaming of escape to distant lands.

ACTIVITY

Note down in what ways the Grade A/A★ opening

- sets the scene **more vividly,** provides **more detail**, and uses **powerful imagery**
- focuses on a **specific item** to make a symbolic link to one of the themes of the story
- **holds back information** about the main character

ASSESSMENT FOCUS

Now write your own opening to the same brief, but this time based on the idea about the girl who is lost abroad in a capital city.

Use this grid to help you plan your opening:

Beginning (go straight into the story)	The faceless, grey streets fanned off from the traffic island where she stood, gazing into the driving rain.
Describe the scene around her in detail	In front of her ...
Focus on one specific detail which could symbolise the ideas of being lost and alone	
Link to story – taxi or taxi driver appearing?	

Focus for development: Sustaining the reader's interest

A good short story begins with the writer engaging the reader's attention, but stories change direction and move on. How is this done, and where can the writer take us?

Here is an example of a writer 'positioning the reader' by taking them back to an earlier occasion and a different scene. Think of the writer holding a camera that can look at things in the present, past and future and zoom in and out.

> *She walked up to the apartment's polished door and inserted the key with the personalised leather tag in the lock. Click. She was standing in the hallway. Ahead, a narrow box of light defined the kitchen so she slowly walked towards it, feeling her away along the wall. Her hand brushed against a frame, a photo she remembered... but she didn't look to the side, just kept moving.*

> *It had been two years ago that she had stood on the terrace for the first time watching Danny Leigh play for United. He had been a distant dot on the pitch, but she knew even at that point that he was the man for her. Now she stared down at him, at her feet, lying flat on his back, a bottle of gin still in his hand. He had a bruise on his left cheek.*

ACTIVITY

Sketch out a storyboard of eight frames which show how the writer has 'positioned' the reader. The first two frames have been done for you.

Now write the next two sentences of this story. The first should be a 'close up' of Danny waking up or responding in some way. The second should switch our attention to something or someone else – it could be a descriptive detail of the kitchen, for example.

Sustaining interest through structure

Ordering events interestingly is another useful way of keep the reader's attention.

Note how, in the story above, the writer above introduces the detail about how the woman met Danny **after** she entered the flat, but **before** he was seen on the floor.

An **alternative structure** could have been:

> Starts with how she met/saw Danny.
> Moves to seeing him on the floor.
> Tells us how she had arrived at the flat.

The structure of the whole story could be told in yet another way.

The writer doesn't tell us anything about how they met, what they said, how long ago it was, how long they have been together. All these things could come later, or earlier.

Here are some further details from the story; move them around to consider the most interesting way of telling it. Think carefully about how you might split some of the ideas up for effect.

- Danny gets a serious injury in the game she watches and his career is ended – she meets him as a doctor at the hospital and they fall in love.
- Danny is already a heavy drinker but gets worse after the injury. She leaves him but he says he needs her, so she returns after a six-month break.
- She realises he will never change so tells him it's over for good.
- He turns up at her house a year later sober and with a new job as a coach of a youth team.
- She asks for time to think – and decides to go back to him.

Plan the whole story as a story board.

Remember

- Structure your story to keep the reader guessing.
- Take them on a visual journey.
- Try out different structures before deciding on the best one.

Extended Assessment Task

A website called All-people-together.com has asked for contributions from young people about friendships or experiences of people or places of a different culture.

> *We would like a short story in which two people from different cultures meet. It cannot be longer than 800 words. It can be based on a real experience or be entirely fictional. We don't want worthy but boring. Make it interesting to read.*

The content – where it takes place and who the characters are – is entirely up to you.

You may wish to continue and complete the girl in a foreign city story, develop the barge story, adapt the Danny story (the woman could be from a different culture), or write your own idea.

Evaluation – What have you learned?

With a partner, use the grade checklist below to evaluate your work on the Extended Assessment Task.

- I can engage and sustain the reader's interest from start to finish, sequencing ideas in original ways, introducing detail and positioning my readers so they look and follow where I want them to go.
- I can meet the requirements of the task in all respects, with rich and original ideas and language.

- I can engage and sustain the reader's interest from start to finish, sequencing ideas, introducing detail and positioning my reader.
- I can meet the requirements of the task convincingly, with interesting ideas and language.

- I can meet the requirements of the task and use a range of techniques to engage the reader and sustain interest, often with rich and varied language use and structure.
- I can use more advanced paragraphing, punctuation and spelling.

- I can meet the main requirements of the task and write in a clear way, making my story ideas coherent and easy-to-follow.
- I can use some language devices and techniques for effect, and engage the reader where possible.
- I can ensure my response is presented accurately.

- I can produce a response and my story makes sense, though it is not well-developed.
- I can use some language devices, write mostly accurate sentences and create some interest in what I write.

You may need to go back and look at the relevant pages from this section again.

Controlled Assessment Preparation
Creative Writing

Introduction

In this section you will

- find out the exact facts, demands and requirements of the Controlled Assessment task for Unit 3 Section B: Producing Creative Texts
- read, analyse and respond to three sample answers by different candidates
- plan and write your own response to a sample task
- evaluate and assess your response and the progress you have made.

Why is preparation of this kind important?

- If you know exactly what you need to do, you will feel more confident when you produce your own response for assessment.
- Looking at sample answers by other students will help you see what you need to do to improve your own work.
- Planning and writing a full sample written response after you have completed the whole chapter will give you a clear sense of what you have learned so far.

Key Information

Unit 3 Section B is 'Producing Creative Texts'.

- The controlled part of the task will last up to **four hours**, and is worth **30 marks**.
- It is worth **15%** of your overall English Language GCSE mark.

What will the assessments involve?

- You have to complete **two** written tasks.
- The total number of words recommended for the two pieces is **1200**. The pieces do not have to be of equal length.

You will choose, or be provided with, two tasks from these three areas:

- Re-creations (transforming a text into a different form)
- Moving images (writing based on moving images)
- Commissions (responding to a set brief).

So, for example, you might re-create a poem as a letter in 500 words and then write an extended commentary on a piece of documentary film in 700 words.

These tasks will be done in 'controlled conditions', in the exam room or in your own classroom over a period of up to four hours.

Here are some example questions based on the three task areas set by the exam board.

Re-creations	Look at the short story, 'The Darkness Out There'. Write a feature article in which you interview Mrs Rutter on the 50th anniversary of the end of World War II and question her about rumours with regard to what happened to the fighter plane.
Moving images	Write a review of a documentary you have seen, analysing how it got its message across, and how effective it was.
Commissions	The web host of a site for teenagers approaches you to submit some writing for it. This month's theme is 'Health = Happiness'. You have complete freedom about how you approach the topic but it must be lively and engaging.

The Assessment

The assessment objectives for this unit (AO4 Writing) state that you must be able to do the following:

- Write to communicate clearly, effectively and imaginatively, using and adapting forms and selecting vocabulary appropriate to the task and purpose in ways that engage the reader.
- Organise information and ideas into structured and sequenced sentences, paragraphs and whole texts, using a variety of linguistic and structural features to support cohesion and overall coherence.
- Use a range of sentence structures for clarity, purpose and effect, with accurate punctuation and spelling.

Targeting Grade A

Some of the key features of Grade C and Grade A/A★ responses are as follows:

Grade C candidates	See example on pages 233–34
<ul><li>adapt one text and turn it into another so that the new form is clear for its new purpose</li><li>use a range of sentences and a varied vocabulary to maintain the reader's interest</li><li>write in paragraphs that are clear and link well, and use punctuation and spelling accurately in general.</li></ul>	(C)

Grade A/A★ candidates	See example on pages 235–36 237–38
<ul><li>write confidently within the new form of text they have been asked to create, understanding the effects of changes of style and tone</li><li>engage the reader's interest immediately and sustain this interest throughout. This is done through well-argued, logical writing, persuasive force or creativity</li><li>use linguistic and structural features skilfully to sequence texts and achieve coherence</li><li>achieve clarity and be imaginative and ambitious in choice of sentence structure, range of sentences, choices of vocabulary, punctuation and spelling.</li></ul>	(A) (A★)

Exploring Sample Responses

ACTIVITY

Read the extract below from a response to this Re-creations task.

> Look at the short story, 'The Darkness Out There'. Write a feature article in which you interview Mrs Rutter on the 50th anniversary of the end of World War II and question her about rumours with regard to what happened to the fighter plane.

As you read it, think about whether it is closer to a Grade C or a Grade A, and why.

Consider these key elements an examiner would look for:

- how effectively the student has transformed the original text into a new version
- how clearly the student's ideas are conveyed
- whether the conventions of the new text type (a feature article) have been followed
- how engaging and interesting the article is – in terms of variety and range in the vocabulary and sentences.

Example 1: Re-creations

Article heading a bit dull and vague →

Uses reported speech →

Punctuates direct speech correctly →

Some variety in sentences →

Gives the facts but does not offer an exciting first sentence

MEMORIES

I went to interview Mrs Rutter who is a lady who lived at the time of World War II and has many memories of the things that happened. I met her at her little house near the woods and asked her what she remembered. **She told me about rationing and how she had lost her husband** but what I was interested in was the rumour about the woods.

The rumour was that a German plane had crashed in the woods and that the local people had killed the crew. Some children have talked to their parents and said Mrs Rutter was involved. Because it was near her cottage it seemed like she must know something.

'**That's not quite true, love,**' she told me when I interviewed her.

I asked her what really happened then, and she told me that yes, a plane had come down, but that the crew were killed. **I wasn't convinced. I asked her again.** Wasn't there a young German crew member who had survived?

ctd.

Mrs Rutter got really angry at that point and told me to leave. She shouted that I didn't understand what it was like back then. She said it was war and the 'jerries' had murdered her husband. So I had to put my note-book away and leave the cottage.

Good change of tense in the questions suits article →

So, what is the truth? *Several local people who didn't want ← Paragraph used to give their names told me that yes, a German soldier survived the crash but he was badly wounded. Mrs Rutter knew she could save him if she wanted to but decided to let him slowly die of his wounds. It took two nights apparently.*

Paragraph used effectively for new point

How come no one heard him? Well, the woods are pretty dark and thick, and **would you** *go out into them if you heard something? Mrs Rutter probably took a gun with her in any case.*

The informal 'would you' is not really appropriate here

The mystery of the crashed plane isn't solved as no one is prepared to say for sure that a soldier was left to die. I have tried to contact Mrs Rutter several times since but she does not answer her door or the phone. Perhaps she is embarrassed about what she did. **But we mustn't judge her. We weren't alive back then so we can't really know what went on.**

Ending is quite good. Gives a sense of a conclusion

Examiner feedback

This is quite a successful re-creation.

- We can see the 'bones' of the original short story here with a new perspective and the article is reasonably well-structured, clear and easy to follow.
- There is some variety in the sentences, but in other respects it is a little bit dull and predictable.
- The title is poor and, whilst the use of questions tries to engage the reader, much of the rest lacks originality in terms of how language is used.

Suggested grade: C

Read the response below to this moving images task.

> *Write a review of a documentary you have seen, analysing how it got its message across and how effective it was.*

Looking carefully at the annotations, decide how this is an improvement on Example 1.

Example 2: Moving images

Clever and funny heading establishes viewpoint →

WATCH OUT! GREAT WHITE IDIOT NEARBY

'SHARK WATCHER' [9pm, Discovery channel]

Animal documentaries are, unlike sharks, not dying out. ← Nice tongue-in-cheek first sentence continues mocking tone

There are huge numbers on television and it seems that, if you want to guarantee viewers, the television companies think all you have to do is take a camera to some exotic location and stick a celebrity in front of it where they will moan about how much they will miss the **Lesser Spotted Green Horny-backed Toad.**

Good use of humour for effect →

From sit-com to sharks ← Sub-heading not usually used in reviews but ok

Basic facts of programme →

'Shark watcher' is a new documentary presented by Dominic Doran, who we all know as a comedy actor in brainless sit-coms. The first time we see him in this new documentary, he is sitting on a **lovely** boat in **lovely** sunny weather. Next moment he is telling us how dangerous it is watching sharks. Yes, Dominic, very dangerous when you are sitting on a huge boat with a camera crew. Next, he tells us, 'The Great White Shark is under threat from mankind'. **Really? You're kidding!**

Repetition used for effect ←

Quite nice ironic, sarcastic tone →

The programme then proceeds to follow Dominic as he fails to actually see any sharks at all. Instead we get long shots of Dominic looking thoughtful as the sun goes down. Or we get close-ups of him going to sleep with sad music playing. **It**

This does not add anything to the review →

drives me mad!

ctd.

Old ideas

The programme is also irritating because it uses the same old ideas: Dominic interviewing a conservationist but clearly not understanding a word he is saying; Dominic phoning home and telling his girlfriend he misses her (does he think he's on I'm A Celebrity Get Me Out Of Here?) and Dominic pretending to read a difficult book all about sharks.

Good use of brackets for an 'aside'

The only moment in the programme worth watching is when the camera crew actually do get some footage of sharks. There are dozens of them and they look in great condition. Unfortunately, they are not Great Whites, which gives Dominic another excuse to repeat the fact that they are under threat.

Paragraphs well used for each point

What is most worrying about this programme is that it is only the first episode in a six-part series, which means we will have to face another two and a half hours of Dominic's stupid pale face looking concerned!

Well, **I won't**, because **I won't** be watching this rubbish again. I just pity the poor Great Whites if they actually meet up with Dominic. One look at his face and they will probably sink lifeless to the bottom of the sea-floor. **All I can say is, 'Bring back David Attenborough'!**

Unnecessary repetition

Good, firm conclusion

Examiner feedback

This is generally a very successful and engaging piece of writing on moving images.

- We get a good sense of the reviewer's opinion, and this is supported by some funny and well-argued points about the documentary.
- The writer usually uses appropriate language such as 'location', 'close-up' and 'long shot' and, although it is not necessary to see these in a television review, here they add to the points being made.
- In general the student has tried really hard to engage the reader through humour and some good uses of language (bracketed asides, questions, exaggeration).

All-in-all, a well-structured and persuasive text with some odd moments of creativity and flair.

Suggested grade: A

Read the response below to this Commissions task.

The web host of a site for teenagers approaches you to submit some writing for it. This month's theme is 'Health = Happiness'. You have complete freedom about how you approach the topic but it must be lively and engaging.

Looking carefully at the annotations, decide how it is an improvement from Example 2.

Example 3: Commissions

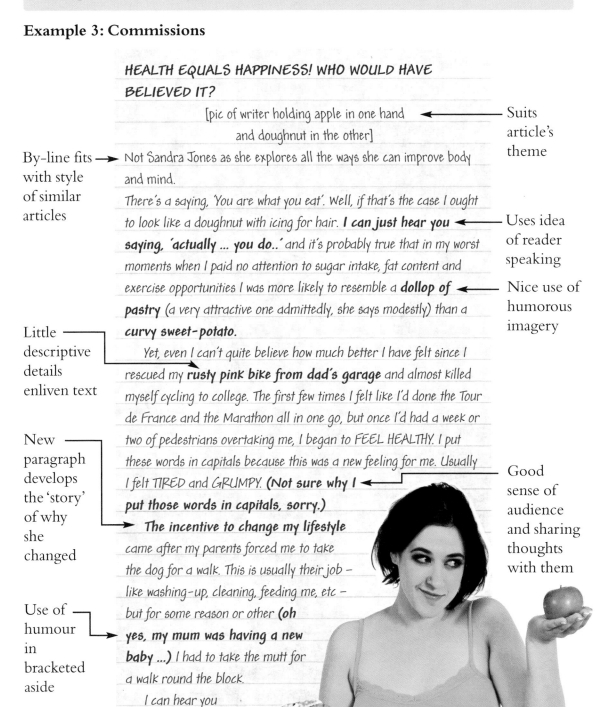

HEALTH EQUALS HAPPINESS! WHO WOULD HAVE BELIEVED IT?

[pic of writer holding apple in one hand and doughnut in the other] — Suits article's theme

By-line fits with style of similar articles → Not Sandra Jones as she explores all the ways she can improve body and mind.

There's a saying, 'You are what you eat'. Well, if that's the case I ought to look like a doughnut with icing for hair. **I can just hear you** ← Uses idea of reader speaking **saying, 'actually ... you do..'** and it's probably true that in my worst moments when I paid no attention to sugar intake, fat content and exercise opportunities I was more likely to resemble a **dollop of** ← Nice use of humorous imagery **pastry** (a very attractive one admittedly, she says modestly) than a **curvy sweet-potato.**

Little descriptive details enliven text → Yet, even I can't quite believe how much better I have felt since I rescued my **rusty pink bike from dad's garage** and almost killed myself cycling to college. The first few times I felt like I'd done the Tour de France and the Marathon all in one go, but once I'd had a week or two of pedestrians overtaking me, I began to FEEL HEALTHY. I put

New paragraph develops the 'story' of why she changed → these words in capitals because this was a new feeling for me. Usually I felt TIRED and GRUMPY. **(Not sure why I** ← Good sense of audience and sharing thoughts with them **put those words in capitals, sorry.)**

→ **The incentive to change my lifestyle** came after my parents forced me to take the dog for a walk. This is usually their job – like washing-up, cleaning, feeding me, etc –

Use of humour in bracketed aside → but for some reason or other **(oh yes, my mum was having a new baby ...)** I had to take the mutt for a walk round the block.

I can hear you

ctd.

Informality ok here as she is trying to make article sound as if talking to a friend →

saying – 'around the block? That's not very demanding'. **Well, I can tell you that walking up Fisher Avenue is very demanding. OK, it's not exactly Ben Nevis,** but by the time I got to the top I was all ready to plant a flag in the ground. In fact, if I had had a flag I would have, but the truth is I was too out of breath to plant anything. **I asked the dog if I could have a rest and he said,** ← **Silly idea used to entertain us**
'**yes,** provided you promise to exercise properly, cut out iced doughnuts except for Fridays, and eat the odd salad'. I nodded my head (I couldn't speak as I was too knackered), and after a rest on the kerb walked back down Ben Nevis ... er, Fisher Avenue.

Good link words →

Since then I am a changed girl/woman (what do you call yourself when you're almost 15? A girl-man?). I do still yearn for doughnuts and still have the odd one – like after I got my mock Science results (I didn't know 'U' meant 'ungraded', I thought it meant 'utterly brilliant') – but I am now an **avid cyclist, salad**

Two 'patterns of three nouns' stress point here ⌐→

freak and general lover of fresh air, food and fitness. I can't wait to get out of the house, although that could be more to do with the smell of nappies than the need for activity.

What is really funny is that I feel more confident. I was quite confident when I looked like a ring doughnut so I must be unbearable now. **There's this boy in Year 11** who keeps on looking at me strangely, too. I think he fancies the new me, but actually my best mate Cara says it's because I hadn't realised I still had my cycle-helmet on when I was chatting to him. Oh well, 'c'est la vie' as they say in Germany... or is it Italy? **Must go and practise for my French oral. It's all about healthy living, so I should be OK.**

Ends with comic anecdote which cleverly brings together school life, mind and health ⌐

Examiner feedback

This is an excellent piece of feature writing which gets the tone and style spot on for the audience. It meets the commission almost perfectly.

- There are lots of references to the writer's own life which have been exaggerated and played with for entertainment value and creative delight.
- The language really affects and shapes the reader's response; the comic asides (in brackets) when talking to the reader as a friend, the little vivid details about the writer's life, even the well-judged use of informal or chatty language such as 'Oh well', 'OK' and 'knackered' is fine.
- There is also real variety in the sentence structures which give us a clear sense of the writer's own personality.
- In most places, the vocabulary is varied and thoroughly engaging.

Suggested grade: A★

EXAM PRACTICE TASK

> **Commissions**
>
> *A television company is commissioning a new reality show featuring teenagers. It wants the show to have a serious message, issue or idea to explore. It will be on for one hour every night for 14 days, ending on a Sunday evening.*

You have been approached by the producer to suggest what the show might be about, what its format might be and who might be involved.

Write a proposal of **no more than 600 words**

- explaining your ideas clearly
- giving a clear vision of the look and feel of the programme
- saying why it would appeal to teenage viewers.

If you only do five things...

1 Prepare fully for your Controlled Assessment task by drafting your response carefully in line with the type of creative text you are writing.

2 Watch, read or listen to the full range of texts you are likely to have to write or respond to.

3 Make sure you use the main conventions that fit the style or form in which you are writing.

4 Take every opportunity to show off your creativity through your ideas, richness of language or detail. Include a variety of vocabulary, paragraphs and sentences. Use imagery, vivid description and detail where appropriate.

5 Think carefully about the structure and sequence of your ideas – you don't have to tell the reader everything straight away. Begin brilliantly, engaging the reader straight away. End brilliantly, by satisfying or surprising the reader.

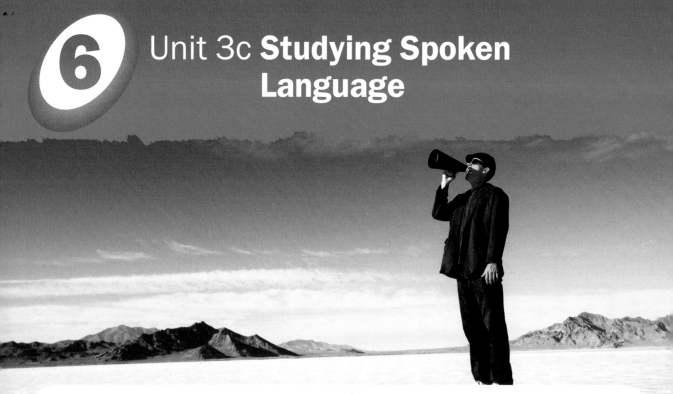

6 Unit 3c Studying Spoken Language

What's it all about?

Spoken language defines who we are, our relationships and our lives. We use talk to communicate feelings, influence others, tell stories, convey information and exert power and control… amongst other things. But what do we know about our own talk? And what rules, if any, govern the way we speak?

How will I be assessed?

- You will get **10% of your English Language marks** for your ability to write about spoken language.
- You will have to complete **one** Controlled Assessment task of **800–1000 words** over the course of **2–3 hours**.
- You will be marked on your written response to **one** of these three topics:
  - **Social attitudes to spoken language**: how we and others respond to, and are affected by, the way people speak
  - **Spoken genres**: the different patterns, conventions and features of talk in particular situations (for example, in television interviews or in speeches)
  - **Multi-modal talk**: the way talk is changed or affected by a range of media (for example, mobile phones or the internet).

What is being tested?

You are being examined on your ability to

- show your understanding of how spoken and written language evolves as a result of changes in society and technology
- explain how these changes in language reflect our own identity and culture
- engage with the different ways language is used in 'real life' – for example, attitudes to accent and dialect, or how language is used in the workplace or between particular groups or individuals
- reflect critically on your own and others' uses of language in different contexts and how you and others adapt to different listeners, contexts and situations.

However, your response will only have to focus on one or two of these areas, depending on the topic you choose.

Talk – What's it all about?

Introduction

This section of Chapter 6 helps you to

- explore the types of research and data collection about spoken language that will be useful for your own investigation
- learn about transcribing talk
- investigate your own and others' spoken language.

Why is learning about talk important?

- Understanding how talk operates can help you improve your own communication in everyday situations and with different groups of people.
- Talk has its own conventions and ways of being analysed. It requires specific approaches which may be different from the way you approach written texts. Learning about these differences enhances your understanding of both spoken and written language.

A **Grade C** candidate will

- describe their own talk and explain some of its features
- explain clearly how they and others use and adapt spoken language in different situations, such as with friends or in formal contexts.

C

A **Grade A/A*** candidate will

- analyse their own talk and its specific features in fine detail, using appropriate terminology, exploring a range of influences and background information
- analyse in detail how they and others use and adapt spoken language in different situations, exploring influences on their spoken language.

A A*

Prior learning

Before you begin this unit, think about

- what you already know about your own spoken language
- what you know about other people's spoken language.

> How does it change when you are talking to parents, friends or teachers? Do you have an accent?

> Do any friends or family members have a different accent? Do they expect you to talk in a certain way? Why?

What is special about my talk?

Learning objective

- To explore your own talk, and understand some of your own attitudes to it.

ACTIVITY

Discuss your own 'talk' for a few minutes in a group.

- **How do you speak with your friends?** Do you have special 'in-words' or phrases that you all share? What are they? Where did they come from? Would you use them in writing?
- **How does your talk with others vary?** Do you speak differently to adults, other friends, people you don't know so well? How do you feel when speaking in public or to unfamiliar audiences?
- **How would you describe your talk?** Do you have a particular accent? Is this related to where you live – or lived?

All these things that make up your own talk – including pronunciation, grammatical patterns of speech, dialect and vocabulary – can be referred to as your **idiolect**. For example, you might say, 'My idiolect is characterised by my Yorkshire accent and my habit of saying 'like' lots of times. I also use a range of local dialect words.'

Key terms in spoken language study

Term	Meaning	Example usage
accent	pronunciation of words according to the place, society or culture you are from	I have a southern accent which is noticeable in certain words like 'grass' which I pronounce with a 'long' A.
non-standard dialect	vocabulary and grammar distinct to a place, group of people or, sometimes, country	My dad (from Somerset) still says 'Where's that to?' instead of 'Where is it?' and uses 'gurt' meaning 'very' or 'really' as in 'that's a gurt big burger you've got'.
standard English	the most widely-used form of language which is not specific to a particular location or region	In standard English I'd use 'we were going' not 'we was', and in terms of vocabulary I'd use 'argument', not 'barney' or 'tiff'.
formal and informal	the types of language you would use in a professional or business situation or talking with a friend or people you know well	I use more formal language when I'm doing my Saturday job. If customers come in, I have to say, 'Can I help you, sir?'. Of course if a friend came in I might suddenly be more informal, and say, 'All right, mate? What d'you want, then?'
register	the particular language used for a specific social situation or subject	I use quite an informal register when my friend comes in, dropping letters from the end of words, and using the odd bit of slang – and swearing!
transcript	written-out version of a conversation or talk as it actually occurred (including pauses, hesitations and repetitions)	Well. I met our lass in, I mean, I fell, I mean, why, it sounds, it might sound old-fashioned, but I fell in love with her.

Focus for development: Researching idiolect

Your discussion so far has been based on what you think about your talk rather than **evidence**. But are you right? What is your spoken language really like? One way of finding out is to record some spoken language from your everyday life.

Read this short piece of conversation which one student recorded and then transcribed. (A is the student; B is his brother.)

> **A:** here (.) give me the remote
> **B:** er why
> **A:** this is rubbish (1) um are you going to give it to me ? or not
> **B:** ((*mimicking*)) are you going to give it to me or not ?
> **A:** oh you[h]'re so [funny
> **B:**   [here it is
> **A:** (loser)

Examiner's tip ⭐

It is helpful to use the term 'utterance' for any complete unit of speech in a dialogue. It doesn't have to be grammatically correct. Notice also that **verbal fillers** like 'er' and 'um', often linked to hesitations, are also noted in transcripts.

Here is the key to the symbols in the transcript.

(.) or (1)	a very short (only just noticeable) pause. A longer pause is indicated by a number to show length in seconds.
↑ talk/↓ talk	onset of noticeable pitch rise ↑ /or fall ↓
A: talk talk [talk B: [talk	square brackets aligned like this denote the start of overlapping talk.
?	gradually rising intonation to the point at which the question mark symbol is used, not necessarily an actual question
[h]	'laughter' within a word
(talk)	a guess at what was said, if the recording is not clear
((*sobbing*))	anything difficult, or impossible, to write down is shown in italics in double brackets

ASSESSMENT FOCUS

- Although the sample transcript is very short, what could you conclude about the brothers' relationship – and their talk?
- Write at least one paragraph making specific reference to the transcript. You might comment on things such as the 'interjection' when B interrupts A's answer.

Remember

- You will need to refer to at least three pages of transcription as part of your study.
- It doesn't have to be your own, but your own talk is a good place to begin.

How others speak

Learning objective

- *To practise using different types of source material to research the spoken language of others.*

Standard English: the most widely-used form of English. You would say 'I'm not' rather than 'I ain't' and you would talk about a 'child' not a 'kid' or a 'nipper'.

ACTIVITY

Articles can be a good source of data on spoken language. Read the web text below and make brief notes about the regional dialect being explained.

- How widely is 'Geordie' spoken?
- What variations, if any, are there in local dialect?

What is Geordie?

The word Geordie refers both to a native of Newcastle-upon-Tyne and to the speech of the inhabitants of that city. There are several theories about the exact origins of the term Geordie, but all agree it derives from the local pet name for George. It is sometimes mistakenly used to refer to the speech of the whole of the North East of England. Strictly speaking, however, Geordie should only refer to the speech of the city of Newcastle-upon-Tyne and the surrounding urban area of Tyneside. Locals insist there are significant differences between Geordie and several other local dialects, such as **Pitmatic** and **Makkem**. Pitmatic is the dialect of the former mining areas in County Durham and around Ashington to the north of Newcastle-upon-Tyne, while Makkem is used locally to refer to the dialect of the city of Sunderland and the surrounding urban area of Wearside. Although only 10 miles apart, the difference between Sunderland and Newcastle-upon-Tyne is, of course, extremely important locally, not least because of the rivalry between supporters of the two football clubs. For many people these different identities are expressed in the way they speak. To the south, speakers in rural County Durham and North Yorkshire are sometimes affectionately referred to as **Farm Yakkers**, while **Smoggies** – the inhabitants of Middlesbrough and the surrounding urban area of Teesside – have their own distinctive dialect, too.

http://www.bl.uk/learning/langlit/sounds/case-studies/geordie/

Discuss with a partner:

- Why do you think locals would 'insist there are significant differences' between how they and others speak, even in quite a small area of the country?
- When you speak to someone from your area, how do you tell exactly where they come from – maybe a town nearby, or a different part of your county? Are there clues in their accent or vocabulary?

Focus for development: Research from transcripts

Data can also come from transcripts from actual speakers. Read this extract from the same website as the article on page 244.

> **Mark:** Well. I met our lass in, I mean, I fell, I mean, why, it sounds, it might sound old-fashioned, but I fell in love with her. You know. I still, I still, I'll always love our lass. I mean I love her stronger each day. I mean, you, the, them days you didn't, you didn't live with lasses. If, if a bloke was ganning with a lass and they weren't married, she, she had a bad name. You know. And everybody looked, looked down on people like that. And if a lass had a bairn, even if a lass had a bairn out of wedlock, she was, look, frowned upon, you know. I mean, I'm not saying that's right. But at the time they seemed right. I mean, people's att, your attitudes change now. I divn't think they're right now anyway. You know, when they live together. And they're having kids and, and they divn't want to get married and, I think you're, you're better being married. I mean it worked for me. But saying that, mind, uh, I got the right one. I was lucky; I got the right one. And it didn't work for my brother; he got the wrang one. So you cannot speak for other people really, can you? You know what I mean? I cannot. But I mean, I'm lucky. I've been lucky; dead lucky.

ACTIVITY

With your partner, note down from this transcript

- any examples that show this is a record of a 'spoken conversation', for example repetitions, hesitations and pauses
- examples of where local vocabulary has been used which might be phrased differently in standard English (see **Key terms box** on page 242)
- what you know about Mark by the end and how you made these decisions, based on the way he speaks and what he says.

Using your notes from both texts decide what you have learned about variations in accent and dialect in the North East.

ASSESSMENT FOCUS

Consider the two topics you have looked at so far, 'My talk' and 'Other people's talk'.

Decide for each which sources from the list above you would choose to research if you were going to base your spoken language task on them.

These two sources – the web article and transcript – provide a great deal of information about local dialect. Other sources to consider for your own research include

- video or audio clips of people speaking, for example podcasts, internet, television or film clips
- print-outs of text messaging exchanges
- transcripts or recordings of 'live' everyday speech situations, for example speeches or conversations
- questionnaire results, for example, on attitudes to talk
- charts, graphs or other data patterns, for example, a map of UK dialects.

Remember

- **Talk – and information about it – is all around you; capture what is interesting and then select data or source material that fits your topic.**

★ **Examiner's tip**

*When you prepare your questionnaire, the headings and the way you write the questions are up to you. It is easier to analyse the results if you give a statement to which people 'strongly disagree/ disagree/not sure/ agree/strongly agree', or give a scale of 1 to 5 in which 5 means 'strongly agree'. You may also want to record some basic details about the **respondents**, such as age and gender, especially if in this case you were asking people between the ages of 25 and 85.*

Checklist for success

- You need to **engage** with the subject matter in a practical way. That means finding areas that interest you and which you can research.
- You need to **reflect critically** about your own and others' use of language, especially their particular 'idiolect'.

Conducting your research

Select an area that interests you and consider how you will collect useful information. One way is to create a questionnaire or survey which you could personally carry out, or give to people to complete. Look at this example about the way in which young people's speech has changed over the years.

Question	Definitely not	Probably not	Probably yes	Definitely yes
Do young people today speak differently to their parents from the way that you did?				
Do young people swear more today?				
In your opinion, do young people today find it easier to talk to adults than you did when you were young?				

ACTIVITY

Write two more questions of your own for this questionnaire.

Make sure they can be answered using the columns on the right.

Focus for development:
Following up key points

Any survey you carry out could be separate from any interviews you do, or you could use interviews to follow up key points that emerge from your survey. For example, here are some interview questions that lead on from the survey above.

1. You agreed that young people today talk differently to their parents. How did you talk to your parents when you were young?

2. What was considered swearing or unacceptable?

3. Were there occasions when you were told off by adults because of how you spoke? Why? And what did you say?

By asking 'open' questions like this you should get some longer answers so it may be a good idea to record the interview and play it back later. Also keep some basic details about the interviewee.

ASSESSMENT FOCUS

Once you have conducted your interviews and questionnaires, you need to decide what they tell you.

- First, **record the results of your survey in measurable ways**, such as, 'Four out of five people questioned felt that they didn't speak with an accent.'
- Then, if you can, **draw some conclusions**, such as, 'This demonstrates that we treat our own speech as "normal" unless we have moved to a new area or region recently.'
- In addition, comment on **specific statements from interviews**, such as 'My grandfather's way of speaking showed his local accent, for example when…'

ACTIVITY

Select an area you would like to investigate – it could be as broad as 'how others talk' or 'other people's idiolect' – and develop a questionnaire to give to other people. This might be two friends, a brother/sister, parent or adult you know well, and a grandparent or older adult.

Decide on some basic questions, such as:

- Do you think you have an accent?
- Do you change your talk according to who you speak to?

Then develop more open questions for an interview, such as:

- How do you change your way of speaking with different people?
- What sort of accent do you think you have? What dialect words do you use?

Examiner's tip ★

For the highest marks, try to link your specific analysis to wider reflection on language variation and change, for example how greater social mobility has meant a wider variety of accents in cities.

Remember

- Use interviews and questionnaires to gather evidence for your study.
- Keep clear records – both written (surveys or transcripts) and spoken (recorded conversations).
- Analyse these carefully, and draw conclusions.

Grade Booster

Writing up your research

Having selected an area of spoken language to research related to 'my talk' or 'how others speak', and gathered your data and materials, write up what you have found out.

- Introduce the area you focused on.
- Explain what you did and the research you carried out (interviews, surveys, questionnaires, source materials).
- Write about your findings:
  - What were the outcomes (the results you produced)?
  - What did these tell you about your – or others' – language use, and how it varies?
- Write a short conclusion which makes some broad points, if possible. Relate what you've said to wider ideas about language variation and change.

Evaluation – What have you learned?

With a partner, use the grade checklist below to evaluate your work on the Extended Assessment Task.

- I can write up my research in detail, clearly analysing what I did, drawing specific and broader conclusions, perceptively interpreting and evaluating what I have learned and reflecting on language variation as a whole.

- I can write up my research in detail, clearly analysing what I did, drawing specific and broader conclusions, and developing an interpretation of what I have discovered.

- I can write up my research in detail, clearly explaining what I did, and draw conclusions based on each part of my research.

- I can write up my research clearly, explaining what I did and what it told me.

- I can write up my research, detailing what I found and making some points about it.

You may need to go back and look at the relevant pages from this section again.

The Spoken Language Study Topics

Introduction

This section of Chapter 6 helps you to

- explore the three areas of spoken language study: Social attitudes to spoken language, Spoken genres, and Multi-modal talk. Each of these topics will be explained clearly as you progress.

Why is learning about these three topics important?

- The tasks in the Controlled Assessment will be based on research and response to the three areas; you need to be clear about what each one entails.
- The three areas overlap and influence each other. For example, social attitudes can be observed in the area of multi-modal talk – in different groups' perspectives on the language of texting, for instance.

A **Grade C** candidate will

- explain what the main issues are with regard to each area
- use research evidence in an effective way to support their explanations.

C

A **Grade A/A*** candidate will

- analyse and evaluate specific features and issues related to the three areas in fine detail, using appropriate terminology
- select apt and specific examples, evidence and references to support analysis and interpretation.

A A*

Prior learning

Before you begin this unit, think about

- what you already know about attitudes to different social groups and the particular way they talk

- what you know about different types of talk that take place in everyday situations

- what you already know about types of talk influenced by technology.

> Does your language change when you are with a particular group of people?

> Do you use certain phrases when you complain in a shop or restaurant or when you visit the dentist?

> Do you chat on social networking sites? How does chat change when you are texting?

Social attitudes to spoken language

Learning objective

- To understand how the way we and others speak can both include and exclude, and that we all make judgements based on how people talk.

What does social attitudes to spoken language mean?

Many of us use language differently with different groups of people. For example, with our families and friends we might use pet names, silly phrases or invent different meanings for common words. These make sense to that group, but they could be a barrier to outsiders. It is these types of language use that you will be exploring through this topic.

ACTIVITY

Discuss with a friend or in a group:

- When you meet someone for the first time, what do you notice most? The way they look? The way they speak? The way they dress?
- Now role-play the two extracts below with a partner. Discuss what conclusions (rightly or wrongly) you might draw about the speaker in each case, for example about their age, their culture or background or their social group.

Speaker A

> Gosh, Jemima. I am absolutely flabbergasted that Simon Cowell complimented that quite awful singer.

Speaker B

> No way, Jem! I mean get real Simon. She ain't no singer, innit?

A student writes…

I don't like talking about this sort of thing. It makes me feel snobbish, or like I have a downer on some people.

Answer…

Our attitudes to talk go very deep; but that doesn't mean they automatically make us racist, ageist or sexist. Most of our social attitudes to language use are based on what we have heard or experienced. Reflecting on these attitudes helps us become aware of any prejudices we might have.

Focus for development: Others' attitudes

Read this range of comments from people that show their attitudes to other people's talk.

Employer: When I interview someone and he or she starts dropping his/her 't's, like 'wha' I did', or he/she says 'we was' instead of 'we were', they weaken their chance of getting the job.

Teenager: There was this funny sketch on *The Armstrong and Miller Show* where these two World War Two pilots are talking in posh accents, but using modern teenage slang and talking like teenagers.

Pupil in school in Cornwall: I hate it on TV when they use a west-country 'yokel' accent to show someone is slow or stupid. It's like an easy laugh, but I don't think it's funny.

Newsreader: When I first started working on television you had to have a Received Pronunciation accent – no regional voices at all. When I questioned this, because I had a naturally strong Welsh accent, they said people trusted the RP voice – that if the accent was too strong then it made the news less believable. Of course, now regional accents are everywhere and that's great.

ACTIVITY

Look at each example and make notes about the attitude displayed by the speaker. Decide

- whether the attitude is a positive one
- what we learn about their attitude to accent, dialect and non-standard English.

Can you think of any examples where a way of speaking has been used for comic effect? Does the humour stem from

- the situation (for example, is the accent out of place?)
- the particular language? (For example, does it match the character? Is it unusual or silly? Does it come as a surprise or shock?)

ASSESSMENT FOCUS

Write two paragraphs in which you comment on attitudes to accent, in particular when they are used to convey a stereotype or idea about someone.

- Give particular examples.
- Explain your own attitude to the accent and why you might have that attitude. (Be honest in your views!)

Remember

- We all have attitudes to spoken language; it may just be that we don't stop to think about them very often. 'Unpicking' what we feel, and explaining it in a clear and informed way, is a key to getting a higher grade.

Hip, or just plain wrong?

Read this article from the *Daily Mail*. It reports on a new production of *Julius Caesar* in street talk.

Friends, Romans innit? Shakespeare is given a makeover in street slang

Schoolchildren argue over an iPod, actors talk like gangsters and rapping mixes freely with spoken words. Welcome to Shakespeare's Julius Caesar, rewritten for 2009.

A group of young actors has reinvented the play, described by its director as the 'ultimate knife crime', as a tale of urban violence by rewriting the script into street slang. Out goes The Bard's nuanced Renaissance language. In its place come chatter and text-talk from the streets of modern-day London. The play, retitled *Wasted!*, is being put on by Intermission, a youth theatre group based in Knightsbridge in London that works with young people who have committed crimes or are at risk of getting into trouble. The plot loosely follows the original.

Trouble begins when Caesar moves from Harvey Nicks Grove school to nearby Harrods High. He is marked out as a threat for wanting to become head prefect and knifed to death.

WILL THE BARD BE TURNING IN HIS GRAVE?

How the young actors have rewritten Shakespeare's Julius Caesar:

OLD – Marullus: You, sir, what trade are you?
Second Workman: I am but, as you would say, a cobbler.
NEW – Miss Portia: Jamie Cobbler?
Cobbler: Yeah blood.
OLD – Soothsayer: Beware the ides of March.

NEW – (Rapping) Fix up, look sharp, beware the ides of March.
OLD – Mark Antony: I speak not to disprove what Brutus spoke but here I am to speak what I do know.
NEW – It ain't no lie that we're dying in our endz but here we are to speak what we do know to keep us alive.
OLD – Mark Antony: Friends, Romans, countrymen, lend me

your ears. I come to bury Caesar, not to praise him.
NEW – Friends, mandem, roadmen, give me a second. I come to bury Caesar, not big him up.
OLD – Mark Antony: But Brutus said he was ambitious and Brutus is an honourable man.
NEW – But that waste-man Brutus said he was ambitious.

Instead of adults in the Roman court, it is set in the classroom and all the teenage actors wear uniform. The vast majority of the first half is embellished with street slang, although the balance tips back towards Shakespeare after the interval. Director Darren Raymond, 27, said street talk was an important aspect of the play because language formed a large part of young people's identities. He said: 'This is not dumbing down. Shakespeare was creating words that nobody had heard of, and these young people are doing nothing different. I didn't relate to Shakespeare at all when I first read him but if you strip the language away the themes are much easier to grasp.'

Wasted!, being performed at St Saviours Church in Knightsbridge, has sold out every 50-seat performance since its four-week run opened last week. Dr Peter Swaab, a reader in English at University College London and an editor of the Penguin Shakespeare, said: 'This is another way into Shakespeare and if it has the fortunate effect of causing those involved to read further then that's a good thing.'

Daniel Bates, Nov 23 2009

ACTIVITY

Discuss the extract in groups:

- How has *Julius Caesar* been updated in the version of the play described? Give some good examples.
- In what ways is the article positive or negative about the use of street language?
- What do you think the reasons were for including street language?
- In your opinion, is there any downside to this approach?

ASSESSMENT FOCUS

Write your own personal view of teenage slang. You could comment on

- particular examples you know and when and where they are used
- why you think it has become popular – if it has
- how much you use teenage slang yourself and your view of it
- what adults think about it in general
- where it comes from (friends, TV, music, films?)

Remember

- Analyse attitudes in your source material in terms of how words and phrases include or exclude people.
- Show how the language used adds richness and variety or make it less appealing.
- Show what impact or effect the language has.

Spoken genres – the media

Learning objective

- To understand that there are different 'spoken genres' and that these often follow routines or have certain conventions.

What are spoken genres?

- Just as there are different genres or forms of writing, such as a novel or newspaper article, so there are also recognisable 'genres' of speech.
- Talk varies according to the **context** or situation. However, certain areas of life – the media, for example – often have their own patterns or **conventions** for speaking which we recognise very quickly.

ACTIVITY

Read these three extracts with a partner. For each, try to identify:

- what the context is (where it take place)
- who is speaking (the type of person or their role)
- how you know these things.

Extract 1

And that's a fantastic ball to Henry....back to Ibrahimovic....he crosses....oh....here's a chance....brilliant block from Pepe....but Madrid can't clear, it's back in....corner to Barca. [pause] Graham, what do Madrid have to do to improve after half-time?

Extract 2

X: With due respect, you haven't answered the question, have you?

Y: I repeat what I said earlier. The government will take all necessary steps to ensure that incidents like this never happen again. We have appointed a committee...

X: [*interrupting*]....the committee you objected to, the committee you said...?

Y: Let me finish....an independent committee who will report to Parliament and make recommendations which we will act on. That is what the Prime Minister announced today, and that is what we're doing.

X: Harriet Burden, thank you.

Extract 3

X: Look, I have to say, it wasn't your fault. It was a terrible song choice.

Y: Hang on a minute, I thought it...

X: Don't listen to him, it was terrible. It was like a dog had got stuck in a cat-flap.

W: I don't agree. I thought you nailed it.

Focus for development: Speech patterns and routines

Each of the extracts uses a variety of different **routines** or **conventions**. Each also has its own **semantic field**. For example, look at this analysis of the live TV football commentary from Extract 1.

Context	Talk	Example	Speech conventions
Studio – presenter faces camera; guests on sofa	Presenter introduces game and studio guests; then switches to the stadium	*Presenter: We're live at the Nou Camp to see Barcelona take on Real Madrid. With me, I have former England player, Robbie Smith…* *Guest: Hi there.*	Shared understanding with audience of what 'Nou Camp' (stadium name) is. Convention of introducing the guest 'With me…'
Inside the stadium	Introductory voiceover from presenter; then interview between reporter and manager in tunnel	*Presenter: Now over to Gerry who is in the tunnel…* *Reporter: So, Pepe, how are you feeling about today's game?*	Typical live presentation phrases: 'Now over to…' Typical conventions of 2-3 questions from reporter and brief answers from manager.

ASSESSMENT FOCUS

- Transcribe a short section from a radio phone-in programme using the techniques explained on page 243. You will need to listen to the recording a number of times to make sure you capture everything that is said, as well as pauses and hesitation markers like 'er' and 'um'.
- Reflect on any challenges you faced in making the transcription.
- Next, make notes on:
  - the kinds of speech routines in the language that are particular to this type of talk, for example: 'And on line one we have…' 'Carrie, what's your view on…'
  - any words or phrases that are part of the semantic field for radio journalism.
- Write a short analysis of the transcript you produced, based on your notes.

Remember

- Refer to the fact that all talk follows routines or has conventions, especially in different media genres.
- Discuss any terms that are part of the semantic field for this spoken genre.

The power of talk

What does power of talk mean?

- In some contexts, one speaker will have more power or a higher status than another (for example, a manager talking to a trainee). You can get a clear sense of the attitudes and interaction in such 'power' relationships by considering the way the people speak.

ACTIVITY

Read this extract from a soap opera about a police station. You may want to work in a group and each take a part to gain a better idea of how it sounds.

Once you have read it aloud, make detailed notes on the types of talk going on in the extract, for example:

- the purpose of each conversation
- the register (degree of formality) each person uses
- any clear routines or patterns of language
- the status or power of each speaker.

Examiner's tip

Make sure you base your analysis on evidence from the extract and use technical terms (for example, status, speech routine, formal, register) to show your understanding.

Glossary

'twoc': taking without owner's consent

Enquiry desk, 11.27a.m.

Desk sergeant: Yes, madam? How can I help?

Woman: I've lost Henry. We were on the high street… well, Henry was; I'd left the back-door open, and…

Desk sergeant: Sorry, madam. Could you tell me who Henry is?

Woman: I have had him years… he's got curly hair…

Desk sergeant: *(aside to colleague)* We've got a right one here. She's nuts… oops, here comes the Super…

Woman wanders off.

Superintendent: Dave. My room, five minutes. Get someone to cover you, OK?

Desk sergeant: Yes sir. *(to colleague)* You down the club tonight?

Colleague: Nah. SOCO want to see me. You know that kid I pulled up?

Desk sergeant: What, for twocking?

Colleague: Yeah, him. Well, he reckons it weren't him. An ARV was in the area and they saw an older guy driving the car earlier. Kid reckons it was his old man.

Focus for development:
Spoken genres in everyday contexts

We tend to think of talk as being spontaneous and unplanned but many types of talk follow routines. For example, a boy chatting up a girl for the first time is likely to start by saying 'Hi' not 'Do you want to go out with me?'

ACTIVITY

- Choose one of these everyday situations to explore: a hospital or a school.
- List the different types of talk that might happen in the situation and make notes about each in a grid like this.

Situation	Speakers	Content / Purpose	Conventions of talk in this situation
First-aid room	First aider and pupil	Find out why pupil is there Comforting sick pupil	Questions from first-aider Single word/short responses from pupil
Assembly	Head of Year	Give out information	Addressed to whole group – 'you' means the year….

ASSESSMENT FOCUS

Once you have done some research into your chosen everyday situation, write the opening to a study about it. Start by introducing the range of speakers and the talk that takes place there to give a flavour of the diversity and range of speech practices. For example:

A police station is a melting-pot of different dialogues, conversations, situations and speech practices. In it, you will hear chatty, informal conversations between friends and colleagues, as well as highly patterned routines such as interrogations and enquiries...

A student writes…

Couldn't I just watch Holby City or Waterloo Road to learn about speech in these situations?

Answer…

In fact, writers of these series are keen observers of 'talk' but be aware that they often exaggerate or emphasise certain things and, unlike real speech, there are few hesitations or interruptions in these scripts.

Remember

- Comment on the diversity and range of speech situations.
- Explain how these different situations affect the language and structures of talk.

Multi-modal talk

Learning objective

- To understand what multi-modal talk is and how it differs from other forms of speech.

What is multi-modal talk?

- The term 'multi-modal' refers to the many (multi) different ways (modes) through which we can express ourselves in talk or something that is close to talk. It particularly applies to the new modes of 'talk' available to us through new media such as the internet or mobile phones.

ACTIVITY

Discuss with a partner:

- Why do we choose to call the sorts of communication that take place on social networking sites, and in other digital contexts, 'talk' or 'chat'? After all, in most cases we are actually writing, not 'talking'!
- Does such 'talk' have more in common with speech or with other writing that you do?

Now look at this text message from a university student to his mother and write answers to the questions below.

> From: SAM
> Yeh got it thanx pressie is gr8
> c u 2moro luv 2 dad

- How does the content differ from a conventional letter a son might send home from university?
- How is this text **more like chat** than a written letter?
- In what way are these differences a result of the technology?

ACTIVITY

In pairs, quickly role-play a conversation between a son phoning his dad to check his birthday present has arrived. Begin…

> **Son**: Hi Dad, it's Adam. Happy birthday!
> **Dad**: Thanks.
> **Son**: Did you get my pressie?

Then discuss:

- What does the spoken talk have that the 'text talk' doesn't?
- Can you 'read between the lines' about the present in the text-talk?

Focus for development: Talking the talk

In order to write about multi-modal talk, you need to use professional and specific language to help you. Here are a few terms you might find useful.

Term	Meaning	Example
interactive	Where the medium or user responds to input.	'the interactive site updated itself in response to my comments.'
medium	The means or place through which communication happens.	'I used the medium of a networking site to contact friends.'
operation	An act or event that occurs a part of communication.	'A number of language operations such as tweeting and then mobile texting took place during the session.'
passive	Non-active, not participating.	'I was very much the passive user, just checking Wikipedia for information.'
download	Transferring data (usually a file) from another computer or server to the computer you are using. The opposite of *upload*.	'I downloaded the song to my phone.'
community	Group of people with shared interests.	'As a community all interested in the same band, we read and responded to his tweets after the show.'

ASSESSMENT FOCUS

Write two paragraphs:
- one explaining some of the particular features of text language
- one discussing whether texting is closer to real talk or a written letter.

Remember

- Many terms used for written texts also apply to spoken ones, such as 'audience', 'purpose', 'content', 'form'.
- However, where words or phrases particular to multi-modal communication are needed, make sure you use them, such as 'user', 'community', 'site'.

Online conversations

Learning objective

- To understand how 'talk' varies when a range of voices contribute in a multi-modal environment.

Exploring group multi-modal talk

Multi-modal talk gets more complicated when a range of voices is involved.

ACTIVITY

Look at this example of an online chat sequence in response to an album release by Leona Lewis.

<u>Aleyshaa4</u>

Last album sold millions howcan you say that? theyre both great and this one evn better!!! BEST of luck Leona your album sounds amazin

<u>Cally9112</u>

STOP CRYING YOUR HEART OUT!! AMAZING

<u>ADY5a</u> (58 minutes ago) Show Hide

Reply   0

umm someone down said her last album has variety? O.o lol its pop tune after pop tune xD Tthis album has variety, It has rock driven songs, r&b, ballads, and uptempo. this is variety :} and it sounds really nice tbh,

<u>MKY33</u> (1 hour ago) Show Hide

Reply   0

No one can say she can't sing... (apart from miserable youtube pests)... Pure British diva... Goes to show, what London can do one of the Biggest talents in the world...

<u>Pollypc67</u> (1 hour ago) Show Hide

Reply   0

wow love her version of stop crying your heart out. could be big as run xx

<u>jann76</u> 1 hour ago) Show Hide

Reply   0

<u>Aleyshaa4</u>

"I got you" or "Outta my head" should be her next single!!!! Like last album lots of vAriety just great songs
(1 hour ago) Show Hide

Discuss and take notes in a group:

- How is this talk different from normal/offline chat? How is this different from normal writing?
- What is the general subject of the 'conversation'?
- What different points are being made in the conversation? (Are **all** the contributors saying what their favourite track is?)
- How are specific contributors responding to others?
- What do you notice about the order of the conversation?
- Does the technology make it easy or hard to follow and take part in the conversation?
- How important do you think it is to spell or construct sentences 'properly' on this sort of site? Explain your view.

The Leona Lewis and the 'birthday present' conversation on page 258 give some insights into the sorts of exploration of multi-modal talk you can do.

- Read through this grid which offers some more areas you could explore.
- Evaluate what you already know about each of these and decide on what you might research further.

Focus	Already know about	Need to find out more
How multi-modal talk differs from both real talk and printed text on paper • How is online conversation different from one between friends at school in terms of its length, time limits, and longevity (time remaining 'out there')? • Is chat online like a printed text (such as a newspaper or novel)? In what ways, other than in spelling and grammar, is it different?		
How we establish our identity in online or digital communication • How does printed onscreen text both allow us to hide our identities and also 'be ourselves'? • How might our feelings be hurt as a result of online communication?		
How multi-modal talk is changing the way ideas are communicated or created • How are certain television shows or ideas now prepared for 'multi-platform' use, which involves multi-modal talk? For example, a show might have a website, viewers might influence the content of the show by texting or emailing to contact the show live or even to change the storylines – in other words, be interactive. • Are these changes a benefit to the user or not?		

ASSESSMENT FOCUS

Using the notes from your discussion of the Leona Lewis text, write your views on

- how online chat is different from real talk
- how the technology influences the language and structure of the conversation.

Remember

- Whichever area you choose to explore, you need to find suitable research or source material.
- Use key terms in your analysis relating to the appropriate assessment objective – whether this is 'language variation and change', 'adapting spoken language' or 'different contexts'.

Analysing talk

Select a typical genre of speech from this list.

- a radio phone-in programme with an agony-aunt
- a sports coach giving a half-time team talk
- a receptionist at a hotel welcoming guests.

Write an analysis of the sort of talk that takes place, commenting in particular on

- the status of the speaker(s)
- the semantic field (what sorts of vocabulary, grammar and patterns of speech there are)
- any other set conventions that typically occur in such a situation.

Evaluation – What have you learned?

With a partner, use the grade checklist below to evaluate your work on the Extended Assessment Task.

- I can analyse the context in an impressive way, commenting perceptively on all three bullet points, showing a real confidence in what each means, and supporting what I say with specific and apt references.
- I can understand the subtle shifts in status and power between speakers in any given situation.

- I can sustain the analysis of my chosen context in a detailed way and comment on all three bullet points, offering evaluation and supporting what I say with some apt references.
- I can show some understanding of the subtle ways talk reflects people's status.

- I can explain clearly and in detail my chosen context and what occurs.
- I can analyse all three bullet points.
- I can support what I say with relevant examples.

- I can make clear points about the ways people speak in my chosen context referring appropriately to all three bullet points and showing some confidence in my ideas.

- I can write about the ways people speak in my chosen context, dealing with all three bullet points, though without developing ideas or offering detailed explanations.

You may need to go back and look at the relevant pages from this section again.

Controlled Assessment Preparation
Spoken Language Study

Introduction

In this section you will

- find out the requirements of the Controlled Assessment task for Unit 3 Section C: Studying Spoken Language
- read, analyse and respond to three sample answers by different candidates
- plan and write your own answer to a sample task
- evaluate and assess your answer and the progress you have made.

Why is preparation of this kind important?

- If you know exactly what you need to do, you will feel more confident when you take part in the Controlled Assessment
- Looking at sample answers by other students will help you see what you need to do to improve your own work
- Planning and writing a full sample task response will give you a clear sense of what you have learned so far.

Key Information

Unit 3 Section C is 'Studying Spoken Language'.

- The controlled part of the task will last between **2 and 3 hours**, and is worth **20 marks**.
- It is worth **10%** of your overall English Language GCSE mark.

The Controlled Assessment task

- You have to complete **one** written task.
- Your single task will be chosen from the three topic areas:
  - Social attitudes to spoken language
  - Spoken genres
  - Multi-modal talk.
- You will write between **800 and 1000** words.
- You will choose, or be provided with, a task to respond to from the three topic areas.
- You will then produce a Spoken Language Study that involves analysing source material and data on your chosen topic and drawing some conclusions based on your evidence.
- The task will be done in 'controlled conditions', in the exam room or in your own classroom, over a period of up to three hours.

Here are some example questions based on the three task areas set by the exam board.

Social attitudes to spoken language
Reflect on some aspects of your own personal talk (idiolect) perhaps including criticisms made of it by adults.
Spoken genres
Investigate a type of media talk, such as sports commentary, celebrity or news interviews, or game-show presentation.
Multi-modal talk
What devices do people use to maintain brevity when messaging/texting? How does this relate to the way we speak?

The Assessment

The assessment objective for this unit (AO2) states that you must be able to do the following:

- Understand variations in spoken language, explaining why language changes in relation to contexts.
- Evaluate the impact of spoken language choices in your own and others' use.

Targeting Grade A

Some of the key features of Grade C and Grade A responses are as follows:

Grade C candidates	*See example on pages 265–6*
• give a clear explanation of how they themselves and others use and adapt spoken language for specific purposes • explore features found in some spoken language data (i.e. transcripts) • explore some of the issues arising from public attitudes to spoken language.	

Grade A/A★ candidates	*See example on pages 267–8 (A) 269–70 (A★)*
• provide detailed analysis and evaluation of how they themselves and others use and adapt spoken language for specific purposes • give sustained and sophisticated interpretation of features found in a range of spoken language data (i.e. transcripts) • offer analysis and evaluation of key issues arising from public attitudes to spoken language.	

Exploring Sample Responses

ACTIVITY

Read the extract below from a response to this task on social attitudes to spoken language.

> **Reflect on some aspects of your own personal talk (idiolect) perhaps including criticisms made of it by adults.**

As you read it, think about whether it is closer to a Grade C or a Grade A and why.

Consider these key elements an examiner would look for:

- how well the writer has focused on his/her own talk
- how well he/she has explained attitudes and given appropriate examples
- whether this response does more than just explain, and begins to look more deeply at attitudes.

Example 1: Social attitudes to spoken language

Me, my parents and grandparents:

Part one

I come from south-east London so I don't really think I have an accent though when I go to other places on holiday or to visit mates, they say that I do. I think I get my way of speaking from my dad and mum. They were both born in London near where we live so I think I just grew up to speak like them.

Some people think that because we come from London we would use cockney rhyming slang, like 'apples and pears' for 'stairs' but actually we don't. My dad says that when he worked in the City there were some people who did talk like this, but that it's a bit of a stereotype that you hear in the media that people from London talk like this. Officially you have to be born 'within the sound of Bow Bells' to be a cockney. St-Mary-le-Bow is a church in east London.

The main difference between my idiolect and my parents' is nothing to do with my background but more to do with my age. Me and my mates use all sorts of language when we are talking, probably a lot which has come from using mobiles or the internet. For example, my friend Danny is called 'Dammy' cos when one of our friends was typing his name on hotmail he spelled it wrong and hit the 'm' key. Then one of our other mates saw this and sent a message saying, 'DAMMY? Who's that?' and we all picked up on it so he's called that now. Even my mum and dad call him 'Dammy'.

However, they do pick me up on the way I speak. Sometimes I use words like 'blood' to mean 'mate'. I know that it comes from street language and urban music and stuff like that so I'm not being serious really, but I like using it. They don't. They say, 'why can't you speak properly?' but for me it's just the way I speak with my friends. I know it's not how to speak when I am in posh situations or serious situations, like jobs or interviews. But then, I also notice that there's a difference between how my gran and grandad speak, and my mum, dad and me. My grandad says 'Crikey!' when he's cross, which I don't say, and my gran uses words like 'condiments' when we are laying the table for tea. In the interview I did with them, they talked about lots of words and phrases that aren't used anymore, like 'courting' to mean 'seeing someone'. My mum and dad don't understand what 'got with' means (which I use) as they used to 'get off' with someone. It all means the same really...

Examiner feedback

- The candidate has answered the task set: he/she has explained some particular personal uses of language and how they differ from parents and grandparents.
- Better use of source material, giving more examples and exploring how these reflect attitudes would have helped. For example, the candidate could have explored how use of talk reflects a higher or lower status, or written more on the origins of certain types of talk. The issue of accent was raised but then not really pursued – why doesn't the writer think he or she has an accent?

Suggested grade: C

ACTIVITY

Read the extract below from a response to this spoken genres task:

> *Investigate a type of media talk, such as sports commentary, celebrity or news interviews, or game-show presentation.*

Looking carefully at the annotations, decide how this is an improvement on Example 1.

Example 2: Spoken genres

Sports commentary: Part one, tennis match

    To prepare for this task I chose to examine an extract from the transcript of the Federer/Roddick Wimbledon final commentary.

    One of the key things about a sports commentary is that it **assumes a shared vocabulary with the audience**. For example, words and phrases like 'passing shot' or 'lob' or 'drop shot' aren't explained by the commentator or expert, they are just stated. They know because the audience are already interested that these terms are understood. This means that the **context – a commentary on a tennis match – affects what is said and how it is received by the listener**. Someone with no interest in tennis would be confused and probably turn off.

    Several key features of spoken language emerge in the transcript. The first is that often the commentators don't speak in full sentences, so we have **the commentator saying, 'Wonderful smash!' (line 22)**, which you could argue we don't really need as we see it on screen, but it adds to the atmosphere. Of course, because this is on television, we don't get running commentary like on radio: sometimes we get a series of words or exclamations: 'Roddick approach shot... Backhand return... Crosscourt... (pause)... magnificent!' At other times we just watch and get a summary at the end of the point.

    On radio, because listeners can't see the actual match, the commentator has to make everything much clearer:

        'Serve down the centre, good return by Roddick but Federer down the line, back by Roddick... and ooohh Federer with a smash down the centre!'

Annotations:

- Good point which is then explained
- Reference to the 'context' links to Assessment Objectives
- Detailed analysis of data
- Contrasts types of commentary

In this case, the drama is being created for us, so we picture the scene and become involved in the excitement. The pause (…) makes us hold our breath; then **the 'ooohh Federer' is an emotional gasp introducing** ← Precise analysis of what is said and the effect created
the climax ('a smash down the centre') as the commentator's voice rises and the crowd applauds. The listener might just feel that she is there, seeing it first hand.

However, there is more to the commentary than just describing the points. The commentator's role is also to ask the expert summariser what he or she thinks. These comments will usually be connected to the **lexis** ─── Good use of language terminology
for tennis. This means that there are expected things or ways of speaking that we would hear in a tennis commentary. These include:

'So, what has Roddick got to do to get back into this match?' (line 44).
'He's really pumped-up now' (line 48).

Typical question openings, like 'so… what… ?' are quite common, as are sports or game-related verbs and adjectives **like 'pumped-up',** ← Excellent examples to back up point
'belting the ball' (line 49), and 'stay focused' (line 50).

These are also quite informal sometimes but work very well as commentary because they are what we expect and it's like the commentator and expert are talking as friends…

Examiner feedback

- This extract takes a detailed look at a particular genre of speech, and gives some good analysis of how it is constructed and what makes it specific to this area (the reference to sports terminology, for example).
- The candidate makes an interesting distinction between television commentary and radio commentary and offers analysis on the effect of the words and sounds (for example the interjection, 'ooohh', in the middle of the commentary).
- The candidate begins to explore and analyse the complex area of semantic field with regard to tennis commentary and is moving on to discuss the way the commentator and expert talk to each other.

Suggested grade: A

Read the extract below from a response to this multi-modal talk task:

> **What devices do people use to maintain brevity when messaging/
> texting? How does this relate to the way we speak?**

As you read it, consider these key elements that an examiner would look out for:

- how well the writer has addressed the focus of the task
- examples of technical language related to speech and talk
- whether there are any examples of detailed analysis or original thinking and interpretation
- whether there are any areas that are not fully explored.

Example 3: Multi-modal talk

Part one: text, chunks and age

Clearly sets out the situation →
A number of language operations are taking place when people text. For a start, the means of communication itself partly defines what the user can do; restrictions such as cost (at least initially), space – you tend to type within the limits of the screen space – and the need to communicate rapidly, all shape the way the language is built up. So, in the examples I researched I noted:

Abbreviations which use letters, or letters and numbers, can

Includes appropriate details →
be seen, such as 'lol' **('laugh out loud') '4eva' ('forever')** *and* **'omg' ('oh my god').**

Abbreviations where symbols replace common phrases such as '?' meaning 'I don't understand', 'why?' 'explain!', etc.

However, what the research I did also showed was that the usage of text abbreviations was by no means universal, in that some users used hardly any (see

Good use of data →
example A) *but others used it all the time. I also conducted some research when I talked to the texters and it was clear that in most cases, they didn't particularly think about their target audience; in other words, their fingers took over and they*

Shows a clear development of thought in response to the evidence →
used what they had become accustomed to doing, so one user (Julie–see example) texted in the same way to her gran as to her friends. **I wondered if this was the same** *when she*

spoke to her friends and grandmother and, in fact, she said she probably adapted her spoken language slightly more than her texting.

Drawing conclusions → *Clearly, the 'chunked' nature of texting does reflect, however, much of the way that some people, especially teenagers, talk. So, chunked expressions, such as 'I went, like, hello?' with an accompanying tone, replace longer grammatical clauses such as, 'I told her she must be joking!' This can be seen as linking with the '?' abbreviation for 'what do you mean?'.* **However, the sorts of omissions and utterances we** ← **Perceptive comments** **hear in a lot of dialogue ('er', 'well', 'um') are largely absent from texts.** *Probably because although we text quickly we can erase, go back, reword – which we can't once we've spoken!*

Challenging approach → *But does this mean that we are worse at expressing ourselves? Older people, for example, might object to this sort of chunked usage but this might reflect the fact that they simply don't understand it, not that it is inferior – although they may feel it is. Variations and change in language almost always bring with them status or power but this can lead to certain groups feeling excluded. This is particularly true of multi-modal language which not only uses new ways of expressing ideas* **but, because it is linked to technology, also creates another** ← **Extends sophisticated ideas** **barrier for some users.** *If you are an older person who can't email or use predictive text then that is a barrier to the language.*

Extended comment with a clear view of what happens → *However, it is easy to think that it is just a matter of age. As the third transcript (from my gran to my mum) shows, the use of texting can be quickly and enthusiastically learned. In fact, the abbreviations, which my gran would not dream of using in speech, are useful when not wanting to type laborious letters onto her mobile...*

Examiner feedback

This is a sophisticated response to a complex area.

- The detailed examples given shed light on the world of texting, and links to speech, and the candidate draws out both similarities and differences, although the point about omissions and utterances in dialogue could be exemplified more thoroughly.
- The language used is generally very technical and analytical, with common linguistic terms utilised such as 'utterance', 'chunks' and 'omissions', etc.
- The candidate does jump around a little in terms of points made and the diversion into discussing technology in a wider sense is interesting but could equally apply to written as spoken language, so a little more focus here perhaps needed.

However, this is an impressive, detailed analysis.

Suggested grade: A★

EXAM PRACTICE TASK

Social attitudes to spoken language

Reflect on some aspects of the personal talk (idiolect) of someone you know well (for example, your form teacher, a television presenter or sports coach), perhaps commenting on:

- similarities and differences in how you both speak
- attitudes to your, and your chosen person's, way of speaking.

If you only do five things...

1 Think carefully about the different forms of spoken language used around you – by anyone from your friends to radio DJs to politicians – and recognise the features of how they speak.

2 When you are preparing for your Controlled Assessment, your success will depend upon the quality of your data, so carry out any research activities carefully. Always analyse your research findings: in themselves, they are only a starting point.

3 Plan what you are intending to write because it is almost certain to improve the quality of the mark you receive. Set down your findings logically: open with a statement of what you are examining and why, and come to a definite conclusion at the end. Analyse closely, because a detailed analysis of a relatively brief extract or a set of findings is likely to lead to a higher grade than a very generalised and superficial examination.

4 When you are writing, always give examples, analyse them and use key terminology whenever possible.

5 Don't forget that responses to different topics will require different approaches:
   - Social attitudes to spoken language will require an appreciation of the linkage between what people say and how they are perceived.
   - Spoken genres are likely to deal in detail with the conventions of how people speak within contexts and situations.
   - Multi-modal talk will involve writing analytically about the way we 'talk' to each other electronically – it will not be enough to simply identify significant features.

Published by Collins Education
An imprint of HarperCollins Publishers
77-85 Fulham Palace Road
Hammersmith
London
W6 8JB

Browse the complete Collins catalogue at
www.collinseducation.com

© HarperCollins Publishers Limited 2010

10 9 8 7 6 5 4 3 2 1

ISBN 978 0 00 734212 9

British Library Cataloguing in Publication Data.
A Catalogue record for this publication is available from the
British Library.

Editor: Catherine Martin
Design and typesetting by EMC Design
Cover Design by Angela English
Printed and bound by L.E.G.O. SpA, Lavis, Italy

ACKNOWLEDGEMENTS

The publishers gratefully acknowledge the permission granted to reproduce
the copyright material in this book. While every effort has been made to
trace and contact copyright holders, where this has not been possible the
publishers will be pleased to make the necessary arrangements at the first
opportunity.

Chapter 1 p5, 'Picks of the day', from *The Observer*, 26 July, 2009. ©
Guardian News & Media Ltd 2009; p5 website reprinted with kind
permission of The Coventry Building Society; p6, 'Flood victims will suffer
trauma of a war zone, says GP' by Russell Jenkins, *The Times*, 25 November,
2009 pg 13. © NI Syndication; p7, 'After the rain, here comes The Sun' *The
Sun*, 25 November, 2009. © NI Syndications; p9, courtesy of Sky News; p10,
extract from *New York Encounter* Lonely Planet 2007 © 2007 Lonely Planet;
p11, Text and images courtesy of NYCVP (New York City Vacations Packages)
website; p12, extract from *Withnails: the Film Diaries of Richard E Grant*
published by Picador Macmillan; p14, 'Birth of Asian Elephant is trumpeted
by Zoo', *The Times*, 29 July, 2009. © NI Syndication; p15, Marriott Hotel
courtesy of Marriott Hotels; p16, Transun Arctic Spirit advert reprinted with
kind permission; p18, extract from *The Backwash of War* by Ellen la Motte
published by Dodopress; p23, 'The day of the vulture' *The Independent*, 5
September, 2009; p24, 'Er, does this thing have a reverse gear?' *Daily Mail*,
27 July 2009. Reprinted with permission of Solo Syndication; p25, WaterAid
ad reprinted with kind permission of WaterAid; p27, 'It's wonderful to see
you all: re-united with the evacuees' by Chris Green, *The Independent*, 5
September, 2009; p28, problem page from *Woman's Magazine Annual*,
1935. Reprinted with permission of IPC Media; p30, 'Barbed Ire - Allotment
fence 'might injure vandals' *Daily Mirror*, 5 September 2009; p36, Harley-Davidson advert © Harley-Davidson Europe. (Prices are not
current, this is an old advert.); p40, 'Academies are the only way forward'
Oldham Advertiser, 24 September 2009. Reprinted with permission of MEN
Syndication; pp42-43, 'Let's Rejoice in the Rain' by Andrew Grimes,
Manchester Evening News, pg 8, 31 July 2009. Reprinted with permission of
MEN Syndications; p43, 'What a He Row' by Ben Ashford, *The Sun*, 25
November, 2009. © NI Syndication; p45, Dracula leaflet for Northern Ballet
Theatre's production of Dracula at the West Yorkshire Playhouse, 2009;
pp46-47, screengrab courtesy of Folk Alley homepage; p50, 'Champion of
the word: Keith Waterhouse' (written by Anton Antonowicz), *The Mirror*, 5
September, 2009; p50, 'Farewell Keith, King of Fleet Street' (written by Sam
Greenhill) *Daily Mail*; p55, 'Grizzly bears starve as fish stocks collapse' by
Tracy McVeigh, *The Observer*, 20 September, 2009. © Guardian News &
Media Ltd 2009; p56, 'From Russia With Love' from *Sky Magazine*, October
2009; p57, extract from *A Short History of Nearly Everything* by Bill Bryson
published by Random House; **Chapter 2** p74, Short extract from 'TV dinners:
Chops, mash and Mad Men' by Julie Myerson, *The Observer*, 21 June, 2009.
Copyright © Guardian News & Media Ltd 2009; p88, 'Oceans of Clichés' by
A.A. Gill published by *The Times* November 16 2008; p89, Short extracts
from 'To Groom or not to groom' by Kathy Lette, *Good Housekeeping*, August
2009. This was written by Kathy Lette, author of ten best-selling novels;
p100, extracts from 'The right to die or not' by Brendan O'Neill, *The Big
Issue*, August 17-23 2009; **Chapter 4** pp168, 170 Extracts from MARTYN
PIG by Kevin Brooks, published by The Chicken House. Copyright © Kevin
Brooks, 2002; pp168, 188 and 189, extracts from *Lord of the Flies* by
William Golding published by Faber & Faber; pp169 and 174 extract from
'The River God' by Stevie Smith published by Faber & Faber; p172, 'Medusa'
by Carol Ann Duffy, from THE WORLD'S WIFE by Carol Ann Duffy published by
Macmillan; pp177and 178, Short extracts from 'The Darkness Out There' by
Penelope Lively from A PACK OF CARDS published by Penguin. Reprinted
with permission of David Higham Associates; p191, extract from
KINDERTRANSPORT by Diane Samuels, published by Nick Hern Books;
Chapter 5 pp208 and 209, extract from Leila Aboulela 'Something Old
Something New' from *Scottish Girls About Town* published by Pocket Books;
p210 Tanzania Today website extract courtesy of Tanzania Tourist Board;
p219 extract courtesy of Peter Drew Voiceovers; p225, extract from
www.frootsmag.com reprinted with permission; p226, extract from
www.frootsmag.com written by Kevin Boyd reprinted with permission of the
author; **Chapter 6** pp244 and 245, extracts from www.bl.uk (British Library)
reprinted with permission; p252, 'Friends, Romans innit?' by Daniel Bates,
Daily Mail, 24 November, 2009. Reprinted with permission of Solo
Syndications.

The publishers would like to thank the following for permission to reproduce
pictures in these pages:

Advertising Archive: p35; Alamy: pp62, 64, 67, 107, 110, 118, 127, 139,
150a, 150b, 162, 237, 265; Alton Towers Resort: pp115a, 115b; Modern
Television, copyright Alan Peebles: p256; BBC: pp152b, 251b photographer
Jeff Overs, 254a, photographer Anthony Todd; Erik Boomer: p24b; Caroline
Green: p218; Cavendish Press: p43b, Corbis: pp19, 75, 79, 202, 203, 206;
Sam Drevo: p24a; Getty Images: pp23, 43a, 55, 112, 113, 114, 116, 120,
123, 132, 141, 145, 157, 170, 188, 209, 225, 242b, 244, 246; Hat Trick
Productions Ltd: p251a; iStockphoto: 10, 12, 13, 37, 38, 44, 69a, 69b,
72a, 72b, 74, 76, 77, 78, 82, 85, 86, 87a, 87b, 90, 92, 93, 95a, 95b, 97a,
97b, 98, 100, 101, 108, 124, 125a, 125b, 134, 136, 140, 148b, 148c,
151a, 151b, 167a, 167b, 173, 175, 176a, 176b, 186, 187, 200, 207, 208,
209, 212c, 214a, 214b, 214c, 216a, 216b, 216c, 226, 227, 228a, 228b,
229, 235, 240, 242a, 244, 252, 258, 269; Ian Lloyd: p 27; Mary Evans
Picture Library: pp21, 191; Movie Store Collection: p160; NERC/BGS: p7;
News Team International: p7tr; North News and Pictures: p 7cl; PA Photos:
7br; Photolibrary: 2, 66, 83, 91; Rex Features: 14, 26 (Kelly Hancock/UCF),
50 (Ray Tang), 89, 118 (CSU/Arhcv/Everett), 122 (Steve Hill), 130, 144
(c.20thC.Fox/Everett), 147a, 147b (c.20thC.Fox/Everett), 148 (Alastair
Muir), 152 (Brian J. Ritchie), 158 (Giuliano Bevilacqua), 164 (Donald
Cooper), 168 (Lynne McAlley), 183 (SNAP), 185 (c.MGM/Everett), 195
(Alastair Muir), 196 (Donald Cooper), 222a (Back Page Images), 222b (Ray
Tang), 253 (Owen Sweeney), 254 (Giuliano Bevilacqua), 260 (Action Press),
267 (Sipa Press); Ronald Grant Archive: pp165, 182, 212 (top);
Shutterstock: p8; Solent News: p30; TalkbackThames: p256; Topfoto: p204
(The Granger Collection, New York).